20
DISCIPLINARY
STRATEGIES
for Working With
CHALLENGING
STUDENTS

20

DISCIPLINARY STRATEGIES

for Working With

CHALLENGING STUDENTS

WILLIAM N. BENDER

LearningSciencesInternational

1400 Centrepark Blvd, Suite 1000
West Palm Beach, FL 33401
717-845-6300

email: pub@learningsciences.com
learningsciences.com

Printed in the United States of America

20 19 18 17 16 15   2 3 4

Library of Congress Cataloging-in-Publication Data
Bender, William N.
  Twenty disciplinary strategies for working with challenging students / William N. Bender.
    pages   cm
  ISBN: 978-1-941112-22-9 (pbk.)
  1. School discipline—Handbooks, manuals, etc.   2. Teacher-student relationships—
Handbooks, manuals, etc.   3. School children—Discipline.   4. Classroom management.
I. Title.
LB3012.B46 2014
  371.5—dc23

                                                    [2015931655]

Table of Contents

Acknowledgments

Learning Sciences International would like to thank the following reviewers:

Stephanie A. Bowling
Seventh-grade math teacher
Henry Scott Middle School
Denison, Texas

Angela Humphrey Brown
Professor of Education and Secondary Education Coordinator
Piedmont College
Athens, Georgia

Michael J. Coco
Instructor
Mississippi College
Clinton, Mississippi

Alisa Janiski
2014 Maryland Teacher of the Year finalist
Prospect Mill Elementary
Bel Air, Maryland

Adam Schechter
2014 Virginia Teacher of the Year finalist
Mark Twain Middle School
Alexandria, Virginia

Shauna Snyder
Kindergarten teacher
Eastanollee Elementary School
Eastanollee, Georgia

Justin Taylor
2009 Connecticut Teacher of the Year
Bulkeley High School
Hartford, Connecticut

Jennifer Toledo
2013 California Teacher of the Year finalist
A. L. Gauldin Elementary School
Downey, California

About the Author

 **William N. Bender, PhD,** is a national leader on the general topic of instructional tactics for the classroom, with special interests in discipline, project-based learning, technology in the classroom, differentiated instruction, and response to intervention. He has written twenty-four books in education, many of which are leading sellers in their respective topics. He currently presents numerous workshops each year for educators around the country and in Canada, using humor and his down-to-earth personal style. His focus is always on practical strategies and tactics that will work in real classrooms, and his work is firmly based on his experience teaching public school special needs students in eighth and ninth grades. After earning his PhD from the University of North Carolina, he spent a career teaching educators at Rutgers University and the University of Georgia.

Introduction

This is the first truly "modern" book on school discipline. While strategies for effective discipline continue to evolve and thousands of books have been written on class discipline, there has been since 2014 an increased emphasis on using fair, effective disciplinary practices in schools (Duncan, 2014). For the first time in history, the federal government challenges schools relative to disciplinary practices that are widely used, such as suspension and expulsion of students, in particular students of color and minority students.

Teachers are, today, expected to become much more involved in disciplinary management, as the response to intervention initiatives has now become best practice around the nation and in Canada (Algozzine, Daunic, & Smith, 2012). Also, the recently evolving instructional practices such as the flipped classroom, project-based learning, response to intervention (RTI), and technology infusion only create different and increasing disciplinary challenges for teachers today. This book, unlike any other yet available, discusses all of those recent issues and trends in order to provide practical disciplinary strategies for each. Further, the book is intended to provide advanced disciplinary strategies for the modern classroom, with serious consideration given to these new disciplinary challenges. The book presents information both on preventative, whole-class/whole-school strategies and more intensive, targeted interventions for practicing teachers to implement.

Many of these strategies have been created recently, and may be new to some practicing teachers, while others may be something teachers have learned about but not directly implemented in their own classes. Still, to be clear, this book is not intended as a level-one book for class management of relatively easy-to-manage behaviors. Rather, this is a practical, how-to guide for tough disciplinary challenges in real classrooms in today's schools. One thing is certain: no teacher can have too many disciplinary interventions or too much knowledge of preventative disciplinary techniques, and more intensive, focused interventions that are research proven can help almost all teachers manage the more unique or challenging disciplinary situations experienced in classrooms today.

THE BASICS OF DISCIPLINE

In preparing this book, I assume that the readers know the basics of discipline. For example, consistency in how one manages students is much more important than whether one is hard-nosed on disciplinary matters or more relaxed in one's disciplinary style. While consistency in disciplinary management is absolutely critical (Bender, 2007), most teachers get that concept during their training in college. Likewise, other basic techniques for discipline, such as setting up one's classroom to minimize problems (i.e., using the physical space to separate students) or using proximity control to manage mild behavioral disturbances (e.g., kids talking in class), are typically mastered prior to being hired in a teaching position. I do not discuss herein those level-one class-management strategies at length.

Also, this book is not heavily based in any one discipline theory. Too often in the literature on school discipline, one finds either a book dedicated to generally positive class-climate/classroom-management strategies (the feel-good disciplinary books) or focused, highly targeted behavioral interventions for very difficult-to-manage behaviors. In this book, I avoid that either/or approach to discipline. While I discuss classroom management and interventions for more challenging behaviors, I do not wish to dilute this focus on discipline by a "camouflage" of false choices between the feel-good, positively oriented management techniques or intensive behavioral interventions. Quite frankly, both are essential in classrooms today, and both are included here. I also present the teacher not with theory, but choices from both areas that he can use in real classrooms to alleviate his hardcore disciplinary issues.

> Consistency in how one manages students is much more important than whether one is hard-nosed on disciplinary matters, or more relaxed in one's class management style.

This book will be somewhat different from other discipline and class-management books in several ways. First, this book draws from the work of Marzano (2003, 2007) in its emphasis on the efficacy of various disciplinary and class-management interventions. Much of Dr. Marzano's research in this area as well as the earlier work in discipline I have personally done (Bender, 2007) informs this work. Specifically, Marzano identifies various questions and several design elements that focus on the areas of class management and discipline, including

- demonstrating "withitness" (intense awareness of all aspects of class functioning)
- applying consequences for lack of adherence to rules and procedures
- acknowledging adherence to rules and procedures.

I stress these in each section of this book. Further, I certainly focus on the emphasis within Marzano's (2003, 2007) work on showing how teachers adhere to innovative strategies as well as showing evidence of student behavioral change based on those interventions. For all of these strategies, I discuss indicators that allow teachers to measure direct evidence of student behavioral change and provide a number of case studies to help teachers implement these strategies, while generating specific evidence of effectiveness.

DIFFERENTIATED DISCIPLINARY STRATEGIES

This book presents strategies that are differentiated based on both the severity of the disciplinary problem and the specific types of behavioral problems the students exhibit. For example, clingy or attention-seeking students often require different strategies than verbally violent or physically aggressive students (Bender, 2007). Also, strategies for unmotivated kids differ from strategies teachers use with oppositional-defiant or bipolar students. In each case, I present the discipline strategy under discussion as either a "whole-class/whole-school" strategy or as a strategy that is effective for specific types of disciplinary problems. As this indicates, some strategies are effective for some types of problems but not others. In the literature on behavior management and/or class management, this differentiated approach to effective discipline is relatively unique.

Also, the severity of the disciplinary issue may dictate the severity of the intervention strategy necessary. Specifically, you may manage with some minor behavioral problems (e.g., blurting out answers, spreading rumors about others, or whispering in class) by holding daily morning meetings, using teacher's proximity, or setting clearer behavioral expectations in the class rules. However, more challenging disciplinary problems (overt violence, fighting, verbal assault) often require specific intervention strategies coupled with ongoing, individual behavioral monitoring. So, the level of severity of the disciplinary infraction may indicate the level of intensity of the required intervention. This book presents disciplinary strategies for both less severe and more severe disciplinary problems.

> This book presents strategies that are differentiated based on both the severity of the disciplinary problem and the specific types of behavioral problems exhibited by the students.

Finally, the book is intended for use in the elementary and middle school grades, but most of these strategies work just as well in the high school classroom.

A THREE-STAGE DISCIPLINARY APPROACH

Every veteran teacher realizes that different disciplinary situations require different teacher responses. For example, two students fighting in the classroom require a different disciplinary response compared to several kids whispering in the back of the class. As this indicates, disciplinary problems do differ in their severity as well as in the students' emotional intensity, so these disciplinary problems are likely to require a variety of approaches on the part of teachers. This book addresses that concern with a focus on a three-stage approach to effective discipline. Strategies are in three broad categories:

1. Whole-class/whole-school preventative disciplinary approaches
2. Immediate disciplinary defusing strategies (disciplinary Band-Aids)
3. Targeted disciplinary interventions to decrease specific behavior problems

Stage One: Whole-Class/Whole-School Prevention

The whole-class/whole-school strategies, described in Section I of the book, are preventative strategies established in advance of disciplinary problems, and teachers generally use them with the whole class. Preventative strategies simply must be the backbone of school discipline in today's world, as these are much more effective and time efficient than strategies that take place after a discipline problem occurs. Of course, many of these strategies may serve as a basis for a targeted intervention for one or more students in the class, but in general these are considered more preventative in nature. Further, most of these strategies are quite effective when undertaken as whole-school strategies. Research shows that these whole-class/whole-school strategies alleviate many minor behavioral infractions as well as some major ones.

> Because disciplinary problems do differ in their severity, and require a variety of approaches on the part of teachers, this book will focus on strategies in three broad categories: whole-class prevention strategies, defusing strategies, and individual disciplinary interventions.

In my professional development workshops on discipline, teachers often provide various examples of problem behaviors that are a challenge for them, and, as discreetly as I can manage, I then question which of these preventative strategies the teacher has used prior to the problem. While most teachers used some of these ideas, some teachers used them only occasionally and some not at all. Such oversights lead to more discipline problems in these classes.

While this book describes a number of preventative, whole-class/whole-school strategies, teachers should not use them all. Rather, teachers should select the strategies that they are most comfortable with, and implement those, but the key is that all teachers—indeed, all schools—should have one or more of these preventative strategies in place.

The efficacy of the whole-class strategies in the first section can be measured most easily by whole-class indices such as the total number of times a teacher has to "call out," for attention or by simply charting the number of overt class disruptions for the whole group. In Section I, several examples are provided for

> All teachers and all schools should have one or more of these preventative strategies in place.

using these preventative strategies to target specific problem behaviors of specific students.

Of course, if these strategies are undertaken as a whole-school effort, many measures of school-wide discipline may be used to assess the efficacy of these strategies. These generally include measures such as reductions in in-school or out-of-school suspensions, disciplinary referrals to the office, reduction in dropouts, and crime on campus. Again, the whole-class/whole-school strategies are a first line of preventative defense against overt discipline problems.

Again, while these strategies are preventative in nature, any of them can likewise be the basis for a targeted intervention for a specific student. One case study in the first section of the book illustrates the use of a whole-class strategy as a targeted intervention. Also, this book presents a chart a bit later in the Introduction, with some general suggestions for use of all of these strategies in particular grade levels.

Stage Two: Triggers and Band-Aids

Stage two in this three-stage disciplinary process involves the teacher's immediate response to misbehavior. Teachers often need to respond to immediate disciplinary infractions in two ways: avoiding triggers that set off disciplinary problems and using immediate response techniques to avoid power plays with students. Therefore, I present guidelines on how to avoid behavioral triggers and provide a set of options on how to respond to an intense disciplinary problem in class such as students cursing each other, fighting, or other critical situations. In such situations, teachers are at a disadvantage in that they are responding to students' immediate, and often intense, misbehavior. In these cases, teachers must use quick thinking and appropriate tactics to de-escalate a potentially explosive situation, and there are a number of things teachers can do.

While these quick response tactics (I refer to them as disciplinary Band-Aids) are not likely to effectively curb disciplinary problems over the long term, they can very often prohibit further escalation of potentially explosive situations. This book discusses these tactics at the beginning of Section II.

Stage Three: Targeted Interventions for Serious Behavioral Problems

Stage three of this three-step disciplinary plan involves targeted interventions. The disciplinary problems that are the most vexing for teachers often involve extreme misbehavior of only a few students in the class, and specific interventions should be aimed at those disciplinary problems. In today's classrooms, most teachers have between two and five students with overt disciplinary problems, and it seems they can count on those students to disrupt the flow of teaching and learning in the classroom almost every day. Those students' disciplinary issues often require specific, targeted interventions to alleviate the disciplinary concerns. These interventions are, in general, individual in nature and more intensive, and generally require specific daily measurement of behavioral change prior to and during strategy implementation. These individual interventions, in Section II of this book, are therefore intended for the most challenging disciplinary issues that teachers face. Presenting disciplinary strategies in this differentiated fashion allows this book to address the entire range of disciplinary issues teachers face in today's classrooms.

> The disciplinary problems that are the most vexing for teachers often involve misbehavior of only a few students in the class.

This book describes each strategy in five to thirteen pages. Strategies in the first section of the book are presented as recommendations for the whole class, and all teachers should seek the two or three tactics here they wish to employ in their classroom. Strategies in the second and third sections are intended as individual applications for specific target students, and several of these present more developed case studies to demonstrate strategy application, complete with a data chart showing the results on the specific individual student's intervention. Also, each strategy section will include implementation instructions or guidelines for that specific strategy, and these are generally presented in a sidebar or box adjacent to the text.

CHALLENGES AND SOLUTIONS IN MODERN DISCIPLINE

The third section of this book presents various trends and issues impacting discipline in the 21st-century classroom, and strategies for each. In today's classes, the only constant seems to be continual change. With the ongoing move to transform disciplinary policy nationwide (Duncan, 2014), teachers are seeing increased pressures on their time. Further, the infusion of technology, flipped classrooms, and the growth of project-based learning all must be discussed in terms of the specific types of disciplinary issues these trends involve. Clearly, the disciplinary challenges teachers face in these newly developing instructional areas will be changing.

Therefore, the book's third section presents several challenges for today's educators, as well as one or more innovative instructional and/or disciplinary approaches to address each challenge. In fact, most teachers may find themselves involved with these challenges in various ways. Again, Section III draws from the seminal work of Marzano (2003, 2007) and Hattie (2013) as well as other influences on discipline such as the recent "Supportive School Discipline Initiative" (US Department of Education, 2011), as Secretary of Education Arne Duncan (2014) promotes.

Section IV of this book includes my recommendations for educators. This is intended to provide guidance as to how teachers and/or administrators might consider disciplinary issues for the next decade. Specifically, I make recommendations as to how administrators may wish to challenge their faculty to master the increasing complexities of discipline in the classroom, or even consider a shift to one of the innovative instructional approaches that helps address discipline problems in a preventative manner (school-wide morning meetings, flipping the classroom, fully implementing project-based learning or RTI in behavior, etc.). Using these recommendations promises to revitalize the entire school, both in terms of academic achievement and class discipline.

RECOMMENDED APPLICATIONS OF THESE STRATEGIES

Authors can always get into trouble making specific grade-level recommendations for certain strategies or discussing various strategies for specific purposes and not others. For example, as I previously mentioned, almost all of the whole-class/whole-school strategies can serve as the basis for a targeted intervention for one student, even though such implementation is not the basis for most of the descriptions in the literature about those strategies. The plain fact is, you can use almost all of these strategies across a wide grade range and for a variety of purposes, including both preventative measures and targeted interventions.

With that concern noted, I do wish to provide the reader with general suggestions for strategy application in various grades and for various uses. Of course, the book structure addresses that issue in one sense, in the four sections described earlier. However, the chart shown later does provide general guidance on grade-level application and uses for each strategy. These are based on my reading of the collective applications in the literature on discipline, but I also use some educated judgment, and of course, other professionals may make other determinations as to appropriate strategy applications.

Strategy 6 provides a good example of the pitfalls of making these types of recommendations, so it presents a variety of quiet-time and meditative interventions. Both quiet time and meditation have been recently discussed as whole-school interventions for the middle and upper grades, whereas one early version of the same strategy (Turtle Time) was discussed as a whole-class strategy from kindergarten through grade three. But while this strategy is primarily a preventative strategy, you could certainly use it for a targeted intervention as well. Therefore, in the upcoming chart on page 9, I include information for possible uses and recommended uses for each strategy, and if a strategy lends itself to use as a targeted intervention, I show that also.

USING THIS BOOK

This book is intended to be a resource of strategies for class management and discipline for teachers and administrators at various grade levels, and as such, I encourage teachers to skip around and select those strategies that they wish to employ based on the different disciplinary challenges they face. However, newer, somewhat less experienced teachers often assume that specific disciplinary challenges may be more serious, so I do encourage all teachers to give some attention to the whole-class/whole-school management strategies section, as these management practices can very often alleviate even some of the more serious disciplinary infractions. For example, holding a morning meeting and encouraging open discussion of ongoing disciplinary problems in such a meeting can help alleviate discipline problems of even the toughest youth, as those students see and hear their peers respond negatively to their behaviors in the meeting discussion.

Next, teachers should use the reference list to further explore strategies they wish to implement. Each strategy includes references, typically as a name and date in parentheses. Using those, and the full reference list at the back of the book, teachers can easily find the online references, online videos, or other articles that discuss the strategy. Using information in this book and those references, teachers will be prepared to implement any of the strategies herein.

Next, the response to intervention (RTI) initiative has swept across the United States since 2005 (Bender, 2012a), and almost all teachers in the primary, elementary, and middle grades have now received some professional development on RTI. This book should be helpful for RTI in behavioral improvement for individual students because the strategies and interventions herein are very appropriate for use in RTI procedures. For example, the interventions and data-charting procedures I demonstrate, particularly in Section II, are exactly the types of interventions and data collection recommended for progress monitoring of RTI interventions to curb inappropriate behaviors. More on this in Section III.

Finally, I do invite all educators to communicate directly with me on their thoughts relative to these strategies. I use a Twitter account as a professional learning network (@williambender1) exclusively for educational content. There, I provide recommendations for teachers to read online articles and interesting strategies, with a focus on a number of topics including discipline in the schools, project-based learning, response to intervention, technology in the classroom, and so on. To book me for professional development around this topic, contact me at bookings@ learningsciences.com.

I hope this book is helpful to you. You do a critically important job, and I'd like to be of some small assistance in that. Also, I'd like to thank you for allowing me to play a small part in the important work you are doing for your students across the United States of America, Canada, and around the world!

Strategy Applications for Specific Grade Levels

Strategies	Preventative Applications		Targeted Interventions	
	Possible Use	Recommended	Possible Use	Recommended
Class Climate	K–12	K–12		
Morning Meetings	K–12	K–7	K–12	
Teaching Movement	K–12	K–5	4–12	
Respect Policy	K–12	K–12	K–12	
Adult Mentoring	K–12	4–8	4–8	
Quiet Time/Meditation	K–12	6–12	6–12	
Conflict Resolution	3–12	6–12	6–12	6–12
Peer Mediation	5–12	5–12	5–12	5–12
Triggers and Band-Aids	K–12	K–12		
Peer Pressure	5–12	5–12	5–9	
Group Contingency	K–12	5–12	5–12	
Self-Regulation/Goal Setting	K–12	3–8	3–8	3–8
Personal Responsibility			5–12	5–12
Video Monitoring			5–12	5–12
Let's Make a Deal!			5–12	5–12
Restorative Justice	K–12		4–12	4–12
Response to Intervention	K–12	K–12	K–12	K–12
The Flipped Classroom	4–12	4–12	4–12	
Project-Based Learning	K–12	4–9		
Technology	K–12	K–12	K–12	K–12

SECTION I
Whole-Class/Whole-School Preventative Strategies

A teacher's ability to manage students is as critical in teaching as the teacher's knowledge of the subject. Without effective management of students, little learning will take place, even when the teacher is highly knowledgeable of the subject content. While most teachers pick up the basics of class management in their teaching preparation courses, most veteran teachers would agree that they often face disciplinary situations in the real world of teaching that they have never encountered previously in their student teaching internships. Simply stated, a one-semester student teaching rarely offers the opportunity to deal with as many types of disciplinary problems as today's teacher will encounter.

In this section, I present a variety of preventative whole-class/whole-school strategies that will help curb disciplinary problems before they occur. I primarily describe these strategies as whole-class because it takes the entire class to implement them. For example, teachers cannot implement a morning meeting (see Strategy 2) without the involvement of the whole class. Further, individual teachers can undertake any of these strategies in his class, even if other teachers in the school are not doing so. Therefore, these are techniques that teachers should consider building into the fabric of their classes from the first day of school. I do not recommend that teachers should employ all of these techniques in any single classroom. Rather, teachers should find two or three of these preventative class-management strategies and build those into their class, as the basis of preventative discipline.

However, I also recommend for school-wide implementation each of the strategies in this section of the book. In most examples in the literature (e.g., descriptions of quiet time, conflict resolution, and peer mediation), these strategies tend to be implemented school-wide rather than in a single class, which is why I use the phrase whole-class or whole-school.

Because these strategies are generally preventative in nature, I recommend that educators begin school-wide implementation of at least two or three of them. I cannot overemphasize the importance of preventative strategies in today's schools.

In today's education climate, all schools must spend the time and resources to undertake the preventative strategies of their choice. Given that these strategies are considered best practices in the 21st-century school, every member of the school faculty should implement at least a few of these strategies school-wide, as use of best practices places one in the most defensible position should some negative "news-catching" disciplinary event occur in the schools. I therefore have a dual specific recommendation here: First, administrators should ensure that they implement at least two of these whole-class/whole-school disciplinary strategies school-wide. These preventative efforts will alleviate many behavioral problems and show that the school is ahead of the curve in managing disciplinary issues.

Next, teachers should individually work to implement at least two of these whole-class/whole-school strategies, if these are not done on a school-wide basis in that particular school. Also, I suggest that teachers in such situations approach their department chairpersons and school administrators and recommend two or more of these strategies for school-wide implementation.

The specific class-wide/school-wide strategies include

Strategy 1: Creating a Positive Class Climate for Effective Discipline

Strategy 2: Morning Meetings to Improve Behavior

Strategy 3: Teaching With Movement to Curb Problem Behaviors

Strategy 4: A Classroom Respect Policy: Rules for My Class

Strategy 5: Adult Mentoring to Reach Unreachable Kids

Strategy 6: Quiet Time and Meditation

Strategy 7: Conflict Resolution Training

Strategy 8: Peer Mediation in the Schools

═══ Strategy 1 ═══

Creating a Positive Class Climate for Effective Discipline

WHAT IS CLASSROOM CLIMATE?

Perhaps no single aspect of discipline captures Marzano's concept of withitness better than class climate (Marzano, 2003, 2007). Withitness represents an intense, immediate awareness of, and response to, various situations within the classroom. Teachers who practice withitness are highly aware of and respond immediately to situations in which problem behaviors may occur (Marzano, 2003). Sometimes this is referred to as situational awareness and involves not only understanding the overt relationships in the class (teacher/student) but also the more subtle relationships (student/student). This also includes the teacher's understanding of how students in the class actually perceive the class interactions (Hattie, 2013), because students will behave in a certain way based on their perceptions of the dynamics of the class more so than the obvious class roles (Hattie, 2013). Certainly, a full knowledge of the class climate and the impact of that climate on each student in the room is one expression of withitness.

"Classroom climate" is a construct that has been discussed fairly widely in the educational literature in the past twenty years (Brand, 2011; Hattie, 2013; Miller & Cunningham, 2011; Pianta, La Pero, Payne, Cox, & Bradley, 2002; Sousa, 2009). Sometimes referred to as "school climate," I prefer the term *class climate*, as this term suggests that teacher efforts are primary in the development of an appropriate environment for learning. In general, classroom climate deals with the students' or parents' sense of safety within the class, as well as the emotional impact of a particular learning environment (Bender, 2007). Class climate issues involve such questions as

- Are students and teacher happy to be in the classroom?
- Does everyone seem to enjoy themselves?
- Is the teacher stressing academics and social learning in a positive, enjoyable way?
- Does everyone feel valued in the class?
- Do all students feel that they can contribute meaningfully to the class?

While the class climate construct is typically limited to the emotional impact of the classroom, the term *school climate* is much broader and encompasses issues such as teacher/administrator relationships, bus supervision of students, and other outside-of-class social interactions (Brand, 2011; Loukas, 2007). For this book, I limit the discussion to class climate because that is the environment in which teachers exert the most influence over behavioral issues.

Classroom climate deals with the students' or parents' sense of safety within the class, as well as the emotional impact of a particular learning environment.

Another aspect of class climate involves student perception. Classrooms that students perceive to be predominately punitive in nature will not facilitate the development of positive, respectful relationships and are quite likely to involve more disciplinary infractions than classes in which teachers have attended, carefully and strategically, to class climate issues (Hattie, 2013). In such punitive classes, students will not enjoy their learning as much—if at all—and teachers will be much more likely to burn out in their profession much more quickly. Rather, in effective classrooms, the teacher is likely to be very concerned with how students and other teachers perceive their own value in the context of the classroom (Hattie, 2013; Loukas, 2007; Sousa, 2009). In fact, the most effective classrooms are those in which everyone feels valued and where the various emotional needs of all the students and the teacher are met (Bender, 2007; Brand, 2011; Miller, 2011; Pianta et al., 2002).

In effective classrooms, the teacher is likely to be very concerned with how students and other teachers perceive their own value in the context of the classroom.

ASSESSING CLASS CLIMATE

For this reason, effective teachers must be concerned with how students and parents perceive their own value in the context of the classroom. It is important to use various informal assessments that allow the concerned educator to gauge the classroom climate in any setting from the various perspectives of those within that setting (Brand, 2011; Loukas, 2007; Pianta et al., 2002). Therefore, I advocate that each teacher spend some time toward the beginning of each year to actually assess the climate in their classes using one of the procedures below. Certainly teachers can utilize student inventories and questionnaires, but a simple questionnaire for parents who visit the classroom might also provide some insights into class climate (Bender, 2007).

Overall, such assessment is not a time-consuming process and can be accomplished rather informally, but the potential insights such an assessment can provide are critical (Pianta et al., 2002). Teachers may find that these informal assessment data seem to reaffirm insights the teacher already has about how students perceive the class. However, frequently such assessments can show teachers critical areas to which they must attend. For example, teachers might find that the quiet student who rarely demonstrates any disciplinary problems at all is actually feeling quite alienated, and may even be contemplating suicide. In that case, the assessment of class climate can provide critical information on which the teacher can take action.

Further, with some assessment data in hand, teachers can work to improve the climate in their classes. Sometimes simple things can dramatically improve class climate; for example, providing students a choice of assignments or using "peer buddy" learning on some in-class assignments can make a tremendous difference in how connected students feel with each other. Certainly the use of 21st-century social networking in the class will often result in students having a richer class learning experience and valuing their learning experience more highly.

Students' Assessment of Class Climate

A number of authors provide informal assessments for capturing students' perceptions of class climate (Bender, 2007; Brand, 2011; Sousa, 2009). As one option, teachers may consider a simple survey of students concerning how they sense the classroom. The brief informal measure in Figure 1.1 offers the teacher the option of checking on how students experience their classroom environment (Bender, 2007; Sousa, 2009). Of course, using informal inventories also provides teachers with the opportunity to add more indicators that are specific to their own class.

Interpretation of Surveys of Class Climate

Given the way this particular assessment is structured, lower scores are much more desirable and indicate a much healthier class climate overall than higher scores. Teachers may simply wish to average the score for each indicator (taking the average out to two decimal places), and then scan those data to determine overall indications of class climate for each question.

However, another advantage of informal student surveys to assess class climate involves the multiple levels of data interpretation they provide. While teachers should aggregate the data, as I noted above, teachers should also look at individual responses from some of their more challenging students. In particular, teachers should use these data to determine the emotional well-being of individual students with behavioral problems and take action to improve those students' class climate experience, when possible. I present some ideas for that later in this section.

Figure 1.1: Assessing Students' Comfort in the Class

Directions: On this sheet, circle the number that represents the extent to which you are worried about this.

	Not worried about this	Hardly worried about this	Worried about this	Very worried about this
Students picking on me	1	2	3	4
Failing in my schoolwork	1	2	3	4
The teacher not liking me	1	2	3	4
Being made fun of	1	2	3	4
Being different from others	1	2	3	4
Finding classmates for joint projects	1	2	3	4
Not understanding my work	1	2	3	4
Students picking a fight with me	1	2	3	4
Getting into trouble	1	2	3	4
Losing my way between classes	1	2	3	4
Working with peer buddies in class	1	2	3	4
Finding friends to sit with in the cafeteria	1	2	3	4
Being sent to the principal	1	2	3	4
Not knowing what is expected	1	2	3	4
Which clubs/teams to join	1	2	3	4

Parents' Perceptions of Class Climate

Another group of individuals who are highly motivated to explore class climate are the parents of students in the class. While measures of parental perceptions of class climate can help teachers foster positive relationships with parents, these measures are a bit less influential on disciplinary issues within the class than are measures of student perceptions of class climate. However, there are many instances in which teachers may wish to assess a parent's perception of the class, and teachers may use a simple questionnaire or survey for that purpose, such as the one found in Figure 1.2.

Among the things that parents want to see in the classroom, perhaps the comfort level of students is paramount. Parents want to see happy, engaged students interacting with their peers and their teacher. They want to perceive that the students are comfortable in their relationships with the teacher and with other adults (e.g., paraprofessionals) in the class. Therefore, I included on the questionnaire several indicators of student happiness.

Figure 1.2:   Parent Questionnaire on Class Climate

Directions: Answer each question with a yes or no, and then write a brief note on that particular question if you'd like. It is better to answer questions fairly quickly, without intense reflection.

How does the class feel? Welcoming? Intimidating? _____

Who is talking? Teacher? Students? _____

Is the teacher smiling? _____

Are the kids working on their assigned tasks? _____

Are multiple learning tasks ongoing? _____

Are any kids quietly whispering? Does the teacher respond? How? _____

_____

Do students seem happy? _____

Do students seem friendly toward each other? _____

Does the teacher speak respectfully to students? _____

Do students speak respectfully to each other? _____

Do you see any bullying in the class? _____

What disciplinary procedures are in evidence (e.g., rules posted, good behavior charts)?

_____

Are kids of different races working together? _____

Are there displays of student work in the class? _____

Do the students seek out the teacher for help with a problem? _____

Do the students seek out other students for help with a problem? _____

Is the classroom generally pleasing to look at? _____

Are you happy your child is in this class? Why? _____

In general, I do not recommend widespread assessment of parents' perception of class climate, unless the entire school faculty and administration wish to make some changes in that regard. Rather, the teacher can use the questionnaire in Figure 1.2 with individual parents who visit the classroom, particularly if their child is demonstrating behavioral problems. If that parent sees that the class climate is positive overall, she may be somewhat more willing to work with the teacher in helping alleviate some of her child's behavioral disturbances. Of course, parents must realize that this informal measure is not a summation of how effective a teacher may be with all children. Rather, parents might wish to use this measure as a discussion starter with their child's teacher for next year to begin a dialogue about what seems to work with their child.

HOW DO I IMPROVE CLASS CLIMATE?

Collecting data on class climate simply for the sake of collecting data is not at all helpful. Rather, teachers must be in a position to effect change toward a more positive classroom experience for all students.

First, if a particular student's individual responses indicate a negative perception of the class, the teacher should plan instructional opportunities to make the student's learning experiences more positive. If a particular child's responses indicate a sense of aloneness, perhaps the teacher could formulate specific cooperative learning opportunities (e.g., cooperative group work on a major project) for the class that would facilitate more positive social interactions for that student. Teachers may wish to talk directly with the student about forming friendships with others in the class who share similar interests. As another option, the teacher could subtly preselect a potential friend with similar social characteristics as the target student (e.g., perhaps another shy person for a particularly timid student or another "rowdy" person for an active or boisterous student). The teacher may then arrange a special opportunity for the pair to work together as peer buddies.

In addition to individual student efforts, Uhlig (2014) describes a school-wide effort to improve the climate for the entire student body. At D.C. Everest Middle School in Wausau, Wisconsin, when students return for the second school semester, each student is greeted with a "happy note" on his locker. The notes present a positive message such as "Just be you! No one can change who you are," "Stay positive today," "You look great." The notes were written by two school clubs, as part of the anti-bullying effort at the school, and most of the students respond quite positively. The principal, Mr. Casey Nye, says the notes are ". . . one piece to a whole bunch of things we're doing to make this a positive environment. It's about establishing a [positive school] culture in the long run" (Uhlig, 2014).

Other schools in Utah and Wisconsin have also utilized this happy note idea to improve school climate (Uhlig, 2014). In particular, I want to present this idea in this book because individual teachers can easily do this two or three times each year! Teachers may wish to write the first happy notes themselves, but later they could use students in the class to write happy notes for others.

SUMMARY

As these examples indicate, teachers can implement many things to improve class climate, either for specific troubled students in the class or for the class as a whole. One thing is certain: when teachers strive to make the class climate as positive as possible for all students, including those who present disciplinary challenges, everyone in the class will benefit (Brand, 2011; Uhlig, 2014).

Marzano's perspective (2003, 2007) emphasizes withitness as one essential element for effective class discipline, and there are few more impressive ways for teachers to demonstrate withitness than by increasing their own knowledge of how students collectively experience their classroom. In that sense, an assessment of class climate may be the first step for many teachers to become more with-it. Consideration of class climate, and perhaps assessment thereof, is therefore recommended for classrooms across all grade levels. Such assessment may show ways in which teachers can enhance their class climate with relative little effort.

Strategy 2

Morning Meetings to Improve Behavior

CONDUCTING MORNING MEETINGS

When teachers wish to focus on building a more positive class climate, they may want to consider holding morning meetings. Morning meetings can work wonders by helping a teacher set a very positive tone for his class each day (Dabbs, 2013; Ellis, 2009; Kriete, 2012; Layton, 2014; Rohr, 2014). Marzano (2003) indicates that class meetings are an excellent way to teach students personal responsibility for their behavior, and many others recommend this strategy as a foundation for effective discipline (Gold, 2013; Kriete, 2012).

Teachers might begin their morning meeting by greeting students by name and perhaps providing an opportunity for students to greet each other. Next, they might share the daily schedule; answer questions students might have; have students share good news about things they did at home or in school; or discuss issues that arise in that class, including bullying, academic performance, or problem behaviors. In many primary classes, teachers complete a calendar activity (day, month, season), or discuss upcoming holidays (Ellis, 2009; Rubenstein, 2014). Sometimes teachers can include a song or poem or share a daily joke. While various teachers have developed specific activities they include each day, or even specific rules for the morning meeting (Gold, 2013), others use a more open approach to the activities they undertake in the meeting (Ellis, 2009).

Whatever activities the teacher chooses as part of the meeting, the morning meeting is intended to set a tone for respectful learning, establish trust, motivate and excite students, create empathy, encourage collaboration, and finally, support social and emotional learning (Dabbs, 2013). Further, nothing can enhance a teacher's withitness, as Marzano (2003) emphasizes, more than regular morning meetings, because these meetings will highlight things going on with the students more so than other types of classwork. Teachers using morning meetings will be much more in touch with their students' lives.

As these activities indicate, the overall goal for the morning meeting should be to establish a positive class climate. For that reason, teachers should not use most of the meeting time to discuss disciplinary problems in class. However, such a discussion can be part of a morning meeting activity, as it provides an opportunity for students to discuss behavioral issues independent of a specific behavioral infraction.

I strongly recommend teachers use this strategy in the primary and elementary grades, where they control the class for the entire school day. In that situation, they can certainly include a fifteen- to thirty-minute morning meeting in the schedule each day. While teachers in departmentalized schools (indeed, any teacher who is teaching a certain group of students for only one period a day) may have some difficulty scheduling a class meeting, the morning meeting strategy can even be undertaken on a school-wide basis. Teachers can implement this strategy in an extended homeroom period. For example, in all middle schools in Lexington, Kentucky, teachers engage in daily morning meetings with their classes during the homeroom period (Ellis, 2009). Teachers could also implement morning meetings during class time in first period each day, perhaps in a block schedule situation in which the first-period class changes daily. Of course, academic time is critical, and no educator would ever recommend taking thirty minutes of a ninety-minute block each day for a morning meeting. In that case, shortening morning meetings might be an option (limited to ten minutes), or teachers might undertake the meetings two or three times each week.

> The morning meeting is intended to set a tone for respectful learning, establish trust, motivate and excite students, create empathy, encourage collaboration, and finally support social and emotional learning.

THE BACKGROUND FOR MORNING MEETINGS

Glasser's Reality Therapy

William Glasser (1969) suggests the use of class meetings in his approach "Reality Therapy." In that therapeutic approach, Glasser attempts to assist students emotionally and academically as well as build a positive sense of community among students in school. He describes three types of class meetings focused on different class concerns:

1. *Open-ended meetings* to discuss any topic or issue before the class
2. *Diagnostic meetings* to allow the teacher to determine academic understanding
3. *Problem-solving meetings* to discuss students' behaviors, emotions, or troubling situations

Recommendations for these meetings are based on the concept that students should jointly discuss issues in their class, which encourages students to take more responsibility for themselves and others within the class. For the problem-solving meetings, Glasser recommends discussion of behavioral concerns that center around seating plans, class rules, home problems, and recent classroom incidents involving misbehavior. This initial work provides the basis for today's emphasis on morning meetings to enhance class climate.

The Responsive Classroom

Of course, many variations of the class meeting idea have been developed over the years and incorporated into more comprehensive and recent initiatives. For example, the morning meeting is a major component of an instructional approach referred to as the *Responsive Classroom* (Gold, 2013; Layton, 2014; see also several commercially available books from the Northeast Foundation for Children, Inc., and www.responsiveclassroom.org). The *Responsive Classroom* approach is designed to create positive classroom relationships both between teachers and students, and among students. This approach fosters cooperation and a caring attitude among all class members in order to stress that students are part of a caring community. In one randomized, controlled trial that examines the *Responsive Classroom* approach, researchers compare 13 schools using this technique with 11 schools that didn't (Layton, 2014). Results show that children in classrooms where the technique was fully implemented tended to behave better and score measurably higher in math and reading than students in comparison classrooms.

CARE for Kids

One of the most recent iterations of the morning meeting is the *CARE for Kids* program, which was developed and implemented in Louisville, Kentucky. So far, the program is utilized in fifty-five elementary schools and at all twenty-three county middle schools in the sixth- and seventh-grade classes (Rubenstein, 2014). This program is not yet available commercially, but is identified as a model social-emotional skills developmental program (Ellis, 2009; Rubenstein, 2014). Several morning meetings from this program are featured on a video by the George Lucas Educational Foundation as a model program for school improvement (Ellis, 2009; additional information is available at www.Edutopia.org).

The *CARE for Kids* curriculum was spearheaded by Mr. Sheldon Berman, the school superintendent at the time. CARE is an acronym representing four goals of the program: Community, Autonomy, Relationships, and Empowerment. The teacher emphasizes each goal or component in the morning meeting. For example, depending on the activities the teacher chooses for the meetings, students may discuss a behavioral problem that has occurred in class, or may do an exercise in which students are taught to compliment each other. Instruction in a wide variety of positive social skills can be included, and while teachers in this program are provided with several days of professional development training as a component of the *CARE for Kids* program, teachers who do not have access to this training can undertake the morning meeting individually, as one approach to improving their class climate.

AN AGENDA FOR THE MORNING MEETING

Different teachers use different agendas and different activities in the morning meeting, depending on the needs and focus of the classroom. Also, some teachers invest more time in these meetings than others. Time frames for the morning meeting range from ten to thirty minutes daily. Gold (2012) uses the following general structure for a twenty-minute morning meeting in her elementary class, as the *Responsive Classroom* instructional approach recommends (see www.responsive-classroom.org).

> **Greeting:** Teacher greets each child by name with a handshake. After a few meetings, teachers can add a "What's the news?" to the greeting (e.g., "Hey there, Billy. Glad to see you. What's the news?"). (2 minutes)
>
> **Sharing:** Teacher has a few students share something daily. Using five students each day, teachers can have each student share something personal each week. (5 minutes)
>
> **Activity:** Activities are included to teach social skills (e.g., greetings, complimenting others, disagreeing gracefully, etc.) in order to build a community and value each student in the class. (10 minutes)
>
> **Message:** This includes a summary of the goal or moral of the activity above, any class news or class announcements, and schedule for the day. (3 minutes)

In addition to this general morning meeting agenda, two additional sample morning meeting agendas are in Figure 2.1.

While the morning meeting is intended primarily as a preventative strategy rather than a targeted intervention, the teacher can use it to target specific misbehaviors of individual students. That type of targeted application of the morning meeting is in Strategy 17 (Response to Intervention for Behavioral Change), where it is used to improve the behavior of one student.

HOW DO I BEGIN MORNING MEETINGS?

Different advocates of morning meetings recommend somewhat different types of activities (Ellis, 2009; Gold, 2013). Some have commercially available materials associated with the *Responsive Classroom* initiative (Gold, 2013; Kriete, 2012; Rohr, 2014), and others use nonpublished curriculum materials for various activities (Ellis, 2009). Nevertheless, teachers with or without such curricula are encouraged to begin to use this strategy (Dabbs, 2013), and the following steps, adapted from several sources (Dabbs, 2013; Gold, 2013; Rubenstein, 2014), can help provide some guidance for you to begin morning meetings in your class.

Figure 2.1: Additional Sample Morning Meeting Agendas

"Peer-to-Peer Greeting" Agenda

Early in the school year, teachers may wish to begin morning meetings with peer-to-peer greetings in addition to teacher greetings. This helps students focus on others in the class community. Thus, the peer greeting becomes the main focus of the agenda.

Teacher Greeting	Teacher greets students by name as they come through the door. (1 minute)
Peer Greetings	Teacher says, "I want us all to get to know each other, so we'll count off into groups of three students each." Then, have students count off ("One, two, three, one, two, three," etc.) around the room. Teacher then says, "Okay, each group of three students introduce yourselves to one another, and learn one interesting positive thing about one another. Then you will introduce to the class your group members by name and by describing that one important thing." (10 minutes)
Announcements	Teacher thanks everyone and proceeds with any class news or class announcements, and schedule for the day. (3 minutes)

A "Problem to Discuss" Agenda

At times, several members of the class may exhibit behavior problems, and the morning meeting can provide an opportunity to address those problems. A discussion of a general, recurring behavior problem may therefore be the focus of the agenda.

Teacher Greeting	Teacher greets students by name as they come through the door. (1 minute)
Problem Discussion	Teacher says, "We need to discuss a problem I've seen, and several of you have done this, so it's a class-wide problem. Anyone want to guess what that problem might be?" Teacher should solicit several answers, and if students can't identify the problem, the teacher should then describe it. Mention also why and how the behavior problem impacts the class negatively (loss of class time while teacher and students deal with the problem, etc.). Also, briefly discuss why students might do that behavior (i.e., what that student's feelings and needs might be when he does it). That serves as the basis for the next step, generating alternative behaviors. (10 minutes)
Alternatives	Teacher then asks, "Okay, when a student feels that way, can we think of things that that person might do instead of the problem behavior?" Have students generate some alternative ideas that could help a student get her needs met. Have another student write those ideas down on the whiteboard. (5 minutes)
Announcements	Teacher thanks everyone and proceeds with any class news or class announcements, and schedule for the day. (2 minutes)

Engage in some personal professional development.

Set a time for the meeting.

Identify specific sharing ideas and activities.

Introduce the morning meeting concept to students.

Communicate with parents and the administration.

Use a stripped-down morning meeting initially.

Implement more complicated activities and discuss tougher topics later.

Involve as many teachers as possible in your school.

Engage in some personal professional development. Prior to holding a morning meeting, teachers should review all of the references here. A reference list is at the back of the book so, using the author's name found in parentheses for each strategy, teachers can find the actual article and read it; many of the articles are online to make this a bit easier. Teachers should also watch the Ellis video by the George Lucas Educational Foundation (see Ellis, 2009, in the reference list) to get a sense of what morning meetings might involve. I also encourage teachers to review the materials associated with the *Responsive Classroom* (Gold, 2013; Rohr, 2014). Of course, any new intervention will require that the teacher have a good understanding of what he wants to accomplish, and this review of materials in the references should provide you with several ideas for activities you might wish to include in your morning meeting. You might also seek out colleagues who are already using morning meetings and/or collaborate with other teachers as they begin the process (Dabbs, 2013).

Set a time for the meeting. Ideally, the meeting should happen each morning and be limited to less than thirty minutes. Initially, teachers may wish to aim for a fifteen-minute morning meeting and plan several activities for that time frame (students greeting others, complimenting others, sharing a success story, etc.). Dabbs (2013) indicates that teachers will want enough time to connect with students but not so much that students have difficulty staying focused.

Identify specific sharing ideas and activities. At first, the morning meetings should be relatively free of heavy discussions of serious behavioral problems and should focus on more positive activities. Teachers are encouraged to create their own activities for the morning meeting, and various activities are available online (Ellis, 2009; Gold, 2013). Here is one sample activity to consider for your first meeting:

> After you greet each student at the door, you may sit the students in a circle, and then have each student formulate an accurate compliment for the student sitting seven places to their right. Because students tend to sit beside their best friends, this activity typically results in students formulating a compliment for

students they know somewhat less well. After giving them a moment to think about a compliment, have them go around the circle, with each student taking turns, walking to their target student and then delivering the compliment. After that is complete, have a brief discussion of how it felt to get a genuine compliment from someone who is not your best friend.

Again, teachers should feel free to develop their own activities for the morning meeting, and in some cases, the activity may serve as the only component on the agenda for that meeting. Other activity ideas:

- State how we are each feeling today in one sentence!
- Let's all share one success we had in the past week!
- Did you feel sad this week? Why?
- What do you think about . . . ? (This activity allows the teacher to focus the morning meeting on a news item that might be of national significance and might require some discussion at school; e.g., a war beginning that involves American troops or a national tragedy such as 9/11.)

Any of these activity ideas can provide interesting discussion options, as members of the class share something from their lives.

Introduce the morning meeting concept to students. Student participation is critical, and letting them know what you expect is very important. During your first couple of meetings, discuss the idea of a class-wide morning meeting for your class. Tell students what your hopes and goals are (e.g., making all students feel safe and welcome, helping all students in the class make friends, etc.), and also how important each student's contribution is (Dabbs, 2013). This is critical because a major goal for the morning meetings is to let students know you value them and their contributions to your class (Gold, 2013).

Communicate with parents and the administration. Write a brief note to the principal and all parents explaining the morning meeting and what you hope to accomplish with it. Let them know how you intend to use it in your class and the time frame for it. Dabbs (2013) recommends inviting parents to join a morning meeting.

Use a stripped-down morning meeting initially. Hold a few meetings that are fairly brief and include only one or two activities before you get into more complicated activities (Dabbs, 2013). Then, once you are confident with the initial few meetings behind you, share all the possible activities and components of the morning meeting structure with the students. This stripped-down meeting might include only a greeting for students, having students share a success from the day before, and announcements.

Implement more complicated activities and discuss tougher topics later. You'll soon find that the class itself may devise activities as adaptations to the model, and there is a wide array of activities that can be helpful (many articles listed in the References section describe activities). These might include reviewing disciplinary rules and policies, discussing a bullying situation, teaching a particular social skill (e.g., escaping a verbal argument, disagreeing respectfully), asking students to discuss their feelings (anger, fear, etc.), or other, more involved discussions dealing with emotional and social interactions. These tend to be tougher topics to discuss, and students should have a number of morning meetings under their belt prior to tackling such topics. However, both teachers and students typically demonstrate a fairly sharp learning curve when it comes to morning meetings, so after a week or so, you should be able to hold some serious discussions of behavioral issues in the class or deep-seated students' emotions.

Involve as many teachers as possible in your school. While individual teachers across the grade levels are encouraged to use morning meetings (Gold, 2013), efforts to involve other teachers, or perhaps even all the teachers in the school, hold the real payoff in terms of changing school climate overall. Also, teachers working together are more likely to continue this strategy over the long term, making positive, long-term differences in the lives of kids. Finally, in departmentalized middle and high schools, using some time during homeroom for the morning meeting can have a huge impact on school climate overall, and a school-wide implementation of the morning meeting is strongly recommended. Some of the examples here involve every teacher in the school (Rubenstein, 2014).

EVIDENCE FOR EFFICACY OF MORNING MEETINGS

While the morning meeting has not been the specific targeted strategy in any controlled research to date, there is research data documenting the positive effects of various social-emotional learning programs overall (Rubenstein, 2014) as well as a controlled study of the *Responsive Classroom* approach (Layton, 2014). Further, significant anecdotal evidence shows that the morning meeting procedure will improve students' engagement, build a more positive class climate, reduce behavioral problems, and possibly even increase academic performance for troubled students (Dabbs, 2013; Ellis, 2009; Layton, 2014). For example, Sheldon Berman, the superintendent of schools in Louisville, Kentucky, indicates that improvements in school climate, social behaviors, and academic performance have all resulted from implementation of morning meetings in the context of the *CARE for Kids* initiative (Ellis, 2009).

> Significant anecdotal evidence shows that the morning meeting procedure will improve students' engagement, build a more positive class climate, reduce behavioral problems, and possibly even increase academic performance for troubled students.

Other schools have also seen disciplinary improvement when using morning meetings. When morning meetings were initiated at Stewartsville Elementary in Bedford, Virginia, in the 2011–2012 academic year as part of their *Responsive Classroom* initiative, disciplinary referrals to the office were cut in half (Rohr, 2014).

The next year, by enhancing that initiative and focusing on building community within the school, disciplinary referrals were cut again, by two-thirds.

Here is one principal's testimony on what the morning meetings did for her school in California.

> When I first learned about the morning meeting model, I was working as an elementary school principal in Pasadena, California. I was new to that school, so I was skeptical about launching too many initiatives, but also curious about how it could work to transform my school and the lives of our students.
>
> I'd come to a school that was in a bit of trouble. Kids were struggling with behavior issues outside of class, teachers were finding ways to remove kids from their class, and it was clear that I needed to put my faith in something that I believed could improve the culture and climate of the school. I knew that I had some serious work ahead of me if I was going to build a positive sense of community. So I worked with a small team of teachers to launch the morning meeting—and was thrilled with how it spread like wildfire across our campus.
>
> Having been able to observe this school pre- and post-morning meeting, I can tell you that it was transformational. We didn't use a fancy prepared program or spend thousands of dollars on training. We simply rolled up our sleeves and, with the help of this one new teacher (and good resources), we were able to "rebuild" the school community and encourage kids to care for one another. The resulting decrease in bullying and increase in pupil attendance was amazing! Kids began taking ownership of their actions and resolving their own conflicts. They began to feel safe at school and share more about their lives. They were able to meet each other face-to-face and appreciate and honor their differences. *(Dabbs, 2013)*

Another teacher, Ms. Robben Seadler from Breckinridge-Franklin Elementary School in Louisville, Kentucky, likewise provides powerful testimony.

> The better the relationship you have with the kids, the more they're going to want to learn, and the more they're going to take ownership of what you're trying to teach them, and when they feel that way, the behavior problems aren't there. *(Rubenstein, 2014)*

While testimonies can represent one type of proof of efficacy, the schools implementing the *CARE for Kids* program report more concrete evidence. In fact, the hard data on disciplinary problems at various schools confirm the evaluations of these educators. At Breckinridge-Franklin Elementary School, suspensions and discipline referrals fell by 50 percent between 2006 and 2008 when the teachers implemented morning meetings (Rubenstein, 2014).

Carrithers Middle School is another school in the Louisville system that saw a dramatic improvement in discipline. Their in-school suspensions dropped 9 percent in the fall of 2009 and out-of-school suspensions declined, as well, when teachers instituted morning meetings. Further, time-outs fell by 52 percent. Academic performance also improved at Carrithers in that time frame. During the first six weeks of 2008, students failed a total of 411 classes. However, in 2009, the comparable figure was just 195 (Rubenstein, 2014). This represents dramatic, data-based evidence from multiple schools that using morning meetings will help improve class climate and foster greater academic growth.

EFFICACY EVIDENCE TEACHERS SHOULD COLLECT

As the discussion above indicates, individual teachers should collect specific evidence that demonstrates the efficacy of morning meetings, and indeed all disciplinary strategies (Bender, 2007; Marzano, 2003; Sousa, 2009). Further, in school-wide applications of this strategy, the administrator may also aggregate data. Individual teachers using the morning meeting should keep a record for at least one month of how many times they had to discipline or call out certain students with problems, and certainly teachers should note how many times specific students had to be sent from the classroom (these are individual student data but may also be a whole-class count). During that time, the teacher can begin the professional development exploration of the concept of the morning meeting, beginning with the online resources in the references.

After one month, the teacher should begin morning meetings as described herein and continue to note the data above. The morning meetings must be given time to work, so teachers should continue these meetings for at least three months while collecting these data.

> The efficacy of morning meetings should be demonstrated by specific evidence collected by each individual teacher.

For school-wide applications of this approach, administrators may chart the types of data described by various schools in the research results above. At the end of three months, schools are quite likely to see strong evidence of improved school climate and improved school-wide discipline. Some advocates (see above) describe this as a transformative school-wide experience, and certainly schools desiring a more positive school climate should implement this strategy.

SUMMARY

The use of morning meetings as a disciplinary tool is an old idea, but it has been rejuvenated in the *Responsive Classroom* approach as I noted above (Gold, 2013; Layton, 2014; see www.responsiveclassroom.org). While individual teachers can employ this strategy, it may be easier to implement when undertaken as a whole-school type of project. Further, as this discussion shows, many schools are using this approach, and most educators who try it will never teach again without using morning meetings (please see the video in Ellis, 2009). From the perspective of withitness, this strategy will make teachers much more aware of what is happening in their classroom because it provides students the opportunity to open up in a way that typical classroom instruction doesn't. Therefore, this approach is likely to improve the class climate for individual teachers or the entire school.

This approach is recommended for students with virtually any type of behavior problem, ranging from kids merely seeking attention to overt conduct disorders or even highly aggressive students. In point of fact, almost all students will benefit from feeling a sense of community within the classroom, and the morning meeting is designed to emphasize that sense of a caring community. This approach can therefore be recommended for almost any teacher who wishes to devote time to improving class climate.

Strategy 3

Teaching With Movement to Curb Problem Behaviors

MOVEMENT AND BRAIN-FRIENDLY TEACHING

Many veteran teachers realize that the instructional techniques used in class can positively impact class discipline. Specifically, the research collectively referred to as *brain-compatible instruction* has long suggested that representing educational content via movement can help students learn the content, and positively impact behavior (Bender, 2007; Sousa, 2009). In fact, movement that is built into the fabric of the class, as well as regular exercise programs, positively impacts behavior of students who demonstrate hyperactivity, because such instruction provides an outlet for movement in the class (Benelli, 2014; Reed, 2011; Rowh, 2014; Sousa, 2009).

Movement has many positive effects in the classroom (Bender, 2007). First, movement tends to rejuvenate attention among those students whose attention may have wandered a bit (Benelli, 2014; Reed, 2011; Rowh, 2014). Further, movement and exercise increases levels of neurotransmitters in the students' brains (e.g., norepinephrine and dopamine), so physical activity of any type seems to have a positive effect on students' sense of well-being in class (Rowh, 2014).

Further, movement that represents academic content will tend to reinforce mastery of that content and results in longer-term memory for that information (Sousa, 2009). Specifically, when students sit for thirty minutes or more, blood tends to pool in their seat and feet, making less blood available for brain activity (Sousa, 2009), and movement within the class tends to decrease that problem.

> Brain-compatible instruction research has long suggested that representing educational content via movement can help students learn the content, and positively impact behavior.

TWO APPROACHES TO TEACHING WITH MOVEMENT

At least two differing schools of thought advocate use of movement in teaching. First, there is some research to suggest that many types of nonspecific classroom movements, even traditional exercise, assist students with hyperactivity to pay increased attention in the classroom (Benelli, 2014; Reed, 2011; Rowh, 2014). Many teachers use exercise balls rather than desks for students with attention-deficit/hyperactivity disorder (ADHD) in order to help those students cope with their intrinsic need for movement during class, and research is generally supportive of this trend (Rowh, 2014). Other schools use "motor break" boxes, which contain Slinkys, stretch bands, or small plastic balls, in order to provide small-motor stimulation for children with ADHD (Rowh, 2014). Reed (2011) reports on several teachers who reduce behavior problems by requiring twenty minutes of sustained cardio exercise daily, and other research supports the use of exercise to reduce behavioral problems (Benelli, 2014).

In contrast to this "nonspecific movement" school of thought, other researchers advocate use of movements that are specifically intended to represent the academic content of the lessons (Bender, 2007; Sousa, 2009). In this approach, teachers develop movements that represent the content the students will learn, and are repeated over a period of time both to provide movement within the class and reinforce the content the students need to master. Perhaps a content-based movement instructional example will help.

As one example of movement that represents content, one can use one's own body movements to teach longitude and latitude. Students often have difficulty at first, confusing the two (e.g., is longitude the up-and-down lines on the map or the lines across the page?). To help students remember the distinction using movement, a teacher might have students stand up at their desks and raise their arms high above their head, while saying. "This is longitude, lines are long." Next they stretch each arm out to either side of their body parallel to the floor, while saying, "This is latitude, flat across the map!" Students should repeat those movements while chanting those sentences three or four times with each movement, more quickly each time, and the repetition will help lock those concepts into their long-term memory.

> Some researchers advocate use of movements that are specifically intended to represent the academic content of the lessons.

After the students finish the movements, the teacher should conclude the exercise by doing two things: reinforcing the learning and giving the definition of latitude and longitude. While pointing to the map, the teacher might indicate that longitude represents distance from the prime meridian, in Greenwich, England, whereas latitude represents distance from the equator. The teacher should then repeat this movement daily, as long as the students are studying the map reading/interpretation instructional unit, perhaps for a week or two. Thus, the teacher will use the movement in the repeated exercise to teach and continually reinforce the essential content from the instructional unit—longitude and latitude lines on a map.

Other examples of movement to teach content are in literature, including

- using one's body to represent parts of a letter (Sousa, 2009)
- using movement of one's hands to teach locations of all continents (Chapman, 2000)
- moving on giant number lines across the floor of the mathematics class (Bender, 2013)
- movement for a bar graph (Bender, 2013)
- teaching parts of a circle (Bender, 2013)

GUIDELINES FOR TEACHING WITH MOVEMENT

There are some guidelines for teaching content using movement. First, the goal of using movement is to make the content more fun! Teachers can set a tone for the movement by their own level of excitement and by moving around the room as students complete the exercises.

> ### Guidelines for Teaching With Movement
>
> Make it fun!
>
> Use diagrams/pictures for movement ideas.
>
> Select only essential content for the movement.
>
> Partner the movement with a chant, a song, or teaching questions.
>
> Repeat the movement throughout the unit of study.

Almost any content that can be pictured in a diagram can be a basis for a movement exercise. Teachers may begin the use of movement by reviewing the diagrams and visual aids they use during a given unit of instruction and determining which might be appropriate as a movement exercise. Teachers should then creatively develop such movements, perhaps accompanied by a chant such as the one described earlier about latitude and longitude. In some cases, teachers may wish to have a team of students develop such a movement based on an overhead or diagram for use by all members of the class.

However, teachers must selectively determine which content to represent by movement exercises. They should not try a different movement each day, because use of so many different movements is not likely to assist long-term memory. Rather, teachers should develop a movement that represents the most essential content within an instructional unit. They should then teach that movement to the class, emphasizing how the movement represents the essential content.

Next, if possible, teachers may wish to partner the movement with a chant or song that emphasizes essential elements of the content. Repeated questions when coupled with student responses tend to reinforce the content the students need to master.

Finally, teachers should use the movement repeatedly over a two- or three-week instructional unit, repeating it daily. This will reinforce the most significant content in the instructional unit and is quite likely to result in lifelong learning of that content.

EFFICACY RESEARCH ON TEACHING WITH MOVEMENT

Over the past several decades, various exercise- and/or movement-based instructional programs have been shown to reduce behavior problems among students with ADHD and increase achievement in some students (Benelli, 2014; King & Gurian, 2006; Reed, 2011; Rowh, 2014; Sousa, 2009; Yell, 1988). In one recent article, King and Gurian (2006) report on a single school case study in which the school faculty is able to close a 20 percent achievement gap between underachieving young males and their female peers merely by beginning to teach in a boy-friendly manner, emphasizing movement-based instruction, coupled with specific topics of interest to males.

In general, however, less research is available on the efficacy of movements that represent specific content. Although such movements are likely to positively impact behavioral issues within the classroom, because any movements can have a positive impact, there is no evidence to date that content-based movements alone will actually increase retention for specific content.

With that concern noted, one might well ask what difference it makes, since virtually all movements can positively impact behavior, and movements that teach content are at least somewhat more likely to familiarize students with that content. Also, you can easily create these exercises. For that reason, I tend to advocate teaching using movements that are specifically developed to represent academic content.

EFFICACY DATA TEACHERS SHOULD COLLECT: A CASE STUDY

While I recommend this strategy for class-wide application, teachers may on occasion wish to use this tactic to alleviate certain behavioral problems a particular student demonstrates. In such a case, teachers should begin various movement exercises within the class after collecting baseline data on the problem behavior. Next, they should implement a movement-based instructional strategy, while continuing to take data on the ongoing behavior problem. The following is a case study example.

Billy is a fourth-grade student who has, over two years, taken medication for ADHD. While the medication does help, Billy is still quite hyperactive and consistently demonstrates unruly behavior in class, particularly during the morning instructional period that lasts from 8:10 A.M. until recess at 10:15. Billy's teacher, Mr. Palmer, decides to implement a specific behavioral improvement plan for him. First, Mr. Palmer identifies two of the most problematic behaviors Billy demonstrates and take some baseline data on each problem during that time frame each day. He decides that the most disruptive behavior is verbal aggression with other students. Billy also presents many out-of-seat behaviors in the classroom. Therefore, over a two-week period, Mr. Palmer measures these behaviors by noting each occurrence on an index card he keeps at the teacher's desk. Every time Billy gets into a verbal argument with someone, Mr. Palmer notes the date and time, and he also notes each time he has to tell Billy to return to his desk. He then transfers these data to a chart each day. These baseline data are in the first section of the chart in Figure 3.1.

Figure 3.1: Billy's Baseline and Intervention Data

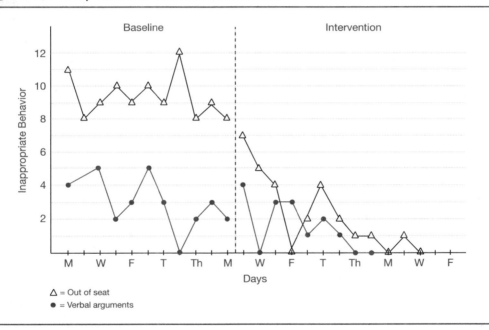

Δ = Out of seat
● = Verbal arguments

As these baseline data indicate, Billy is much more likely to be out-of-seat than involved in a verbal argument. The data indicate that his out-of-seat behavior occurrence averages nearly nine times daily whereas his verbal aggression averages only three times each day. However, both behavior problems are much too frequent and highly disruptive to the class as a whole. For that reason, Mr. Palmer decides to initiate a movement program in his class, while he continues to note the occurrence of these behavioral problems.

As an intervention, Mr. Palmer settles on a twofold movement strategy. He wants to provide both a morning exercise time for the whole class as well as incorporate movement-based teaching strategies once each morning around 9:15. In order to assure that all students have some exercise, Mr. Palmer leads a ten-minute period of calisthenics at 8:10 each morning, consisting of jumping jacks, crunches, and running in place. These are done in the classroom, with each student participating beside her desk. Then he begins his language arts instruction.

Because the unit of instruction in language arts emphasizes the parts of a personal letter, Mr. Palmer chooses a movement-based teaching strategy Sousa (2009) first published. That tactic involves both a movement and a chant describing parts of a letter (see the box below, "Using the Body to Represent Components of a Letter"). Mr. Palmer teaches this activity to his class on Monday of the third week, and on that same day, he begins his ten-minute morning exercise practice with the entire class. When doing this movement, Mr. Palmer has every class member stand beside his desk, do the movement, and repeat the chant. To make it fun, he has the class say the chant three times each time they do it, with each chant being louder and quicker than the last. He finds that the students really enjoy this memory-enhancing technique and that all class members can, in only one week, remember all parts of the personal letter.

Using the Body to Represent Components of a Letter

Have all of the students stand beside their desks and touch body parts in order to represent parts of a letter.

The Movement	The Chant
Touch top of head	Say, "Opening of the letter says the date."
Salute by touching the brow	Say, "This salutation is the greeting."
Touch chest	Say, "The body of the letter includes the message."
Touch knees (as they close)	Say, "The closing of the letter says 'Yours truly'"
Touch feet	Say, "Your signature is the way you say good-bye."

As shown in Figure 3.1, this dual intervention has an immediate impact on Billy's problem behaviors. First, the number of out-of-seat behaviors Billy demonstrates is reduced almost immediately after the intervention begins, and by the second week of the intervention, these behaviors are significantly reduced during the long morning instructional period. Also, these data show a reduction in Billy's verbal altercations by the end of the second week.

SUMMARY

The teaching with movement strategy is useful for all students but is particularly effective for students with ADHD because of their hyperactive behavior (Reed, 2011; Rowh, 2014). With nearly one in ten children in public schools showing some ADHD behavior (Rowh, 2014), the importance of this strategy cannot be overstated. Further, research shows this to be an effective way to curb misbehavior among a variety of students with an array of conduct disorders. In fact, in the case study example above, it is quite likely that the class-wide exercise that Mr. Palmer implements curbs misbehavior on the part of other students in the class as well as assisting Billy with maintaining his improved behavior. For these reasons, schools are likely to be implementing movement-based instruction much more in the near future.

Strategy 4

A Classroom Respect Policy: Rules for My Class

A RESPECT POLICY FOR EVERYONE

Using specific classroom rules to delineate appropriate and inappropriate behavior in the class is certainly not a new concept, but while many teachers set specific rules for their classroom, only a few teachers give this strategy the attention it requires. For example, many beginning teachers post class rules on the board at the beginning of the year and never or rarely refer to those rules again. Other teachers may mention the rules on occasion but fail to show how the rules benefit students in the class. Others spend almost no time in getting students invested in the class rules, and as one might expect, all of these teacher behaviors are likely to make class rules ineffective in curbing disciplinary problems.

In contrast to these examples of relatively minor efforts at implementing class rules, Marzano (2003; 2007) stresses the intensive use of class rules as a basis for effective discipline. Specifically, two elements deal directly with application of class rules:

1. Applying consequences for lack of adherence to rules and procedures.
2. Acknowledging adherence to rules and procedures.

In order to make behavioral expectations explicit, class rules are essential for every classroom. Further, various educators emphasize class rules within a broader "respect policy" through which teachers stress their desire for everyone in the class to show respect for everyone else (Albert, 1996; McGuire, 1999). The driving concern in such classrooms becomes respect for others, and the rules become something more than merely do and don't statements or the teacher's preferences on specific behaviors. In short, class rules should engender and foster a sense of respect for all class members and guests. In that sense, both the respect policy and the class rules become a solid foundation for improving class climate overall (McGuire, 1999). Also, when teachers present class rules as a respect policy that benefits everyone, students are much more likely to buy in to rule compliance, and this will alleviate some of the minor behavior problems within the class.

Of course, the teacher should state all class rules in positive terms, emphasizing how students and others will behave, and not merely what they won't do! Rules are most effective when they are simple, clean, and direct. However, class rules should also emphasize to some degree why rules are necessary and how rule compliance benefits others in the class. Of course, these two statements may appear to be somewhat conflicting, but attention to each of these ideas can result in a respect policy based on a set of class rules that fosters respect for all class members. The box called "Our Respect Policy Rules" shows one set of rules that exemplifies these ideas.

> When class rules are presented as a respect policy that benefits everyone, students are much more likely to buy in to rule compliance.

Our Respect Policy Rules

1. I will respect others at all times, in my speech and behavior.

2. I will show my respect for others by keeping my arms and legs to myself.

3. I will work as quietly as possible so others can accomplish their work.

4. I will always show respect for the ideas of others, even when I disagree.

5. I will quickly comply with all teacher instructions in order to complete my work in a timely manner.

6. Because I show respect to others, I will expect others to respect me.

7. I will report any infraction of these rules to the teacher in order to maintain a healthy and happy class community.

8. I agree that infraction of any of these rules will cost me some of my recess time and may also involve other penalties.

Note that all of these rules are clear in that they state exactly what students should do, rather than what they shouldn't do. Several of these rules emphasize respect as the overall goal for the class community, and a number of them specifically show the relationship between the rules and the overall class experience of other students. Of course, these rules are not etched in stone, and teachers should feel free to develop their own rules or edit these in any way they see fit for their own classroom. Still, this example shows how rules can be the basis of a policy of respect for all in the class. Also, these rules emphasize the why questions of good behavior.

GUIDELINES FOR USING RESPECT POLICY RULES

While class rules may vary widely from class to class, and should certainly vary across grade levels, there are some guidelines for establishing class rules that will help teachers utilize these more effectively as they strive to maintain a healthy class environment.

Guidelines for a Respect Policy Based on Class Rules

Have students develop clear, concise rules.

Refer to the rules repeatedly early in the semester.

Discuss disciplinary issues in terms of infractions of specific rules.

Use language that emphasizes rule breaking as an offense against the class, not the teacher.

Point out when students are following the rules.

Respect policy rules should include possible penalties for rule infraction.

Have Students Develop Clear, Concise Rules

First, students are much more likely to buy into the class rules if they have a hand in developing the rules. Therefore, in almost every teaching situation, there is a benefit in taking twenty or thirty minutes during the first week of school to have the class discuss what rules might help the class overall. Teachers should initiate this discussion using the concept of "respect for others" in the classroom by asking students what rules might help them show respect for all class members. The class can then, collectively, develop their rules together.

Refer to the Rules Repeatedly Early in the Semester

While having students develop the rules is always a great idea, it does little good if the teacher then ignores the rules completely! I suggest that after the class develops the rules, the teacher mention them every day for several days, by saying something like

> Okay, class, we developed these rules for our class together, and I just want to remind everyone to pay attention to these rules so we can all get our work done in class and don't have to finish it as homework.

Discuss Disciplinary Issues in Terms of Infractions of Specific Rules

Next, when a student does misbehave, the teacher should discuss that misbehavior in terms of the specific rule the student failed to follow. I've taught many behavior management classes for pre-service teachers, and in each I've suggested that a teacher literally point to the rules posted in the classroom when he has to speak to a student. In such cases, the student is quite likely to glance at the posted rules and may be more likely to see her own misbehavior as an offense against the class rules rather than merely something that upset the teacher.

Use Language That Emphasizes Rule Breaking as an Offense Against the Class, Not the Teacher

I also recommend that teachers use language that facilitates a sense that the student has offended the class rather than merely offended the teacher. When a student (named Jessica, for example) calls another student a name or curses loudly in class, the teacher might say something like:

> Jessica! We have all agreed to follow rule one in our respect policy, posted on the wall; it says, "I will respect others at all times, in my speech and my behavior." You are not following that rule when you call your classmates inappropriate names! You'll need to remain inside for the first ten minutes of your recess for that rule infraction, and we'll talk about this then.

By using that language and pointing to the rules, the teacher is emphasizing that Jessica's behavior is an offense against the class. Over time, this message is likely to sink in for most students and will make inappropriate behavior less likely.

Teachers should use language that facilitates a sense that the student has offended the class, rather than merely offended the teacher.

Point Out When Students Are Following the Rules

In addition to pointing to the rules when a problem occurs, teachers should also point out when the class rules are helping to create a positive class environment. In fact, when students are following the rules, they enjoy the class more and are likely to complete their work more quickly. For example, after a good discussion on a topic in class, the teacher might say something like:

> Folks, I want to mention how well you guys all talked with each other today. You all showed respect for each other's opinions, including those you didn't agree with, just like rule number four says, so we all enjoyed this discussion today. So, here's a big THANK YOU! to the whole class. Because you got so much done, I don't think we'll need any homework from our history books tonight! How does that sound?

Within this statement, the teacher compliments the class, points out the advantage of following rules, and reinforces the message by rewarding the class with less homework. These are all excellent ways to emphasize the respect policy rules in the classroom.

Respect Policy Rules Should Include Possible Penalties for Rule Infraction

The respect policy should include some mention of the types of penalties that may be involved when students don't follow the rules (McGuire, 1999). While teachers should be careful not to go overboard by delineating the cost of every type of infraction, some mention of the penalties involved can help such penalties seem less arbitrary. Students should see teachers following the guidelines stipulated within the respect policy rules, and although teachers must have considerable leeway in all disciplinary situations—after all, rule infractions differ in frequency, intensity, and level of severity—teachers should note within the respect policy the types of penalties students may expect.

SUMMARY

Again, many teachers post rules for conduct within the classroom and then seem to never refer to them again. Other teachers are quite at ease in a wide variety of disciplinary situations without using posted rules. Still, I do recommend the use of class rules within the broader construct of a classroom respect policy. Further, use of posted respect policy rules can help alleviate some types of minor behaviors and will make teachers' disciplinary decisions seem less arbitrary to the misbehaving students. For beginning teachers in particular, I believe use of respect policy rules can be of great benefit, as all teachers generally struggle a bit in maintaining discipline in the class during their first year or so of teaching.

Finally, respect policy rules such as those described herein can provide the basis for many other disciplinary strategies later in this text, such as personal goal setting and self-monitoring. Therefore, please assume respect policy rules are a backdrop in these discussions.

Strategy 5

Adult Mentoring to Reach Unreachable Kids

ADULT MENTORS IN ACTION

Mentoring programs were a focus of the Clinton administration in the late 1990s and have been a national focus since that time. Mentoring programs in schools have been used with some success as dropout prevention programs and in curbing serious behavior problems (Bender, 2007; Clinton & Miles, 1999; Vanderwerf, 2014). While some mentoring programs involve older students mentoring younger students (this type of mentoring is discussed in Strategy 13: The Personal Responsibility Strategy), I present adult mentoring here. Adult mentoring involves using adults from the local community to partner with troubled students in school-wide mentoring programs.

Adult mentoring has been described as a one-to-one relationship between two people of different ages and who are not relatives, whose relationship is formed to support the younger person throughout their youth (Bender, 2007). Of course, there are many factors that put young people at risk for developing poor social skills or behavioral problems, including violent behavior, but research shows that a caring adult who bonds with a student and is available to the student over time can positively influence the direction of that student's behavior and overall social development (Bender, 2007; Clinton & Miles, 1999; Katz, 1997; Vanderwerf, 2014).

In addition to offering support for kids in crisis, adult mentors can often provide a basis for sustained self-reflection on their behavior. This can work to improve bad behavior, even when other strategies fail (Vanderwerf, 2014).

> Adult mentoring is a one-to-one relationship between two people who are of different ages whose relationship is formed to support the younger person.

A MENTORING MIRACLE

Imagine the following scenario. A school faculty seeks to improve the behavior of the entire student body and curb a growing trend toward misbehavior in the school. Together they approach the principal to ask for ideas. The principal considers the issue, and after a time of reflection and communication with his peers, he indicates a willingness to explore adult mentoring, school-wide. Since no budget is available, such a program requires that every teacher agree to take two additional students in their class the following year. That would allow the principal to free up a veteran teacher's time, and one classroom space as a mentoring center. The principal and faculty then canvas the community for mentors who are willing to undergo a background check and mentor for one hour per week. After two months, they have spoken at and solicited mentors from churches, garden clubs, Rotary, the Pilot Club, the local Moose organization, and many other community organizations.

At this point, the principal has twenty-one names on a list; these are the adults in the community who have said they will volunteer to help the school by mentoring a troubled kid. The principal and faculty are very pleased, and they plan an evening meal kickoff for the school mentoring program. They'll partner these mentors with twenty-one of the most troubled kids at the school, and they believe that curbing the bad behavior of some, even half, of the twenty-one kids in the school will drastically change the school climate. They invite the parents of those twenty-one kids and the prospective mentors to the school for the dinner kickoff.

Now comes the miracle: While the school principal expects twenty-one adult mentors to show up that night, just over eighty adults walk through the doors! These men and women, many retired teachers, others just concerned community members who want to help, walk into the meal that evening, volunteering to give back to their community by helping troubled kids in schools! The principal has two immediate problems, both easily solved. First, he has to quickly order some chicken from a local fast food eatery to feed the multitude, and second, he has to review student folders the next day to find sixty more kids that could benefit from adult mentoring. Wouldn't that be a wonderful problem for every school to have?

Of course, this is a real example. It happened just that way in Green County, Georgia (Clinton & Miles, 1999). At their request, I'll not mention the names of those involved, but I have often visited the mentoring center at this school to observe this adult mentoring program. In fact, adult mentoring in this example drastically improved behavior school-wide. Imagine dramatically improving the behavior of the most problematic kids in school—say 5 or 10 percent of the school population. Wouldn't that result in a drastic improvement in your school overall? This mentoring program continued at that school for the next decade, as long as

> While the school principal expected twenty-one adult mentors to show up that night, just over eighty adults walked through those doors volunteering for adult mentoring!

that principal remained in that location. I interviewed him several times, and as I said, I have visited the mentoring classroom there many times to see for myself the amazing impact that adult mentoring has on very troubled kids. Although not all mentoring partnerships worked out, most did, and the improvement in behavior in the school was tangible; one could sense it walking down the hallways. Each year, the teachers consistently chose to have somewhat larger classes, because no funding was available for this mentoring program (Clinton & Miles, 1999). However, those teachers believed that adult mentoring drastically improved behavior in the school, and therefore this strategy improved their own working conditions!

When a school wishes to dramatically influence the behavior of all students in a positive direction, I repeatedly recommend an involved adult mentoring program as the option of choice. In short, this strategy can and will change the behavior and the climate of your school (Bender, 2007).

> Imagine dramatically improving the behavior of the most problematic kids in school. Wouldn't that result in a drastic improvement in your school overall?

FACTORS TO CONSIDER IN MENTORING

Mentoring primarily involves presenting appropriate role models for students who consistently misbehave, but there are many other advantages of adult mentoring programs. For example, adult mentoring improves behavior of troubled kids regardless of the similarities or differences between the mentor and her charge (Bender, 2007; Vanderwerf, 2014). However, for more serious behavioral problems, mentorships seem to work more effectively when the mentor and the student have a great deal in common. Specifically, psychologists traditionally emphasize the critical influence of a same-sex role model to assist children in becoming successful adults (Bender, 2007). Therefore, if possible, pairing troubled students with mentors of the same sex and race is generally encouraged. In fact, some mentorship programs emphasize the importance of either sex or race in selecting mentors; for example, 100 Black Men of America. This program pairs adult African American males with African American male students. My recommendation is that mentoring should be immediately implemented on a school-wide basis in most schools if possible, and the 5 to 10 percent of students with consistent behavior problems should be immediately paired with a mentor of the same race and sex. If that is not possible, use mentors across race and sex boundaries, but implement this program as soon as possible.

Mentorships also seem to work regardless of the teaching that goes on in the relationship, suggesting that the important aspect of mentorship is not instruction or tutoring, but rather building a positive rapport with a troubled kid (Clinton & Miles, 1999). While many school-based mentorships are initially structured around tutoring on school work (Vanderwerf, 2014), the most effective mentorships move beyond this "teaching only" dynamic to explore the areas of interest or hobbies of the kids and the mentors. Again, it is not content around which a mentorship is structured, but the relationship between the mentor and the student that is most important.

Although this strategy is most effective when administration brings adult mentors from the community into the school, some schools implement adult mentoring on the basis of partnering troubled kids with school personnel. Vanderwerf (2014) describes a successful program in which teachers, school administrators, and others on campus are partnered with challenging youth. While I do recommend this variation of the strategy, the major difficulty with this approach is obvious: there may not be enough mentors and/or not enough mentoring time.

BEGINNING A SCHOOL-WIDE ADULT MENTORING PROGRAM

Getting a school-wide adult mentoring program off the ground can be quite a challenge, but a variety of resources are available to help (Bender, 2007; Clinton & Miles, 1999). Teachers and school administrators can begin by asking the right questions, as listed below.

What is our target goal(s)? Do behavior problems need to be addressed? For example, does the school have a high dropout rate? Is there a high teenage pregnancy rate? Are students overtly aggressive in particular classes or particular areas of the school? Do we, as a faculty, wish to improve the respect our students show to others and/or the faculty?

How many students will participate? Which ones? Does a particular elementary or secondary class need intensive help? Or does a special population (e.g., learning disabled, physically disabled, pregnant teens, etc.) need help? The target population will, to a great extent, determine the number of mentors needed and the role they should play, and I recommend beginning with mentors that administration can pair with the 10 to 15 percent of the kids in schools who seem to be showing behavior problems. For example, an elementary school with 800 students should attempt to identify eighty mentors for the eighty students that show up (nearly every day!) in the principal's office.

How will we lead and coordinate the program? Without good leadership and coordination, any mentoring program is bound to fail. Teachers should be relieved of some teaching responsibilities if they are assigned to develop and guide the adult mentoring program. With eighty new people coming into the school to mentor kids weekly, someone will need to coordinate the program, and the principal and guidance counselor probably already have a full plate.

What resources from the school can we utilize? Is a classroom available for this program? Is a teacher available on a half-day basis to coordinate it? What existing mentor programs are similar in focus such that they can serve as models? It is useful to examine exemplary programs that have served students similar to the students you are endeavoring to reach.

What funding sources are available, if any? Funding can be utilized to pay a veteran teacher for half a day to guide the program, to buy some art supplies for program activities, or to provide get-to-know-you meals for mentors, their mentees, and the parents of those students. Educators may consider Title I funds, state grants, PTA/PTO, Kiwanis Club and other community service organizations, and local corporations or corporate foundations. These organizations are also excellent places to seek out appropriate adult mentors for the school.

SETTING UP A SCHOOL-WIDE MENTORING PROGRAM

A number of sources provide information on mentoring programs (Bender, 2007; Clinton & Miles, 1999; Vanderwerf, 2014), and specific steps vary from program to program. Here are some suggestions to begin.

Establishing an Adult Mentoring Program

1. Select an advisory board
2. Identify a veteran teacher as mentoring coordinator
3. Establish program goals
4. Set measurable implementation objectives
5. Prescribe activities and procedures
6. Provide well-thought-out guidelines for mentors
7. Consider legal issues in adult mentoring

Select an Advisory Board

A steering committee or advisory board comprised of school staff, mentors, parents, and the administrator should be set up. I recommend a smaller group, but there is real work to do for this group initially. With that stated, schools may wish to include others on the advisory board, such as local ministers, business leaders, PTA representatives, and so on, who can help find appropriate adult mentors for the school. These persons should represent the stakeholders in the project; their input, particularly for school-wide or district-wide mentoring programs, is essential.

Identify a Veteran Teacher as Mentoring Coordinator

Within each school, a mentoring coordinator should be assigned to oversee the day-to-day progress of the program and be available to participants whenever problems occur. With eighty new people coming to school each week, a coordinator will be critical. This should be more than a yearly teaching assignment; a longer-term mentoring coordinator will help not only to meet program needs but also to increase program stability year to year. In some cases, a veteran teacher may be relieved from instructional responsibilities for half a day, and that person could coordinate the mentorship program.

The tasks of the mentoring coordinator are many and varied. Working under the supervision of the administrator and the steering committee, the mentoring coordinator will be responsible for a number of tasks. Bender (2007) provides more detail on specific tasks that he must accomplish. These include

- identify students for mentoring (with the administrator)
- recruit mentors (with the administrator and steering committee)
- train mentors
- provide mentor support (as a sounding board for mentors, to alleviate problems)
- match mentors to students
- monitor student progress
- evaluate efficacy of the mentorship program each semester (Bender, 2007), providing a written report on how many students participated, their improved behavior, etc.

Establish Program Goals

Is the focus of your adult mentoring program to be academics or behavioral improvement? Well-articulated program goals, centering on building youth competence in some way, reap benefits in several ways. First, a mentoring effort driven by clear goals will run more smoothly administratively. Clear goals help keep administrative decision making in focus, thus avoiding "mission drift." Next, clear and achievable goals for the program translate into clear and achievable goals for the mentoring partners. For example, the mentor and the student might improve certain academic skills, focus on career or job skills, or merely develop a commonly chosen hobby. Clear goals help the mentoring partnership provide a structure or common task at hand that gives the opportunity for a positive relationship to develop between the mentor and the troubled youth. Moreover, having this structure provides both partners with an understandable purpose for their involvement, which can be a key factor in predicting regularity of meetings. Examples of program goals include

- to decrease office referrals for behavior problems
- to decrease in-school (or out-of-school) suspensions
- to decrease the likelihood of aggressive behavior by a student
- to provide male adolescents at risk for dropping out of school with male mentors in order to increase the students' attendance
- to increase academic achievement

Without well-written objectives as guideposts, program coordinators will lack direction in their work and have no clear means of reporting back to their steering committee what they have accomplished.

Set Measurable Implementation Objectives

In addition to broad program goals, the mentoring coordinator and steering committee should specify measureable implementation objectives, and these typically include a time frame. These objectives may vary between mentorship programs, as some programs emphasize academic development whereas others emphasize reduction in inappropriate behaviors. Specific, concrete objectives are needed to provide the program with a way to assess progress toward reaching its goals. Here are some examples:

- By the fourth week of the mentor recruitment/training period, thirty volunteer mentors will have been screened and enrolled in the program.
- By the October 1 launch date, all mentor/student pairs will be assigned.
- By the seventh week, nine out of ten students will have attended 80 percent of their meetings with mentors.
- By the ninth week, eight out of ten students will have mastered the first vocational skill area assigned (e.g., job application forms).
- By the ninth week, each mentor will report having at least one in-depth conversation with his student about choosing alternatives to inappropriate behavior in specific situations.
- By the end of the first year, elementary students will have increased their reading proficiency by one grade level.
- By the end of the first year, incidents of aggressive or violent behavior involving students in the program will have decreased by 40 percent.

Bear in mind that some of the benefits you seek most for student participants are rather intangible (e.g., wanting them to find meaning in life, becoming more resilient, and recognizing a wider set of solutions to problems). You can never measure these as accurately as you would like, but you can use questionnaires and/or interviews to gather evidence of improvement, even on these less measurable objectives, and incorporate the results into program objectives.

Prescribe Activities and Procedures

I have already mentioned the need for mentoring partners to have an activity they can pursue together besides academic tutoring, as this activity or joint hobby often provides the basis for a positive mentoring relationship to grow. Again, these activities may vary, according to the goals of the program. If the primary goal is academic improvement, some form of tutoring is most appropriate as an initial mentoring activity. If reduction of violence or aggressive behavior is the goal, common interest in a particular hobby may provide a non-threatening framework that will allow the mentor to engage the youth in reflective conversations about choices and values. If the relationship takes hold, the importance of the mentor's influence will make a difference in the student's behavior over time (Bender, 2007).

Provide Well-Thought-Out Guidelines for Mentors

You will also need to delineate procedures for mentors in some detail. You will need to determine the kind of relationship you anticipate between mentoring partners and develop guidelines for mentors. These should specify the types of activities (on campus or off campus? Both?) mentors should engage in with their mentees. Below are some examples that help set the parameters of the mentoring experience (Clinton & Miles, 1999; One to One, 1995).

> **Guidelines for Mentors**
>
> Mentors will undergo a police background check and are expected to relate to their mentees in an appropriate, caring, yet professional manner.
>
> Mentors should schedule a specific day and time each week for their mentoring.
>
> Mentors should call the school on that day to find out if the student is present. If the student is absent, mentors may assist in the mentoring classroom during the student's mentoring period or reschedule their mentoring time when the student returns to school.
>
> Mentors must sign in at the school office when they arrive at school.
>
> Mentors must pick up the student from his classroom, checking with the teacher concerning any special events of concern. Mentors and their students then proceed to the mentoring center classroom, where the mentoring coordinator supervises.
>
> Mentors may give small gifts on occasion. If there is a time when mentors would like to give the student a special gift (e.g., holiday, birthday), the mentoring coordinator must approve the gift (so as not to result in jealousy among the students). We recommend gifts that are small, inexpensive, and serve as a reward for a job well done.

Mentors must realize that all information such as class test scores, behavior problems, and family structure regarding students is confidential. They should be required to discuss all concerns about confidentiality (or any other concerns) with the mentoring coordinator.

Mentors must attend monthly meetings (e.g., all mentors meet on the second Wednesday at 4:30 P.M. in the mentoring center). The mentoring coordinator should hold monthly meetings for the mentors in order to discuss achievements, concerns, plans, and so on. This is how mentors pick up ideas from other mentors on reaching their kids. Training sessions for new mentors will take place during regular monthly meetings. The mentoring coordinator may also invite others (such as additional prospective mentors) to participate.

Consider Legal Issues in Adult Mentoring

In general, administrators are quite familiar with the legal issues involved in bringing adults into the school on a scheduled basis to work with students. I recommend that both parents and mentors be required to sign a letter stating that all mentoring activities will be held on school campus during regular school hours. That letter should further explain that if the mentor and the parents choose to allow the student to spend out-of-school time with the mentor, that such time and activities are not considered part of the mentorship program, and the school takes no responsibility for those activities. With these concerns noted, many of these issues are avoided if the school uses their personnel as the mentors (Vanderwerf, 2014).

Finally, administrators and mentoring coordinators should review literature on mentoring programs that may have already been implemented in their school district or state. They may also wish to have the school board attorney review their adult mentorship planning.

EVIDENCE OF EFFICACY IN ADULT MENTORING

As I noted previously, the mentoring coordinator should provide periodic reports on the mentoring program using data such as the goals and objectives above. The reports should include data on improvements in individual student behaviors as well as any specific evidence for program efficacy teachers provide. Most

> Administrators and mentoring coordinators should review literature on mentoring programs and have the school board attorney review their adult mentorship planning.

principals will have already aggregated the data on office referrals over a given year, and that information should be compared to the same indicators after the school implements adult mentoring.

If mentoring is designated as an intervention for a particular student with behavioral problems in an RTI procedure, individual teachers should keep a record for at least one month of how many times they had to discipline or call out that student as well as note how many times the student had to be sent from the classroom. Also, all the goals and many of the specific objectives above can provide data collection as to the efficacy of this strategy.

SUMMARY

Few school-wide interventions hold the promise of changing the climate of the entire school as does adult mentoring. Of course, many books on such mentoring programs point out additional advantages (e.g., closer ties between the school and community), but if teachers wish to involve themselves in a strategy that will fundamentally transform their school climate, this is one of the first strategies they should consider.

Strategy 6

Quiet Time and Meditation

Some students seem to be consistently verbally or physically abusive, and while they are certainly a challenge, the most challenging students to manage are the explosively violent ones (Bender, 2007). These students seem to get along fairly well, displaying little misbehavior, and then, seemingly over nothing at all, they explode with verbal or physical behavior. They may have never developed any sense of self-control, and often, managing these explosive students in class requires different disciplinary strategies. It seems that some enraged, angry students simply don't know how to chill out! In fact, these explosive students must be taught about their explosive behavior and to learn to reflect on it in order to gain control over it.

For this type of student, relaxation or meditation strategies may be the key (Edutopia.org, 2014; Kirp, 2014; Lopata, Nida, & Marabel, 2006; Machado, 2014; Reed, 2011). The terms *meditation* and *relaxation* here describe a set of strategies that help students relax, reduce stress, and then reflect on their behavior, often helping them gain control over violent, seemingly uncontrollable behavior. Any tactic that effectively relaxes a student, reduces tension, and makes the student aware of and sensitive to stress can provide the student with time for reflection on the rage that frequently underlies the explosive behavior (Kirp, 2014; Machado, 2014; Sousa, 2009).

> Some students seem to be consistently verbally or physically abusive, and while they are certainly a challenge, the most challenging student to manage is the student who is explosively violent.

Self-reflection is crucial in this approach. You can teach students, regardless of their age or grade level, about their explosive behavior; further, you can teach them that they control their own behavior (Bender, 2007; Kirp, 2014; Machado, 2014). The student's willing participation is also critical—the student must believe that he can escape from a behavior that has been quite destructive in his social life. In general, most explosively violent students, once they open up to the teacher about their behavioral problems, will state that they would like to get better control of these explosions. Joint reflection on specific examples of explosive behavior is therefore essential.

This reflective time also tends to build an important bond between the student and teacher, and that bond often lasts well beyond the school year. Of course, application of many meditation or relaxation strategies can be time-consuming. Some are done daily for 15 to 40 minutes (Edutopia.org, 2014). However, even with that time investment, the use of these strategies is infinitely preferable to the alternative—allowing the student's uncontrollable, often violent behavior to set a bad atmosphere for the entire year!

The application of various relaxation approaches for explosively violent and aggressive kids has been common for several decades. Among the meditation or relaxation approaches that have been studied, one will find various exercise programs, specific meditation techniques, mental exercises, physical exercises, and even biofeedback (Edutopia.org, 2014; Kirp, 2014; Lopata, Nida, & Marabel, 2006; Machado, 2014). Some of these tactics are applied in schools on a school-wide basis, though others are not; all have shown promise in school settings in terms of reducing behavior problems with troubled students. Research evidence does support the use of these tactics for a variety of students with significant behavior problems (Carter & Russell, 1985; Kirp, 2014; Machado, 2014). Nevertheless, the rationale for using relaxation strategies for these kids is simple: very few other strategies will work for this group of students.

Here are some options for teachers at various grade levels to consider. We'll begin with a research-proven strategy for young children, and then discuss several strategies for students in middle and high school.

> The rationale for using relaxation strategies for explosively violent, aggressive kids is simple: Very few other strategies will work for this group of students.

THE TURTLE TECHNIQUE

The Turtle Technique is a research-proven relaxation strategy particularly useful in the primary and elementary grades (Bender, 2007; Schneider, 1974). The Turtle Technique can be implemented by a single teacher in her class as well as school-wide. It consists of several components, including the so-called turtle relaxation phase, a problem-solving phase, and peer support, and this has been proven to assist students with serious conduct disorders to gain control over their own explosive behavior. By pretending to become a turtle, students withdraw from the class by placing their head down on their desk and relaxing for a brief time (usually two to four minutes). Students can decide on their own to "do a turtle" when they begin to feel rage or anger or whenever they need a brief break (Robin, Schneider, & Dolnick, 1976). Teachers may also request that students do a turtle for a while, if they see a behavioral problem or some type of altercation developing.

The technique first makes use of the turtle image—of withdrawing into one's shell or protective space when provoked by the external environment. According to Robin and colleagues (1976), you can easily teach young children to withdraw into their shells by placing their heads on their desks, locking their arms under their heads, and closing their eyes. They are told that this is how the turtle protects itself and draws strength to face the outside world. Again, students can decide on their own to do a turtle when they feel rage or anger, and teachers have a right to request that students do a turtle for a while. While in the turtle, the children relax their muscles in order to cope with emotional tensions. After a period of relaxation, the students begin a series of problem-solving tactics that allow them to reflect on their behavior outbursts. You can use the dialogue in the "Turtle Teaching Dialogue" box to teach young aggressive children how to do a turtle.

> ### Turtle Teaching Dialogue
>
> Little Turtle was a handsome young turtle very upset about going to school. He always got in trouble at school because he got into fights. Other kids would tease, bump, or hit him. He would get very angry and start big fights. The teacher would have to punish him. Then one day he met the big old tortoise, who told him that his shell was the secret answer to all his problems. The tortoise told Little Turtle to withdraw into his shell when he felt angry and rest until he was no longer angry. So he tried it the next day, and it worked. The teacher now smiled at him and he no longer got into big fights. (Robin, Schneider, & Dolnick, 1976)

Beyond teaching the turtle response itself, teachers should emphasize several additional aspects of this technique. First, teachers should stress that the turtle is a safe place for students, and they can use the same strategy whenever they need to. When confronted with an argument or potential violence, students need to know that they can withdraw in this fashion, and that can be an important option for many kids. In fact, many troubled students do not learn that withdrawal from a violent or verbally abusive situation is an option, given their home environments, so teaching this skill at school can literally change kids' lives.

After the turtle, the student should engage in some reflective problem solving concerning her behavior (Fleming, Ritchie, & Fleming, 1983). For example, in the study by Fleming and colleagues, the teacher gives four basic problem-solving steps to the students: (1) identify the problem, (2) generate alternative solutions, (3) evaluate alternatives and select the most appropriate, and (4) implement the selected alternative. Teachers should practice both group and individual applications of these steps with the students during the learning phase, and teachers may wish to print out a page that includes these four steps. Students can then reflectively write out their responses.

Finally, it is critical that the other members of the class respect the student's choice to pretend to become a turtle for a few moments. You must instruct the class not to talk to, joke with, or talk about the student who chooses to withdraw into his shell. Support from the class, in the form of ignoring the student during his or her withdrawal, is critical.

A "SAFE PLACE" RELAXATION TACTIC

Application of the turtle metaphor itself should generally be limited to primary and/or lower grades, but variations of this basic idea are appropriate up through middle and even high school. For example, you can teach students in middle and secondary schools the idea of a safe place and that they can enter their safe place by putting up a sign on their desks that says "Time Out" or merely placing their heads on their desk (Bender, 2007; Kirp, 2014). Students may then use this idea when they feel anger, rejection, or simply need a break from the stress of the classroom environment.

Note that in this case, the phrase *time out* does not mean application of the behavioral strategy of time out (i.e., absence of reinforcement). Rather, the phrase and sign indicate that a student needs a momentary escape from the academic and/or social demands of the classroom. The student should then place her head on the desk and peacefully relax for a few minutes. Teachers and students should agree not to call on or ask questions of the student while she is in this time out.

For some secondary students who have never learned to control their own rage and anger (and many veteran teachers have experienced the challenge of teaching such students), this "safe place" concept can be a life saver! Many students have simply never been taught that they can control their own emotions; they believe that they must express their rage and anger via verbal statements or explosive violence. Learning that an option is to escape to a safe place is very powerful for many students with highly disruptive behavior problems. Here is another example of this strategy, as a teacher might use it with middle and secondary students.

> Students in secondary school may be encouraged to place a sign on their desks that says "Time Out" when they need a break from the stress of the classroom environment.

QUIET TIME

Teachers are currently using various meditation practices in nearly a hundred schools in thirteen states across the nation (Edutopia.org, 2014; Kirp, 2014; Machado, 2014). Although meditation may seem a bit esoteric for school disciplinary application, research supports this practice in schools (Edutopia.org, 2014; Kirp, 2014). According to one synthesis of controlled research in schools, meditation can reduce rule infractions in high school by 50 percent, suspensions by 38 percent, class absences by 25 percent, and even aggressive behavior by 8 percent (Edutopia.org, 2014).

Kirp (2014) recently reports on implementation of a relaxation/meditation strategy called "Quiet Time" that is currently used on a school-wide basis in several inner-city schools in San Francisco as an effort to curb problem behavior among students. This is similar to the safe place strategy above. Visitacion Valley Middle School was the first to implement Quiet Time in the San Francisco schools. Beginning in 2007, a gong was sounded twice daily, and at that point, students were told to stop whatever they were doing, shut their eyes, and sit quietly while they attempt to clear their minds.

For some students, the quiet time at school was a revelation. In that community, they heard gunfire nightly, and most students knew someone who had been shot or someone who did the shooting (Kirp, 2014). Families were disrupted and murders were frequent. As one might imagine, the students in years past were largely out of control. Fights were frequent at school and in the community, and graffiti was everywhere. Students often cursed at their teachers during school hours, and both absenteeism and suspensions were very high, even for a large city school system (Kirp, 2014). The faculty began the Quiet Time intervention school-wide for one reason: nothing else seemed to work.

After Quiet Time, the students began to do much better. In the first year of the Quiet Time intervention, the number of suspensions fell by 45 percent (Kirp, 2014), and daily attendance rates climbed to 98 percent, well above the city-wide average. Students, including very troubled ones with chronic absenteeism, valued quiet time enough to come to school much more than previously. Grade point averages also improved markedly. With those results, Superintendent Richard Carranza encouraged the spread of the Quiet Time intervention city-wide, and other schools in the Bay Area now use this intervention school-wide (Kirp, 2014).

> In the first year of the Quiet Time intervention, the number of suspensions fell by 45 percent, and daily attendance rates climbed to 98 percent, well above the city-wide average.

MINDFULNESS

Katherine Priore Ghannam, a yoga teacher who is also a public school teacher, recently created a meditation program called Headstand to assist students in coping with stress and improve social behavior (Machado, 2014). This program is sometimes referred to as "mindfulness" because teachers instruct students to be mindful of their social interactions in the program. Using actual yoga positions as a backdrop, students participate in a training class multiple times each week. Ghannam believes her mindfulness program can serve as an antidote to stress that students feel, and initial student survey results suggest that 98 percent of students in the program reported feeling less stressed and more ready to learn after taking Headstand classes. The curriculum also incorporates character education, using reflective units to consider questions such as "How are responsibility and power related?" or "What does it mean to accept personal responsibility?"

Like many meditative approaches to curbing inappropriate behavior, this program is still the subject of research. Recently, Headstand partnered with the University of California–San Francisco to provide more concrete efficacy data for this program (Machado, 2014), but the anecdotal data, as reported above, look quite promising.

RELAXATION TAPES

As another alternative meditation idea for the higher grades, relaxation tapes have a much longer history in the classroom. Some teachers use audiotapes that help students relax at various grade levels (Bender 2007; Lupin, 1977). For example, a series of audiotapes by Lupin (1977) include fifteen-minute descriptions of imaginary trips to the beach and mountains. The sounds of these various environments are on the tape, coupled with a soft voice describing the scene in a fashion that is designed to foster relaxation. Teachers could easily use these tapes in conjunction with the Quiet Time strategy, and this would help foster increased relaxation among students in highly stressful environments.

EXERCISE TO IMPROVE BEHAVIOR

In addition to meditation training, various other strategies have been used to assist in modifying aggressive and other problem behaviors, including exercise programs, relaxation training, and even biofeedback (Christie, Dewitt, Kaltenbach, & Reed, 1984; Lopata et al., 2006; Reed, 2011). In each of these interventions, similar to the relaxation techniques I just described, the teacher provides the student with an opportunity to become more sensitive to stress in her body and reflect on her anger, rage, or aggressive behavior. Specifically, in both biofeedback and exercise, the student is increasingly focused on a sense of awareness of how her body is feeling (how she is relating to stress) and how she may control that stress without violent explosions (Christie et al., 1984).

Various educators demonstrate that exercise can curb violence and aggression in troubled students (Reed, 2011; Yell, 1988). For example, Yell (1988) is able to use a thirty-minute warm-up and jogging or walking period with six students with very significant behavioral problems. When these students engage in the daily exercise program at the beginning of each day, the data show a reduction in mild inappropriate classroom behaviors (either talking out or out-of-seat behavior) of all six students.

BIOFEEDBACK

Teachers also use biofeedback to teach students to gain control over their own stress levels (Lopata et al., 2006). In biofeedback, the teacher tapes to a student's body a set of sensors designed to pick up the physiological signs of stress. When the indicators of stress increase, an auditory tone increases in frequency. The teacher tells the child, during the biofeedback session, to "think about relaxing things that make the tone go lower." Over a series of practice sessions, the student will subtly learn to reduce his level of stress. Although this strategy may not be useful in school settings since schools are unlikely to own biofeedback equipment, this treatment has nevertheless been demonstrated as an effective treatment in school settings (Carter & Russell, 1985; Christie et al., 1984). Further, for explosively violent kids in clinical or therapeutic settings, this intervention can equip them with the skills they need to foresee their own violent outburst and forestall it. In short, this strategy works, and perhaps it is time to implement this strategy more in school settings.

EFFICACY AND CHOOSING THE RIGHT STRATEGY

You may choose meditative or relaxation strategies in part by the situation. For example, for special education students who live in large cities, implementation of biofeedback may be an option since clinical settings may be available with the appropriate equipment. More common for troubled students are exercise techniques, techniques such as the turtle technique, or quiet time strategies.

In terms of demonstrating the efficacy of any of these relaxation strategies, teachers should collect baseline data on the specific behavior problem or problems they are targeting (e.g., verbal aggression in class, fighting, cursing). Next, they should teach the strategy to the target student (or the entire class) and practice the strategy several times. Finally, teachers should collect data on the targeted behaviors for a month or more while using the selected strategy, as some of these overt behaviors are fairly low in frequency and it may take a month or more for the strategy to take hold and show results.

> Most teachers who wish to use a meditative strategy opt for some version of the Turtle Technique, meditation, the safe place option, or Quiet Time.

A CASE STUDY

Although the techniques presented in Section I of this book are generally considered preventative techniques, teachers can use most of these strategies as targeted interventions in certain situations. For example, if an elementary school teacher wants to undertake one of these quiet time/meditation types of strategies, he could probably schedule a daily time, because most elementary school teachers work with the same group of students all day, so scheduling training time as well as quiet time would not be a problem. Here is an example:

Mrs. Snyder recently realizes that there seems to be more verbal altercations in her fourth-grade class this year than in any previous year. She knows that she has a higher percentage of students coming from disrupted home situations this year, and she wants to find a way to make those students less emotionally explosive in school. First, she counts the number of verbal or physical altercations during the morning instructional period. She chooses that time frame since most of the "specials" (e.g., music class, school assemblies, physical education, art classes, special education pull-outs) are scheduled during the afternoon and she doesn't want those situations skewing her information. Also, rather than targeting one student, she is interested in reducing the number of altercations for the class as a whole, so she collects data on the entire class. Of course, for physical altercations (e.g., fighting, a much more serious problem than a verbal altercation) she does record in her side notes which students were involved. The baseline data in Figure 6.1 presents the overall number of altercations the class demonstrates in a five-day period. The data show an average of five verbal altercations daily as well as two fights.

Figure 6.1:   Safe Place Intervention to Reduce Class Altercations

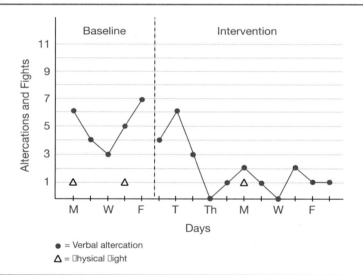

At the beginning of the second week, Mrs. Snyder introduces the idea of a safe place. While she uses the example of doing the turtle and the script above to explain the procedure, she chooses to call the student retreat a safe place given the age of her students. Once in the morning, she tells all the students to go to their safe place, by placing their heads on their desk for three minutes. She tells them to "quietly reflect on something relaxing." This prepares them to be ready to escape to their safe place as necessary. Further, during the intervention period, whenever an altercation of any type is beginning, Mrs. Snyder instructs those involved to "Go to your safe place right now, please."

As the data show, Mrs. Snyder's class-wide intervention works. The verbal altercations decrease rather dramatically over the next week, and by the end of a two-week intervention, most altercations are eliminated. Fighting is also significantly reduced with this intervention. Mrs. Snyder notes that this daily safe place training seems effective from the first day, as she finds that this helps calm her students. Afterward, the students are more ready to begin their work. In addition to reducing altercations in the class, this intervention improves class climate overall.

SUMMARY

Should an educator wish to use any of these techniques, the teacher must select from exercise programs, a safe place approach, Quiet Time, meditation programs, or something like the Turtle Technique. Generally, exercise programs will take more time away from a student's academic study time than other approaches, since dressing and post-exercise showers may take time beyond that required for the exercise. With that limitation in mind, most teachers who wish to use a relaxation strategy opt for some version of the Turtle Technique, Quiet Time, or the safe place. As a practitioner, you should determine which techniques work for explosive students, and use the technique that is most applicable in your classroom.

Strategy 7

Conflict Resolution Training

CRITICAL IMPORTANCE OF CONFLICT RESOLUTION SKILLS

Veteran educators have long recognized that 10 to 15 percent of students in schools create 80 percent of the disciplinary problems (Bender, 2007). These students may be thought of as repeat offenders when it comes to school rules and acceptable school behaviors. Unfortunately, many of these highly disruptive students have learned from their home environment that appropriate ways to resolve conflict include shouting, cursing, or even hitting others. In fact, among students that demonstrate overt, repeated verbal or physical aggression, one might well speculate that these strategies represent their only known options for resolving disputes with both their classmates and teachers. Clearly these challenging students will need to learn new ways to avoid conflict if they are to have any efficacy in life at all, and therefore training in conflict resolution and problem-solving strategies may be necessary for many of these students.

For this reason, schools have been teaching conflict resolution skills to students for a number of years (Drew, 2002; Jones, 2000; McGuire, 1999; Wilemon, 2014; Wolff, & Nagy, 2013), and while these skills are particularly critical for the consistent offenders, all students can benefit from learning more effective ways to manage conflict. Conflict resolution skills are of benefit way beyond the school, and that is one reason that so many work environments now include training in conflict resolution. In many schools, particularly inner-city schools dealing with tough, street-wise kids, conflict resolution training is now common practice.

> Many highly disruptive students have learned from their home environment that appropriate ways to resolve conflict include shouting, cursing, or even hitting others.

In spite of this demonstrated need, however, other schools are reluctant to invest the time that conflict resolution training requires, particularly with the ever increasing emphasis on having students meet and exceed rigorous academic standards. In short, instructional time is now a critical priority in schools, and time for conflict resolution training has not been designated as a priority in many schools as of yet.

This is unfortunate for several reasons. First, conflict resolution skills reduce behavior problems overall, and these programs have become a particular priority for minority students and/or highly disruptive students (Duncan, 2014; US Department of Education, 2011). Next, such skills often stay with students for life, making them more successful overall, because conflict resolution is necessary in almost every work situation. Finally, conflict resolution skills are likely to reduce time spent in conflicts, and paradoxically, these programs may increase academic time overall, resulting in better overall academic outcomes for kids over the long term (McGuire, 1999; Wilemon, 2014).

> Conflict resolution skills are of benefit way beyond the school, and that is one reason that so many work environments now include training in conflict resolution.

STEPS IN CONFLICT RESOLUTION

Different authors suggest varying steps within the conflict resolution process (Drew, 2002; McGuire, 1999; Wilemon, 2014; Wolff & Nagy, 2013), and some theorists include steps that others leave out. For example, Wilemon (2014) describes a conflict resolution procedure teachers use in schools in Nashville, Tennessee, that involves a group role-play activity and even something very similar to the morning meeting idea. In contrast, Wolff & Nagy (2013) describe a seven-step process that involves having students in conflict deal directly with each other rather than extensive group work. For school-based conflict resolution training, it is probably wiser to select an approach with fewer steps for students to master, and Drew's (2002) six-step conflict resolution process is one of the most efficient for use in classrooms. That procedure focuses both on how an angry student manages herself as well as how she might effectively communicate with the antagonists in the conflict situation. This typically involves two or three students in a conflict and the teacher serving as a mediator to help manage the various steps in the conflict resolution process. Alternatively, after students learn conflict resolution skills, they may be able to initiate the conflict resolution process and resolve the conflict on their own without teacher mediation. Of course, that should be the long-term goal for all conflict resolution programs.

Six Steps in Conflict Resolution

1. Cool off!
2. State the problem.
3. Reflectively listen to others.
4. Take responsibility.

5. Brainstorm alternative solutions.

6. Select a mutually acceptable solution and affirm. (Drew, 2002)

Step 1: Cool Off!

To begin the conflict resolution process, the teacher/mediator might invite all students to calmly sit in a circle at the edge of the classroom and close their eyes for just a moment as each student calms down and reflects on the conflict. Assessing one's own emotions is a critical first step in most conflict resolution approaches. Because conflicts result in intense emotions for all participants, each person in conflict must identify and control her own anger, hurt feelings, and emotional intensity. Many tactics can work to help oneself calm down, including making calming statements to oneself ("He's not mad at me. He's angry at something else."), taking a moment to close one's eyes and simply breathe, withdrawing momentarily from the situation (saying, "Let's talk about that right after I get back from the bathroom."), or splashing cool water in one's face. Once one's own emotional intensity is under control, that person is ready to continue the conflict resolution process.

Because this first step doesn't involve engagement between the individuals in the conflict, it may seem more time efficient to overlook this step. However, I urge educators to refrain from doing so. To put matters in simple terms, the students who continually create behavior problems in schools have never been taught this simple, self-calming technique, and devoting some time to teaching them is quite likely to reduce the number of overall behavioral problems teachers must deal with.

> Because conflicts result in intense emotions for all participants, each person in conflict must identify and control their own anger, hurt feelings, and emotional intensity.

Step 2: Stating the Problem

To address a conflict, the participants must first identify the conflict, and while this seems obvious, different students perceiving the same situation differently cause many behavioral outbursts. For example, Terrance, a frequently disruptive student, slaps another student named Billy on the back as he walks by, and a third student, Jason, stands up by his desk and angrily calls Terrance an unpleasant name. Clearly, in that situation a fight might quickly develop in the classroom. While Terrance may have intended his slap on a friend's back as playful, Jason may have seen it as very aggressive. This type of conflict can be resolved if students learn to state the problem as they see it.

The teacher/mediator, Ms. Bowling, begins this conflict resolution step by inviting the first student to state his perspective of the problem by using "I messages" that summarize his perceptions without blaming or accusing others. "I messages" are a powerful technique for conflict resolution (Drew, 2002). They are statements of one's own perspective about the conflict, using the word "I," absent any blame or verbal attack. "I messages" might be contrasted with "You messages," in which the message accuses others of inappropriate actions or blames others for the conflict. "You messages" almost always put others on the defensive, increasing the intensity of emotions in conflict situations and leading to bad outcomes.

> "I messages" summarize a student's perceptions without blaming or accusing others.

In the situation above, Jason might say, "It made me mad because I thought my friend Billy got hit for no reason." In this "I statement," Jason is taking responsibility for his own feelings and his own perception of events without accusing Terrance of misbehavior, and without sarcasm or put-downs of others. As Drew points out, the intention of conflict resolution is to foster a sense of "us against the problem" rather than "us against each other" (Drew, 2002). You must teach students that conflicts are not situations in which one must win and another lose. Rather, students should work toward a solution in which all parties can have their needs met.

Step 3: Reflective Listening to Others

When conflicts in schools arise, they often involve a refusal of one student to listen to the opinions of others about what caused the conflicts. Therefore, teaching students active listening or reflective listening skills is critically important. Active listening skills include such behaviors as looking the person in the eye, adopting an open body position, showing a facial expression of concern, carefully considering the valid points the other person is making, and refraining from interrupting others. Once again, students who are frequently in conflict have rarely developed these skills previously, and taking some time to actively teach these skills, as well as model them repeatedly in the classroom, will reduce conflict in the class over time. To help students develop these skills, teachers should list specific skills (and other such skills they may think of) on a poster on the wall, and then refer to that poster frequently in class discussions.

The third step in conflict resolution involves having each participant in the conflict state their perception of the problem, using "I messages." After Jason uses "I messages" to summarize his perspective on the conflict in the second step, Ms. Bowling invites Billy and Terrance to do the same. The teacher/mediator should always remind all students to use "I messages" and actively listen to the perspectives of others in the conflict. After students learn to use "I messages" to describe their perceptions of a conflict and these active listening skills, which allow them to listen to each other, they are ready to actually participate in significant and meaningful conflict resolution sessions. After students learn conflict resolution skills, they may be able to address each other without mediation. However, early on during the conflict resolution learning process, rather than having students in conflict talk directly to each other, each student should address the teacher/mediator instead of each other. Even in that case, however, the teacher should remind other participants in the conflict not to interrupt until it is their turn. This provides an opportunity for all conflict participants to listen to each other in a more calm fashion (Drew, 2002).

A particularly effective approach to active listening is the phrase, "Let me see if I understand you correctly." You could teach students to listen carefully to their opposition in the conflict resolution process, and then see if they can fairly and objectively restate their opponent's position (Wolff & Nagy, 2013). This will require a high level of active listening skills.

Step 4: Taking Responsibility

At some point, students should take responsibility for their actions and the results of those actions. After each student presents his perspective of the conflict, Ms. Bowling invites Terrance, calmly and without blame, to take some responsibility for the problem. Taking responsibility involves each participant owning one's own actions, and in most cases, this will result in admitting that the other person in the conflict has a point. Consider again the case above. If Terrance can reach this point in the conflict resolution process without experiencing undue anger or blame, he is likely to see that Jason's perspective is valid: The playful slap could have been seen as an unprovoked attack on Billy. In this way, Terrance has owned responsibility for his own actions.

The language and approach of the teacher/mediator, Ms. Bowling in this case, is critical at this step. Ms. Bowling must invite Terrance to take responsibility without blaming him for the conflict. She might say something like, "Terrance, I know you weren't hitting Billy in anger; you were just playing with him. But can you see how Jason thought that you might be starting a fight?"

That sentence doesn't accuse Terrance of any aggression, but does invite his understanding of the perspective of other students. Hopefully, Terrance would be in a calm mental state by that point and able to take responsibility for his actions and their impact.

Step 5: Brainstorm Alternative Solutions

Brainstorming procedures typically involves two emphases: generating as many ideas as possible that might solve the problem, and refraining from discussing or criticizing any suggested ideas. Of course, like the "I messages" and listening skills above, you will need to teach students both of those aspects of brainstorming. The latter emphasis is critically important when brainstorming possible solutions for problems in conflict situations, because both students are likely to be emotionally charged, and angry students will wish to immediately criticize ideas of their opponents in the conflict. Still, with some preparation in Steps One through Four, and a strong guiding hand by the teacher (or other mediator), even students in conflict can typically brainstorm and generate an array of problem solutions.

Teachers can even offer a reward for positive brainstorming (Drew, 2002), such as five extra minutes of computer time/game time for all students in the conflict if they generate four possible solutions in the next two minutes. It is a wise idea to require one student to write down the ideas as the students suggest them so that each idea can be given due consideration in the next step of the conflict resolution process.

In this example, Ms. Bowling invites students to brainstorm an alternative way to play when students pass by the desks of others. Very quickly, Terrance, Jason, and Billy come up with several ideas (e.g., tickling a student's ear or thumping his head, but not too hard!).

Step 6: Select a Mutually Acceptable Solution and Affirm

The final step in the conflict resolution process is the selection of a mutually acceptable solution to the problem from among the ideas the students generate in the brainstorming session. Students at that point have heard others' viewpoints and generated various solutions that might be acceptable. They should be able to select one approach that will prevent conflict in the future in similar situations. In this example, each of the three students agree to "thump their friends behind the ear" when they pass them in the class, as a playful gesture rather than slapping them.

To end the session, it is important that each participant confirm their commitment to the selected strategy. In some cases, they may offer handshakes as a peaceful community-building sign of respect. At times, an apology might be needed, and after a calming conflict resolution procedure is complete, such an apology is typically much more easy to elicit. As each conflict resolution procedure ends, the teacher/mediator might invite an apology, from one or more students. In the example above, the teacher might expect both Terrance and Jason to apologize. The teacher/mediator should always remember to thank each participant in the process, for their work to resolve the conflict.

IMPLEMENTING CONFLICT RESOLUTION IN REAL CLASSROOMS

Initially, teachers must directly teach students conflict resolution skills. The procedure in the example above would take perhaps five to eight minutes in the classroom to complete, but it would take much longer had students not been taught conflict resolution skills. While no teacher likes to take that much time away from teaching the educational standards to the class, most veterans would agree that, had a fight broken out as a result of the conflict above, even more class time would have been lost. Therefore, making time to teach conflict resolution skills is likely, in the long run, to result in more instructional time and not less.

Many educators now suggest that all teachers make the time to teach conflict resolution skills to their students each year (Duncan, 2014; Jones, 2000; O'Brien, 2014; US Department of Education, 2011) as a part of a mutual commitment to 21st-century workplace skills. While the teacher cannot completely cover the topic in three sessions, certainly she can teach the basics of conflict resolution in three twenty-minute sessions during the first week of school. Further, those conflict resolution skills are a major component of, and an important requirement for, success in the 21st-century workplace, a workplace much more dependent on collaborative working relationships than the work environments of the 20th century.

Again, it is easy in today's world of teaching to decide not to make the time for conflict resolution training, and I am very aware of the current time demands made on teachers. Still, I urge teachers to realize two things: first, almost all students need this training as a basis for success in life; and second, this training can be a time-saver overall. Once the whole class has been through three training sessions, and one or more class members was used as a mediator, the teacher will then have various options when a potential conflict erupts. The teacher may place a student mediator in charge of a conflict resolution session in the back corner of the class, while the teacher continues the class work for the rest of the students. Alternatively, the teacher might even decide to assign a five-minute conflict resolution session to two students in conflict, and depending on the students and the level of emotional intensity, not provide a mediator at all.

> Many educators now suggest that all teachers make the time to teach conflict resolution skills to their students each year as a part of our mutual commitment to 21st-century workplace skills.

Of course, student mediators can manage some conflicts in the classroom, but others are likely to require the mediation of the teacher, and teachers can make the determination on whether a mediator can handle a conflict resolution process, given the specific students involved in the conflict. With that in mind, having these procedures in place as a preventative disciplinary approach can help the teacher avoid losing class time.

Here are several more implementation steps for teachers to take.

Prepare the Classroom for Conflict Resolution

First, teachers should teach the skill set of conflict resolution skills. Figure 7.1 presents these main skills and some ideas for teaching them to the class.

Figure 7.1:   Skill Set for Conflict Resolution

Use of "I Messages" and "You Messages": Teachers must instruct students how to use "I messages" when discussing a conflict with others, in order to not make their opponent feel defensive. Show the students that if they wish to have more influence over what happens, then "I messages" are more effective. The teacher can do this through modeling what not to do. She might begin by discussing a conflict she has with a student using "You messages." In such a case, the student is likely to feel defensive, and the teacher might then discuss the same conflict using "I messages." Have the students note how they feel in that later example.

Reflective Listening: Reflective listening, sometimes referred to as active listening, involves an intentional effort to understand the perspective of others rather than merely planning a defensive response to others' perspectives. The teacher should instruct students to actively listen without forming a response at the same time. In such cases, students are likely to better understand their opponents in a conflict.

Brainstorming: Brainstorming involves groups of students trying to get all possible ideas on resolving the conflict on the table for discussion. Teachers should emphasize that during the brainstorming step, she will not allow critiques of any ideas. The goal of this step is merely to get all possible ideas out there for later discussion.

Taking Responsibility: Some students do not know how to take responsibility for negative behaviors. They may believe that if they do take such responsibility, then they are somehow affirming their own worthlessness in general. Those students can benefit from specific training in how to take responsibility. Teaching specific, positive statements can be beneficial for many of those students. For example, teaching students the following statement can sometimes allow them to take responsibility for something negative: "I'm usually a good guy, and most folks like me, but sometimes I might mess up. I may have made a mistake when I. . . ."

In the conflict resolution process, the teacher should encourage and celebrate such statements. The teacher might reinforce such a statement by saying, "That was a courageous thing to say. Thanks for saying that."

Conflict Resolution Steps: Finally, after the teacher instructs on the initial skills, she must teach the steps in conflict resolution. She should model each of these steps using video examples.

To enhance this instruction, teachers might make several posters on conflict resolution to permanently place on their wall. Certainly a poster on the steps in conflict resolution would be a helpful beginning. Teachers may merely copy the six steps above in sequence, and they may add one or two sentences of description of what each step involves. Next, a poster contrasting "I messages" and "You messages," complete with some examples of each, would be useful in teaching conflict resolution to the whole class. A third poster listing and explaining active listening skills would likewise be a useful reminder for students.

Teach Conflict Resolution Steps

Once the class is equipped with those posters, the teacher should directly teach the conflict resolutions steps to the class as a whole. On the first training day, she should teach the steps and then emphasize the specific skills required in some of the steps (e.g., "I messages," active listening). Generally, I recommend a thirty- to forty-five-minute lesson in which a teacher goes through the steps of the process with the class and then provides instruction on the specific skills.

On the second day of training, I suggest that teachers use one of the many online videos to support the steps of the conflict resolution process. After the video, teachers should lead a class discussion that compares the conflict resolution process in the video with the specific steps above. For example, some videos may emphasize different steps or highlight the same basic process in a slightly different order. Teachers may merely wish to use a Google or Bing search for "conflict resolution video examples," and then preview various videos for their own use. Using such a search, I found several examples on YouTube (see the video: https://www.youtube.com/watch?v=yjhauTLFqfM). This follows most of the steps herein.

Role-Play a Conflict

On the third day of training, the teacher may begin by reviewing the conflict resolution steps and then continue with a role-play activity. The teacher should provide a role-play scenario that requires students to actually go through the process. The teacher can ask students to write a three- or four-sentence paragraph about the most recent conflict between students that they witnessed in the classroom. Students will often be more engaged in a role-play that presents a situation that actually occurred in the class.

For grades three and higher, the teacher should appoint a student to mediate the role-play conflict between the other students. Although younger children may require the teacher as a mediator for conflict resolution, older children can learn to do this process themselves. Also, in this fashion, the teacher can train one or more mediators for her classroom so that the teacher's time is not required to mediate every conflict.

EFFICACY FOR CONFLICT RESOLUTION

Conflict resolution receives strong support in research literature, and because of that it is a strategy recommended for all schools (Duncan, 2014; Jones, 2000; O'Brien, 2014; US Department of Education, 2011). In particular, the Department of Education recommends this procedure as one alternative to overuse of suspension and expulsion from schools (Duncan, 2014; US Department of Education, 2011).

Like all the preventative, whole-class strategies in Section I, conflict resolution offers a targeted strategy aimed at improving behavior of specific students as well as an overall preventative strategy for the class. To support this strategy, teachers should record data on how many class disruptions occur for two to three weeks before they teach the strategy to their class. Then, after the training days, the teacher may apply the conflict resolution strategy while continuing to note the number of class disruptions. The distinction between the baseline data and the data after the teacher applies conflict resolution should provide evidence of the efficacy of this strategy in her class.

In contrast, if a particular student disrupts class repeatedly, the teacher might teach the conflict resolution strategy to the class, while taking baseline data on specific behavior of that targeted student. Then, once the class completes the training process, conflict resolution might become the targeted intervention for that student. Each time the student disrupts class, the teacher could undertake a conflict resolution process for the next three to five weeks, while the teacher continues to collect data on the student's frequency of misbehavior.

SUMMARY

Marzano (2003, 2007) has long emphasized the need for students to acknowledge adherence to rules and procedures, and the conflict resolution strategy, perhaps more so than some other strategies, focuses on each student developing an understanding of the perspective of others relative to his own behavior. This helps students to interpret rule violations in the context of how those violations impact others.

Further, this strategy holds advantages that last long after the student leaves the classroom because conflict resolution skills are immediately transferable to classrooms later in the school year and/or subsequent work environments. In fact, long-term success in life may depend as much on one's ability to effectively get along with others as on one's academic success, and conflict resolution skills certainly deserve a place among the skills stressed in the 21st-century classroom.

Strategy 8

Peer Mediation in the Schools

One final preventative disciplinary strategy teachers increasingly use in schools is peer mediation (Cohen, 2014; Duncan, 2014; Harris, 2005; McHenry, 2000). Peer mediation may be best understood as a process that involves using same-aged peers to help students resolve conflicts (Dunn, 2010; NCPC, 2014; Study Guides and Strategies, 2014). The peer mediation process involves many of the same skills in the conflict resolution section, including active listening skills, critical thinking, problem solving, and a willingness to respect the perspective of others in the conflict. Also, like conflict resolution, peer mediation skills readily transfer beyond the classroom, so it is not a stretch to suggest that this set of skills helps prepare students for the conflicts they will face for the rest of their lives (McHenry, 2000).

Critical in the peer mediation process is the understanding that the mediator does not make decisions for the participants involved (US Department of Education, 2014). Instead, the peer mediator is there to help those in conflict work toward achieving a win-win alternative in order to avoid further conflict. Further, when using school students as peer mediators, teachers should give careful consideration to the initial training of the peer mediators and the types of disputes that those peer mediators can handle. Although peer mediators can, if they are prepared carefully, manage a wide range of behavioral problems and conflicts—including somewhat intense conflicts between other students—they should not be used in response to situations in which overt physical violence has occurred or one or more students have broken the law (Study Guides and Strategies, 2014). Sexual abuse, threats of suicide, and certain gang problems also necessitate the use of interventions other than peer mediation. In particular, a school administrator must address any conflict involving danger to students or breaking the law.

> Like conflict resolution, peer mediation skills readily transfer beyond the classroom, so it is not a stretch to suggest that this set of skills helps prepare students for the conflicts they will face for the rest of their lives.

Also of note, teachers frequently implement together the peer mediation strategy and conflict resolution strategy. In fact, peer mediation involves using trained peers to teach and model conflict resolution skills, and this can be an effective aspect of this strategy for many students. The combined use of these preventative strategies is therefore strongly encouraged, even though training in both sets of skills is more time consuming. Because of the concerns with training time, some schools choose to make conflict resolution training available to all students and subsequently train only a small set of selected students in peer mediation skills.

COMPONENTS OF A PEER MEDIATION SESSION

Like the conflict resolution strategy, there are multiple approaches to peer mediation in the schools (Dunn, 2010; NCPC, 2014; Study Guides and Strategies, 2014). Most approaches involve six to ten steps in the peer mediation session (Dunn, 2010; NCPC, 2014). See the following "Eight Steps in Peer Mediation," for an example. This is adapted from various sources (Dunn, 2010; NCPC, 2014; Study Guides and Strategies, 2014).

Eight Steps in Peer Mediation

1. Disputants complete a mediation conflict form
2. Mediator explains mediator's role and mediation rules
3. Disputants describe the conflict from their perspective
4. Disputants describe the conflict from the other's perspective
5. Mediator summarizes facts and agreements
6. Disputants brainstorm possible solutions
7. Disputants select a win-win option
8. Disputants sign a contract of agreement

Step 1. Completion of Mediation Conflict Form

Most peer mediation programs begin by having students in conflict go to the guidance office or the principal's office and there they complete a brief questionnaire detailing the conflict or problem (Dunn, 2010; Study Guides and Strategies, 2014). This is a good first step in the peer mediation process because it provides a cooling down period. Students who may be very angry from a recent confrontation are required to calmly complete the form, answering a series of questions about what caused the conflict. The guidance counselor or principal then assigns the disputants to undergo peer mediation with a specific peer mediator.

At that point, the disputants walk to the peer mediation room, which will usually be staffed by two or three trained peer mediators, because multiple problems can occur in schools at the same time. When students enter, one mediator should take their case, and begin the mediation. Initially, the mediator quickly reviews each student's questionnaire and asks them to commit to the peer mediation process.

Note that the general rules for peer mediation can be introduced on this initial student questionnaire so that the disputants can become aware of how peer mediation works. The form in Figure 8.1 provides a set of typical rules for peer mediation and can be adapted for use in various school situations. Finally, the questions provide an excellent pre-organizer for the conflict resolution steps to follow, by inviting the students to consider the perspectives of others about the conflict.

> The general rules for peer mediation can be introduced on the initial student questionnaire so that the disputants can become aware of how peer mediation works.

Figure 8.1:   Peer Mediation Questionnaire

Mediation Participants Must Agree to Follow These Rules for Peer Mediation

1. Students will attempt to solve their problems through mediation and follow these rules for mediation.
2. Mediators are here to help students reach a mutually acceptable approach to conflict and not to impose a solution themselves.
3. No negative comments about others is allowed. Any shouting, cursing, verbal abuse, or physical violence will result in ending the session and a referral to the principal.
4. Students will not interrupt others. Students may write ideas down as others speak and share those ideas when it is their turn.
5. Students will tell the truth and honor the commitments they make in mediation.
6. Students will show respect for other disputants and the mediators at all times and keep all aspects of the mediation confidential.

Questions: Describe the conflict that you wish to resolve. State exactly who is involved and exactly what happened. It is usually better to answer questions without intense reflection.

State in only two lines exactly what the conflict is. _____

_____

Who is involved in this conflict? (More than one other person? If so, who?) _____

_____

What started the conflict? _____

_____

Did anyone involved in the conflict misunderstand the others? _____

_____

Can you suggest ways to resolve this conflict and avoid the same conflict in the future?

_____

_____

Step 2. Explanation of Mediator's Role and Mediation Rules

The peer mediator begins the mediation session by reminding students of the peer mediation rules. As indicated in Figure 8.1, the mediation form can introduce both the mediator's role and the rules for the mediation process. However, it takes only a minute at the beginning of the mediation session to review those mediation rules and remind participants of the mediator's role in the process, and such a reminder will emphasize the importance of the rules for the mediation session. Should any violation of those rules take place, the mediation session should end immediately, and the disciplinary matter should be referred back to the guidance office or the principal for alternative action.

Step 3. Participants Describe the Conflict From Their Perspective

Have participants use "I messages" (described in the previous strategy) state the conflict from their perspective. This should take only a couple of minutes, and the mediator should take notes on the main points. Once the student is finished, the mediator should paraphrase the student's perception and then summarize the fundamental needs of the student, as demonstrated in the student's own language. Next, the mediator should ask if he has summarized the student's statements, perceptions, and needs correctly. Finally, the mediator should invite the disputant to add any additional thoughts. Once that is complete, the mediator repeats the process with the other student in the dispute.

Step 4. Participants Describe the Conflict From the Other's Perspective

Some proponents of peer mediation (Dunn, 2010) do not include this step. I recommend this process, because it serves as a great way to assist students in becoming more understanding of the perspectives of others. By stating the position of their adversary, students at least have to acknowledge that position. However, the peer mediator should emphasize that summarizing their opponent's position does not mean that they agree with that position. Still, in the best possible scenario, students will summarize the needs and desires of their opponents in this step accurately, and that provides an excellent basis for subsequent steps in the process.

> By stating the position of their adversary, students at least have to acknowledge that position.

Step 5. Mediator Summarizes Facts and Agreements

The mediator should summarize the facts of the dispute, while placing particular emphasis on those points on which the disputants agree. The needs and desires of each participant should likewise be summarized at this point, and the mediator should then note which needs and desires of the disputants seem reasonable. Again, the mediator should highlight any agreements or similarities (Dunn, 2010).

Step 6. Brainstorm Possible Solutions

The mediator invites the disputants to consider the needs and desires of each person in the conflict and brainstorm a variety of possible solutions to the problem. The general guidelines for brainstorming (I discussed this in the previous section on conflict resolution) are useful tools for this step, and the mediator should highlight them at the beginning of the brainstorming step. A poster on the "Rules of Brainstorming" can be quite useful here. Critical to that process is the idea that brainstorming involves idea generation and not critical analysis of any proposed ideas. Also, the mediator should take careful notes on each idea proposed, in order to give each idea due consideration in the next step of the process.

Step 7. Disputants Select a Win-Win Option

Each of the options all participants suggest should be discussed and considered in terms of the needs of each student. Even if the disputants seem to reach an agreement on a possible solution, it is the mediator's responsibility to assure that they discuss all the ideas. Such a discussion may help clarify or refine the solution the disputants chose.

> The win-win nature of mediation should be emphasized, because a win-win scenario is the most realistic hope of avoiding conflict in the future.

Also, the mediator should emphasize that to be successful, both disputants must "Win!" because a win-win scenario is the most realistic hope of avoiding conflict in the future (Dunn, 2010).

Step 8. Sign a Contract of Agreement

The option or options the disputants select through the peer mediation process must be summarized in a contract that they should sign. This contract should state the presenting problem or conflict, and the problem resolution option chosen by the disputants, and display their signatures (Dunn, 2010). A sample peer mediation contract is in Figure 8.2.

Note two things on this contract. First, a follow-up session is recommended, as a critical component of the peer mediation process. For clarity, the mediator should include on the contract a date and time for that session. This lets students understand the importance of their work, because the mediator will review that work with a follow-up of their discussions and how the options may be working.

Next, while the school administrator should not participate in the peer mediation session, it is usually a good idea to have that administrator sign the contract along with the students. That serves to let the administrator know what conflict

Figure 8.2: Peer Mediation Resolution Contract

Date: _____

Peer Mediator: _____

First Student Participant: Name _____ Grade _____

Second Student Participant: Name _____ Grade _____

Problem:
The two disputants listed above came to Peer Mediation with the following conflict: ____

_____

Solution Chosen:

The two disputants agreed to the following:

_____

_____

_____

_____

Contract Follow-Up Session: We understand that in three weeks, the mediator will sit with us again to hold a follow-up discussion of the solutions in this contract.

Date and Time of Follow-Up Mediation Session: _____

Signatures: With our signatures below, we agree to abide by this contract and avoid future conflict by taking the action(s) above.

Student One: _____ Date _____

Student Two: _____ Date _____

School Administrator's Signature: _____ Date _____

---

resolution option the students have chosen, and it provides some basis for the administrator's ongoing work with the disputants, should the same conflict arise again. That signature will also serve to emphasize the seriousness of the commitment made by the students. By requiring that signature, the disputants will see that the principal will be receiving a copy for his signature, and this may persuade them to engage in the selected resolution option should future conflicts arise.

IMPLEMENTATION OF PEER MEDIATION

Because of the challenges in terms of time and resources to develop a peer mediation program, this is one strategy best implemented as a school-wide disciplinary strategy. More specifically, individual teachers can implement a class climate assessment, a morning meeting initiative, or even a conflict resolution program for their

students. However, peer mediation typically requires a set of experienced, trained peer mediators, and a classroom or other room
that is staffed with peer mediators during each period of the day.
This whole-school strategy therefore requires more time and more
resources for the mediator training than do other preventative strategies herein.

> Peer Mediation is best implemented as a school-wide disciplinary strategy.

With that said, the advantages of this initiative are motivation enough to make
the time and secure the resources (mostly time and resources to train mediators, and
space dedicated to the peer mediation sessions). All educators today are encouraged
to pursue this important disciplinary initiative (Cohen, 2014; Duncan, 2014; US
Department of Education, 2011). Below are a number of steps that administration
must take to initiate a school-wide peer mediation effort.

Select a program coordinator

Begin planning and secure resources

Select potential peer mediators

Set initial tasks of the mediators

Train mediators in conflict resolution skills

Begin limited peer mediation and troubleshoot the program

Select a program coordinator. Effective peer mediation programs always involve
management by an adult program coordinator, who is typically a veteran teacher,
guidance counselor, or assistant principal. This person will manage the program,
plan the training, collect data on program efficacy, and determine which students
may be involved as mediators (Study Guides and Strategies, 2014). The coordinator
should devote some time exclusively to the peer mediation program. So if a teacher
has this role, there should be one or two periods daily dedicated to managing the
program after it is up and running, though it will require more time during the first
six months of the implementation effort.

Begin planning and secure resources. The coordinator will need to undertake a
series of initial planning steps. Those duties include developing a proposed planning
document, training curriculum, and schedule for mediator training and program
implementation. Curricula for mediator training is typically found free of charge,
using online sources (the references in this book are a good starting point).

Other initial steps include identifying potential peer mediators and oversee-
ing their training, establishing a protocol for referral to the program, matching
mediators with specific conflicts, assisting with scheduling of mediation sessions,
presenting the proposed peer mediation program to the school faculty, and documenting efficacy of the peer mediation program overall. Finally, the administrators
will typically require progress reports of these planning steps, and preparation
of various planning documents and reports will take some time in the initial

implementation stages. This step alone may take several weeks, depending on the time commitment the coordinator can make to this program.

Select potential peer mediators. Peer mediators that represent the school body at large should be selected, and the program coordinator and the administrator may do this initially. They should select students from all age groups above grade four. They should also include, if possible, students from all races and every identifiable school clique (Study Guides and Strategies, 2014). By selecting students that represent the school as a whole, the resulting peer mediation team is more likely to have someone exactly appropriate for specific mediation situations.

> By selecting students that represent the school as a whole, the resulting peer mediation team is more likely to have someone exactly appropriate for specific mediation situations.

In addition to preselection and invitation, the peer mediation program should be widely publicized across the campus, and students should be encouraged to self-nominate for peer mediation training. Of course, in consultation with administrators at the school, the program coordinator should feel free to not use students who have been nominated if she feels those students may be unsuitable as mediators. For example, students who are enraged, who are frequently violent, or who consistently bully or sexually harass others are clearly not appropriate as mediators. This step should take several weeks.

With those cautions noted, there are advantages to including some at-risk or problem students within the selected group of peer mediators. Cohen (2014) discusses the advantage of teaching students with significant behavior problems the skills they need to become a peer mediator. Further, using some students who are not considered the best and brightest in the school can allow the peer mediation program to reach a wider group of students, including the at-risk population of the school.

Set initial tasks of the mediators. Once the administration selects a group of students, they should review all of the initial planning for the program and modify those plans as determined by the group. This assures wider buy-in to the peer mediation program overall and effectively empowers the student mediators within the program (Study Guides and Strategies, 2014).

Next, the student mediators should prepare a mission statement for the mediation process at the school. The program coordinator may wish to suggest a draft, but the mission statement should come from the mediators themselves, in order to foster their ownership of the program and secure their long-term commitment to it. That mission statement may stipulate specific school-wide goals of the program such as

> The peer mediation program at _____ Middle School will address at least 100 behavior problems during the 2016–2017 school year, with at least 85 percent of those mediation sessions resulting in a successful mediation contract.

Finally, at this point, the mediators should be encouraged to make a long-term commitment to the peer mediation program. Students should know that the training they receive will necessitate their participating in the program for several years, unless they have to withdraw (e.g., if their schoolwork suffers as a result of their commitment). Also, the parents of the mediators should be informed of their student's desire to participate and should sign off on that participation, because participation does involve some time on the part of the student. This step will require a series of perhaps three or four meetings of potential mediators, and depending on the scheduling of those meetings, may take several weeks or longer.

Train mediators in conflict resolution skills. Once students have committed to the program, and have worked through the initial planning, the actual mediator training can begin. Mediation training is not a one-time type of proposition, and different mediators will require more or less training. Typically, multiple training sessions—perhaps four or more one-hour sessions—should be planned to include several steps in the training. First, using a variety of online video resources, the program coordinator should have all students view and discuss several peer mediation sessions. This may take two training sessions or so. Here are a couple of videos from www.YouTube.com that can be used for this initial training. If you cannot find these, feel free to use other, similar videos.

> Mediation training is not a one-time type of proposition, and multiple training sessions—perhaps four or more hour-long sessions—should be planned to include several steps in the training.

www.youtube.com/watch?v=BI5gVrr4lv8

www.youtube.com/watch?v=4gQ0ZLdHlHM

After the trainee group reviews and discusses several videos of peer mediation sessions, the group may move on to role-play specific disputes among students. Role-play can be developed from problems that actually resulted from conflicts in the school, and students should experience these role-play scenarios from the perspective of both disputant and peer mediator. All mediators should be provided the opportunity to serve as mediator several times during the training. Once a student shows significant understanding of the process, he may be considered as a lead mediator trainee and can assist in the training of others. This will take one or two sessions for the training group.

The next step in peer mediation training is serving as co-mediator with the program coordinator in a real mediation of a school dispute. In that session, the student co-mediator should take the lead in the mediation session, proceeding through the specific steps above, and the program coordinator should observe the process, and step in only as necessary. Depending on the skills of the mediator, the program coordinator may wish to hold two or more sessions with the particular mediator serving in the co-mediation role, prior to graduating that mediator to full participation in the peer mediation program.

Finally, at no point should mediator training be considered over! Rather, the program coordinator should regularly schedule monthly meetings for the peer mediators. This allows the mediators to continually discuss problems they encounter in their mediation efforts and also serves as an ongoing training mechanism to improve each peer mediator's skills.

Begin limited peer mediation and troubleshoot the program. Once several peer mediators are fully trained, the program coordinator should assign one or more conflicts to those specific peer mediators. In each case, the program coordinator should debrief the peer mediator extensively relative to how the mediation proceeded and what problems the mediator may have encountered. They can then discuss those problems in the ongoing training meetings.

EFFICACY OF PEER MEDIATION

Research Basis for Peer Mediation

Research strongly supports the use of peer mediation as an effective disciplinary strategy in schools, and many advocates of peer mediation report successes in reducing a variety of behavioral problems in schools using this technique (Cohen, 2014; Duncan, 2014; Harris, 2005; Johnson & Johnson, 2005; McHenry, 2000; NCPC, 2014; Study Guides and Strategies, 2014). For example, Cohen (2014) reports that 90 percent of peer mediation sessions result in contractual agreements that resolve the conflict at hand. In those cases, the solutions peer mediation generated satisfied not only the students involved, but also their teachers and administrators.

> Research strongly supports the use of peer mediation as an effective disciplinary strategy in schools.

In another study, Johnson and Johnson (2005) review the extensive research on peer mediation and concludes that peer mediation programs help students develop more behavioral control in a number of ways. Specifically, they teach students to control their anger and be more effective in developing problem-solving skills, communication skills, and other interpersonal skills after the peer mediation process.

Further, behavioral improvement results from peer mediation can be documented school-wide (Harris, 2005; Johnson & Johnson, 2005; NCPC, 2014). For example, Harris (2005) documents that peer mediation programs are successful for resolving student conflicts and reducing suspensions and discipline referrals in schools. In another example, the National Crime Prevention Council (2014) reports a specific example from a high school in Stow, Ohio. Because of concerns with growing behavioral problems, the school counselors began in 1994 to train a core of twenty-five student mediators to assist with student disciplinary problems. Mediators managed problem behaviors such as hallway confrontations between students, dating relationship problems, student fights or verbal quarrels, or other behavioral problems teachers or principals referred. By 1998, the student mediators were managing over 100 discipline problems yearly, and everyone in the school—students, teachers, and administrators—considered the program a success. Also, those disciplinary problems no longer took up the time devoted to discipline among the teachers and administrators. The study also notes that most students who went through peer mediation demonstrated significant improvements in behavior. The program was so successful that it was extended to all schools in that district, and the high school mediators assisted with mediation in the lower grades (NCPC, 2014).

Efficacy Assessment in Your Schools

As Marzano (2003, 2007) repeatedly stresses, the efficacy of disciplinary interventions must be documented class by class and school by school in order to have long-term impact. When schools initiate a peer mediation program, they must be prepared to document program efficacy in a variety of ways. Because peer mediation is typically undertaken as a school-wide effort, those efficacy data should document a school-wide behavioral impact. Administrators should assess program impact on a variety of variables such as school suspensions, reports of fighting, disciplinary referrals, and crime on school grounds (NCPC, 2014).

SUMMARY

Both the Department of Education and the Department of Justice have recently endorsed peer mediation as an effective disciplinary strategy (Duncan, 2014; St. George, 2014; US Department of Education, 2011), and given that the overall efficacy of school disciplinary practices on the radar of these two federal agencies, they advise schools to implement a rigorous peer mediation program if one is not already in place. This program will empower students within the school to solve their own problems and conflicts, and as such it is a worthy instructional goal within itself. Therefore, my recommendation: all schools with populations older than grade three should consider implementing this program during the next school year. When done correctly, this will change the culture of the school, and greatly enhance school climate.

SECTION II
Targeted Disciplinary Interventions for Challenging Students

While almost all teachers can and do master the intricacies of general class management, there are many students whose behavior is a challenge to even the most experienced teachers (Bender, 2007; Marzano, 2003; Sousa, 2009). Having a set of intervention strategies in hand for these students can make the difference between teachers who enjoy their teaching role and those who, ultimately, leave the classroom. For intense disciplinary situations, teachers must respond to the immediate disciplinary problem in the class (e.g., an enraged student, or several students verbally challenging each other, fighting). Also, teachers must then implement a long-term individual intervention to alleviate that type of behavior in the future. This section addresses each of those needs.

The strategies in this section are not intended to be used by the whole class, but rather as specific targeted strategies for individual students. When a teacher sees a behavioral problem, she must intervene, and often, something more than the typical management strategies such as talking with the student, sending a student to the administrator, or calling a student's parents in for a conference will be needed. While I do strongly recommend that teachers use all of the general class management strategies, there are times when those ideas are simply not enough, and teachers will need to implement other interventions to curb behavior problems.

> There are times when general class management strategies are simply not enough, and teachers will need to implement other interventions to curb behavior problems.

First, this section presents a set of immediate teacher responses to enraged, angry, or misbehaving students—I refer to these as Band-Aid strategies. Teachers should use these to defuse explosive situations and regain control of the classroom. These are in Strategy 9. Next, this section presents a set of individual, longer-term disciplinary strategies that teachers should employ in those more challenging disciplinary situations. In each case, I recommend collecting some type of baseline data on the problem behavior, and collecting data during the intervention itself. In the data-driven world of teachers today, teachers without such intervention data are not prepared to deal with tough kids, and schools may be open to legal action if teachers do not use these best-practice interventions in dealing with various behavior problems. The only way to document the efficacy of disciplinary interventions is data collection on individual students' behaviors (Bender, 2007, 2012a; Marzano, 2003, 2007), so I emphasize such data collection in these strategies.

This section of the book assumes that teachers have implemented one or several of the whole-class management strategies I discussed in the first section, as those often provide a basis for the interventions here. The specific intervention strategies include

Strategy 9: Triggers and Band-Aids: Avoiding Power Struggles

Strategy 10: Peer Pressure to Improve Behavior

Strategy 11: The Group Contingency Strategy

Strategy 12: Self-Regulation and Goal Setting

Strategy 13: The Personal Responsibility Strategy

Strategy 14: Video Monitoring to Improve Behavior

Strategy 15: The Let's Make a Deal! Strategy: Negotiating Power in the Classroom

Strategy 9

Triggers and Band-Aids: Avoiding Power Struggles

One disciplinary challenge almost every teacher faces at some point involves a challenge to the teacher's authority by a misbehaving student. You may think of this as an invitation from an enraged student to engage in a power play. The challenge may come from a student who is in opposition most of the time, or from one who has bipolar disorder. In fact, some students just seem to be ticking time bombs of rage or verbal aggression, and challenge the teacher frequently (Sousa, 2009). Defusing these students early in the situation is critical.

Of course, I'm not talking about mild disagreements (e.g., dealing with students who don't wish to complete assignments). Rather, I'm talking about serious, emotionally charged situations, in which the student is fully invested in challenging the teacher's instructions, or cursing and hurling insults at the teacher. Should a student challenge a teacher in class in a verbally violent, enraged way, that student is often emotionally caught up in the moment and will say and do anything to "win." In that situation, teachers should expect complete noncompliance with anything they say.

In contrast, teachers cannot say or do anything to win a power struggle. We cannot invest ourselves enough to win at all costs, so it is not an overstatement to say that when a power play erupts between a teacher and student, the student always wins (Albert, 1996). Of course, teachers do have the ultimate responsibility for discipline; they can use an array of strategies to send a student out or perhaps recommend future exclusion from class. In that situation, one may well ask, "Who won the power play? Didn't the student win by being excluded from the very activity she was seeking to avoid?"

> One disciplinary challenge almost every teacher faces at some point involves a challenge to the teacher's authority by a misbehaving student.

Engaging in a power struggle with an enraged student can be dangerous for both the out-of-control student and the teacher. Walker (1998) indicates that in 75 percent of cases in which students physically attack teachers, there is some prelude that involves the escalation of a power play. Avoiding power plays with students is therefore not only effective from a disciplinary standpoint, but it is also the safe choice for teachers from a physical standpoint.

The main guideline is simple: teachers should avoid power plays with students at all costs (Albert, 1996; Colvin, Ainge, & Nelson, 1997). Preventing the escalation of a power play with a misbehaving student is like avoiding a ticking time bomb, and teachers are well advised to avoid, if at all possible, the explosion of anger or violence in the classroom. For practical, veteran teachers, this skill is well developed, and they can avoid in such a way to allow the student some space, and maybe even foster the development of a more positive relationship with the troubled student. Numerous authors indicate that the most effective thing a teacher can do is choose not to play the power play game (Sousa, 2009; Walker & Sylwester, 1998).

> Teachers should avoid power plays with students at all costs.

A SITUATION MANAGED BADLY

An example from my own public school days illustrates how I blew up a ticking time bomb of student anger as well as how badly I handled this situation! A student, I'll call her Joanne, enters my class one day fuming; I felt I could almost see smoke coming out of her ears, she was so angry! I was a first-year teacher, and certainly inexperienced. On that day, I try the behavioral idea of "ignoring the behavior to extinguish it," an intervention idea that can work with relatively mild misbehavior. As Joanne sits down, I instruct her to get her book out and begin her work. She looks up at me and says, "I ain't gonna work anymore today, dammit!" Then, she immediately withdraws by placing her head down on her desk.

Being a very inexperienced teacher at that point—which is to say, somewhat idiotic—I nevertheless realize my power has been challenged; I have been invited to a power play. Unfortunately, I respond to the invitation. My authority has been challenged, so I walk toward the student and raise my voice to her decibel level. Both are aggressive moves on my part. I say, "Oh yes, you will, Joanne. Now get that book open and let's get started!"

Immediately, I begin to back up as I see her head pop up; she is enraged, and I witness the fire shooting from her eyes. She begins to rise, and I think she is going to come over the desk at me! I really don't want a physical fight with a student, and needless to say, I'm wondering what in the world I could do next!

> I saw her head pop up; she was enraged, and I witnessed the fire shooting from her eyes. She began to rise, and I thought she was going to come over the desk at me!

In reflecting on that many times over, I realize I responded very badly to a power play. To make matters worse, recall that her head was already on her desk, after her verbal aggression and cursing. Why could I not have been smart enough to just let her leave it there for a while?

I could have just walked away after she cursed. I could have begun the class with the other students, and given Joanne a bit of time to calm herself. I could have then talked with her later. Remember, her head was already down on her desk! My actions here were truly stupid, and stemmed from inexperience.

Again, I can only plead the relative ignorance of an inexperienced teacher. I managed this situation about as badly as possible, and within a minute, Joanne and I were both marching toward the principal's office. I was feeling pretty lousy, and was sure that I'd mismanaged a bad situation. Who really won that power play? As it turned out, Joanne was mad at something said to her before she even entered my room that day, and I have wished a thousand times over that I'd dealt with that student and her explosion of anger differently.

Again, teachers should learn to avoid power plays with students at all costs, and they can prepare themselves in two ways. First, teachers must learn to avoid actions that may trigger misbehavior among oppositional-defiant or bipolar students. Next, teachers need to arm themselves with a variety of responses that will help them extract themselves from a building power play, before it escalates. Guidelines for each of these areas are below.

AVOIDING THE TRIGGERS

Some students display behavioral problems when triggered by certain events in the classroom. In particular, students with bipolar and/or oppositional-defiant disorder often burst into angry behavior because of specific triggers or environmental events. In fact, the trigger may be seemingly insignificant to others. Sometimes merely changing subjects is enough to cause an outburst. Therefore, in addition to learning the Band-Aids below, all teachers should give some consideration to noting, and ultimately avoiding, emotional triggers that set students off (Hall, Williams, & Hall, 2000; McIntosh, Herman, Sanford, McGraw, & Florence, 2004).

Avoiding triggering students is not terribly difficult, and although it is not a disciplinary strategy per se, these behaviors can be considered best teaching practices. This list comes from a variety of sources (Hall, Williams, & Hall, 2000; McIntosh et al., 2004; Salend & Sylvestre, 2005; Zuna & McDougall, 2004).

Call troubled students by name. Often calling troubled students by name, using a soft, easy tone of voice, will help calm them, and this will often help ease transitions. Here is an example: "Brittany, I can see that you are working hard today, and I just want you to know that I appreciate that! I'm really glad to have you in my class, Brittany!"

Stand next to troubled students. I suggest that, for each transition in class, the teacher position himself near their challenging student. At times, being within an arm's reach can alleviate any problem. Also, when unexpected events occur, teachers should physically move toward specific students with behavioral problems.

Use pre-warnings. Simply letting students know that a transition is coming can help reduce some behavior problems. In that way, the students who are overly sensitive to change can get mentally prepared first, and are less likely to feel frustration if it takes them a few seconds longer to get through the transition.

Here is an example of a pre-warning. In preparing for a coming transition, a teacher might pre-warn the class using a statement such as, "We'll be starting our math in about five minutes, once we all finish writing our paragraphs. Sometimes you guys get too loud when we change subjects, so for the next three minutes everything in class has to be said as a whisper! That way, we'll avoid any problems."

Compliment troubled students. Although teachers should always avoid false praise, they should make a habit of complimenting students with behavioral challenges at least as often as they do other students. This will help build a positive relationship, and generally helps foster improved behavior.

Provide students with some choice of activities. Offering choices can empower students with behavioral challenges and may prevent class disruption. Teachers might give students a choice of which assignment they wish to do, and having some choice reduces the incidence of defiant behaviors.

Here is an example: Teachers frequently develop various versions of the same general assignment in order to differentiate the work for students in the class who may need more of a challenge. To an advanced student who frequently disrupts class by making jokes, the teacher says, "Jamie. I usually give you a few more problems than some of the other students, but today I'll give you a choice. If you promise that you won't make any jokes or disrupt class by talking out during our next work session, I'll let you complete this assignment using either pen and paper or on the computer. Can you make that commitment, and if so, which assignment would you like to do?"

Use peer buddies. Use a peer buddy system that partners students together. In most cases, a partner of a student with behavioral issues will assist in curbing misbehavior.

Teach behaviors for transitions. Many students appear disoriented when asked to simply form a line and teachers are left wondering how a student can manage to not understand that request. Of course, such behavior doesn't result from a lack of understanding the instructions but rather may stem from frustration ("I have no friends") or social isolation. Students may then wonder, "Who should I stand next to?" They end up standing in the middle of the hallway, while everyone else lines up nicely along the wall.

Here is an example for teaching specific transition behaviors: A teacher is asking young students to line up along the wall. He should give troubled students specific lining up instructions such as, "Jamie, I always want you in front of the line and close to me. You're strong and I might need a strong young man to help me!"

Give clear instructions. Teachers should get in the habit of giving clear, short, directive commands and using pauses to break up multiple instructions. Rather than stringing different transition tasks together, teachers might say, "Please put away your math worksheet and get out your English book." Pause for about ten seconds, then say, "Turn to page 138."

Establish clear class routines. Knowing what comes next is essential for some students, so, I always recommend that teachers in the lower grades post a daily schedule (what subjects teachers will teach and when) on the whiteboard. Also, if at all possible, teachers should not change that schedule. Changes in class routine are sometimes necessary and may even enrich the class, but they also may be a trigger because students with oppositional-defiant or bipolar disorder gain security from the structure of the class routine.

DISCIPLINARY BAND-AIDS FOR EXPLOSIVE STUDENTS

In addition to the avoidance of triggers, teachers must learn to extract themselves from power plays by angry and defiant students, if possible. In one sense, the teacher cannot manage these situations with disciplinary interventions. In the power play situation above, I was merely responding to a student's anger and explosive behavior. Unfortunately, that is a situation teachers often find themselves in, and disciplinary interventions are not particularly useful at that precise moment. Rather, effective disciplinary interventions are not situational responses. The most effective disciplinary interventions are planned in advance and take time, so teachers cannot immediately apply the most effective interventions in situations such as this.

However, in addition to avoiding triggers, teachers can learn certain avoidance behaviors that they can use to avoid the escalation of a power play. These techniques can prevent, in many cases, the explosion of verbal abuse or violence (Bender, 2007; Sousa, 2009). If teachers manage the power play by avoiding it, they can then deal with the misbehavior later by talking with the student and/or planning a longer-term behavioral intervention. In that sense, you may think of the tactics below as Band-Aids to alleviate the power struggle right away. Teachers can apply them immediately to contain a situation, and then plan and implement a longer-term behavioral intervention. As the situation above demonstrates, Band-Aids are important, indeed critical, in the teacher's arsenal of responses to misbehavior.

> The tactics presented here may be thought of as Band-Aids to immediately alleviate a power struggle.

To avoid power plays, teachers should use one or more of the avoidance techniques, or Band-Aids, below. Effective options for the teacher to use in defusing the ticking time bomb greatly enhance the teacher's ability to manage the situation and hopefully prevent an escalation or overt explosion of verbal or physical violence. Managing such situations wisely may even help teachers build a more positive relationship with the student over time (Bender, 2007).

I recommend that all teachers become comfortable with several of these Band-Aids, and if the first attempt to calm an enraged student doesn't work, try another! Almost anything is generally preferable to an explosion of verbal or physical aggression in the classroom. Therefore, teachers should be prepared, on a moment's notice, to use these Band-Aids as defusing techniques. These ideas come from a variety of sources (Albert, 1996; Colvin et al., 1997; Sousa, 2009; Walker, 1998; Walker & Sylwester, 1998) and generally allow the teacher to escape power struggles with students and defuse the time bomb of student anger.

Defusing an Explosive Student

- Repeat the instructions
- Offer a joke
- Call the student's first name
- Inquire about a student's anger
- Use a calm voice tone
- Respect students' personal space
- Share power
- Postpone the discussion

Repeat the Instructions

When a teacher gives instructions and a student challenges them or disrupts class in some other way, one option is to merely repeat the instructions rather than respond directly to the student's challenge. It is hard to argue with someone who is not addressing the challenge point but is merely saying the same thing over and over again. After two or three repetitions, students might stop making counterarguments since the teacher is not responding to those anyway. They then will generally, often reluctantly, begin their work.

Teachers should therefore merely repeat the instructions, word for word if possible, in a calm voice two or three times after each challenge. Here is an example: A teacher gives the directions, "Please put your math book away and take out your history text." A disruptive student says, "I don't want to do history today!" This challenge holds the potential of becoming a transition disruption in the class, so the teacher responds by moving toward that student and repeating it in a slightly louder voice, "I said, please put your math book away and take out your history text."

Sometimes the student persists with another verbal challenge such as, "Do we have to?" Again the teacher should repeat the instructions. "I said, please put your math book away and take out your history text."

This idea works for one simple reason. It is difficult to argue with someone who is merely repeating themselves! After three or four such gently spoken repetitions, the student will, in most cases, desist in the challenge. At that point, the teacher should then turn, walk away, and begin to assist another student. This will sometimes allow the offending student to calm down a bit. However, teachers should never turn their back on an angry student, and if an explosion occurs, they will need to use another, stronger defusing idea.

Offer a Joke

Well-timed humor that is not directed in any way at the student can often defuse a student's anger (Albert, 1996). In the situation involving myself, in which a student named Joanne cursed at me, I could have merely replied, "Well, that's one way to go." That humor, if directed at anyone, would have been directed at my own ability to control my classroom and not at the student's cursing. Still, such a joke may have allowed me to escape an overt power play with Joanne, and perhaps, continue the lesson with other students.

Again, please do not interpret this recommendation to use humor as an opportunity to joke at the student's expense. In fact, I try to never use humiliation or shame as a disciplinary tool (though some of the strategies in this book do involve some humiliation, as an unintended side effect). Still, a bit of humor, unrelated to a problem behavior, can sometimes defuse a behavioral outburst.

Call the Student's First Name

Softly calling a student by her first name in a potentially explosive situation can have a calming effect on the student (Sousa, 2009). This is a mechanism that hostage negotiators are trained to use because for almost everyone, hearing one's own name in a calm voice tends to calm us down. Actually, there are certain neurologically based reactions to hearing one's own name that induce calmness. The teacher should use a quieter, softer voice each time to call the student's name, and that may help alleviate the potential explosion. The teacher can then continue class and/or inquire about the student's anger later.

Inquire About a Student's Anger

Occasionally, teachers should take a moment and inquire about the cause of a student's anger (Bender, 2007). The teacher might say something like, "I can see that the assignment upsets you. Is it something we can talk about?" Clearly, teachers would rather take a moment and have a brief discussion about the student's concern than have to deal with an anger explosion or other power play in class. Teachers should, however, be cautious with this tactic because it might lead to a lengthy discussion with the student. In fact, if students learn that teachers are willing to talk about problems, some students will intentionally use this strategy to avoid assignments.

Use a Calm Voice Tone

Using a softer tone with less volume, a teacher's voice can sometimes help defuse highly charged emotional situations (Sousa, 2009). This is another technique police forces worldwide use, because it is very effective. Human beings are hardwired neurologically to match those we are talking to in a variety of areas including voice volume, voice tone, emotional intensity, physical stance, and even facial expressions (Bender, 2007). In some intense classroom situations, perhaps a noncompliant student shouting curses at a teacher, the teacher will have a natural inclination to match the voice tone, volume, and emotional intensity of the student, and that will often escalate the situation, resulting in an explosion of violence.

I sometimes give a rather tongue-in-cheek assignment to teachers in my workshops in order to illustrate this point. I tell the teachers to prove this to themselves; they should go home and begin an argument with their spouse about anything, shouting loudly, just to see if they can have their husband or wife shouting back in less than thirty seconds. I then quickly tell them NOT to do that assignment! Such an activity is never recommended, but it does illustrate this point very well; we all match others on these variables in emotionally charged situations.

By knowing about this voice-matching tendency, teachers are empowered to respond better to angry students. Rather than match an angry student's voice tone, volume, and emotional intensity, teachers should train themselves to set a calmer tone and more gentle emotional intensity. That, in turn, is an invitation for a student to match the teacher on that calmer, less intense level. Teachers should always use a voice tone and volume that is somewhat softer than the student's in a potential power struggle.

Respect Students' Personal Space

Teachers are not usually taught about students' physical or personal space, but they should be because such insight can frequently prevent the escalation of violence when dealing with most violent students. For that reason, almost all police officers have some training about the personal space of perpetrators and/or other angry individuals they might have to confront. This training empowers them to manage explosive anger much more effectively than most teachers.

In most westernized countries such as the United States, physical space extends in an oval shape, about two and a half feet in front of the body, but only six inches to one's side and rear. Most persons who are raised in the United States, Canada, and Western Europe become quite uncomfortable if another person enters that personal space; we might feel as if the other person is invading our space, and we even feel threatened.

Personal space, however, is quite different in certain Middle Eastern and Asian cultures. In those countries, there is generally much less personal space, and individuals often stand quite close to each other during a social discussion—perhaps as close as a foot or so from each other. For most Westerners, that distance is an invasion of personal space, while it is quite usual in the Middle East. Given a number of international students in schools today, teachers must become more aware of these personal space differences between cultures.

One constant among cultures is that they view invasion of personal space as aggression. In almost every culture on earth, entering the personal space of an enraged person almost always increases the intensity of the aggression, and may even encourage a physical attack from an angry student. Therefore, teachers should stay out of the personal space of students at all times and find other means to deal with the situation (unless of course, the student is attempting to harm himself or others).

As an example of using personal space appropriately, let's return to the situation I shared in which I managed a behavioral disruption so poorly. Recall that a student, Joanne, challenges my authority and that I respond verbally as I walk toward the student. To make matters worse, I raise my voice to her decibel level and say. "Oh yes, you will, Joanne. Now get that book open and let's get started!"

> Entering the personal space of an enraged person is an act of aggression, and will often encourage a physical attack from the angry student.

Both those moves on my part—matching her decibel level, and moving toward her, thereby invading her personal space—exacerbated a bad situation. I should have done the exact opposite. Rather than move toward her, I could have responded just as well by only looking directly at her—a much less aggressive move on my part. Next, I should have asked a question in a softer voice tone (not matching her level of voice intensity). I could have said, "Joanne, I can see you are upset, and I'm sorry if I've done something that upset you. Can you help me understand why you're angry?"

Had I been taught to use personal space awareness and voice tone in my disciplinary practices, I am confident I would have managed that situation better. I believe I could have defused that explosion and would not have marched that student up to the principal's office. Again, knowing these simple techniques—avoiding triggers and avoiding power plays—will help all beginning teachers and many veteran teachers as well.

Share Power

I also recommend that teachers be prepared to share power in the classroom, up to a limit, with students. If a student challenges you on an assignment or task, and mentions something else he would like to do, the teacher should be in a position, at least some of the time, to negotiate with the student, and therefore share power concerning when the student may do the tasks (Colvin et al., 1997). Even a small acknowledgment of the student's power can often improve class climate and might avoid a major explosion for many kids. Offering students choices between various assignments and activities is, in today's class management pedagogy, strongly encouraged!

Postpone the Discussion

Finally, postponing a discussion of a student's misbehavior or anger may be an appropriate tactic (Albert, 1996). Realizing this is directly contradictory with an earlier suggestion, teachers will have to determine, nearly instantly, which response might work to defuse a difficult situation. If a student is highly emotionally charged or clearly enraged, the teacher might let the student know that she wants to discuss the problem at a later time, perhaps at the end of the period. Sometimes, merely knowing that a caring adult is interested can defuse a student's anger or rage.

A CASE STUDY

In general, these trigger avoidance and Band-Aid tactics are not typically implemented as behavioral interventions in and of themselves. Rather these are general guidelines for avoiding specific triggers of misbehavior or guidelines for a teacher's immediate response in a power struggle type of situation that should allow a teacher to avoid a power struggle with the confrontational student. After the teacher avoids the immediate power struggle, the teacher should then plan on using over the longer term one of the targeted intervention strategies in the rest of this section in order to help the student improve his behavior.

With that noted, in certain cases, teachers may wish to use one or more of these tactics as a targeted intervention. Here is an example: In Mr. Beddard's eighth-grade mathematics class, Mr. Beddard finds himself in numerous power struggles with a student named Jessica. In some cases, Jessica simply refuses to complete work in class, while in other situations, she states that she is not doing any homework the next night. In fact, she makes that statement exactly when Mr. Beddard is assigning homework. He says, "I want you folks to do the three rows of problems at the top of page 289 for homework." While he is completing this sentence, Jessica says, "We shouldn't have any homework tonight. We have a home football game this afternoon!"

Of course, on the face of it, that statement sounds reasonable, at least from a student's perspective. But Mr. Beddard responds to the objection by saying, "Okay, guys, get real! Most of you don't even go to the football games." Being a veteran teacher, as soon as he says it, he knows he has made a mistake. He has, in effect, issued an invitation to everyone else in the class to protest that they are indeed going to the game that afternoon. Within a few seconds, no fewer than seven other students are protesting that they planned on going to the game!

That afternoon, Mr. Beddard reflects on the matter, and he realizes that he had fallen into a student's trap. He'd participated in a power struggle with Jessica. Further, he realizes that, all too often, he responds to a student's point in such situations when, in reality, the student is not trying to make a reasonable request but merely trying to avoid work. So, Mr. Beddard decides he needs to break his habit of responding to such student comments..

For the next three days, Mr. Beddard jots down the number of times that Jessica objects to work or homework in his class or disrupts the class in any other type of power struggle challenge to his authority. He then places that baseline data on a chart, which is in Figure 9.1. As those data show, Jessica is issuing power struggle challenges to Mr. Beddard between three and seven times each day!

Mr. Beddard decides that, for Jessica, the appropriate intervention is to refuse to discuss her supposedly reasonable request, and merely repeat the instructions. He begins that intervention on a Monday and continues to note the number of times Jessica issues a power struggle challenge. For example, if Jessica issues the same power struggle challenge as above, Mr. Beddard uses a softer voice and repeats the instructions: "I want you folks to do the three rows of problems at the top of page 289 for homework." Then, of course, Jessica objects a second time, challenging his fairness: "That's not fair! We want to go to the game!" Mr. Beddard is prepared and again lowers his voice volume and repeats, "I want you folks to do the three rows of problems at the top of page 289 for homework."

Figure 9.1: A Repeated Instructions Intervention

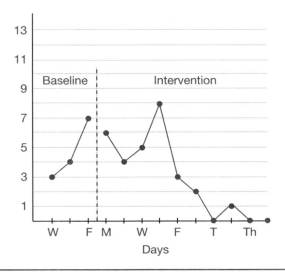

As the intervention data show, Jessica was fairly quick to respond to this intervention of repeating instructions. It is a fact that few students will continue an argument when the teacher is using a soft voice and merely repeating the same thing over and over again. In some cases, the teacher might have to repeat the instruction three or four times, but in most cases that will be enough to get the students back on track. In this instance, the data show that within five days, the number of power struggle challenges Jessica presented was beginning to fall. By the end of the second week, Mr. Beddard's repeated instructions intervention had all but eliminated Jessica's attempts at having a power struggle with the teacher.

Further, Mr. Beddard also noticed that other students had reduced their verbal challenges to his assignments also. In that sense, not only had Mr. Beddard curbed a potential problem with Jessica but indirectly improved behavior of several other students as well.

SUMMARY

Again, these trigger avoidance and Band-Aid guidelines are not typically used as interventions themselves. However they can prepare a teacher to respond to power struggles in the classroom. Also, these trigger avoidance guidelines and Band-Aids can be very effective for students who are consistently enraged as well as the student who only explodes into overt aggression and range occasionally. Of course, all teachers should make a habit of avoiding triggers that set students off. Also, while most teachers will need the Band-Aid tactics at times, it is a fact that teachers do not typically learn these defusing strategies in pre-service classes. Of course, most veteran teachers do pick up many of these tactics on their own over time, but all teachers will need some of these tactics.

Further, the tactics in this strategy should not be considered disciplinary intervention strategies like those covered elsewhere in this book; teachers will never collect data on the efficacy of the tactics in this strategy. Rather, these tactics represent immediate teacher responses to potential power plays, or emotionally explosive situations. That is why I present this strategy first in the section on dealing with highly challenging students.

Because all teachers hope to establish a positive relationship with challenging students over time, they should never engage in power plays the student creates. Rather, all educators must find ways to avoid the initial power play and positively influence these students toward less emotional intensity. While I may have faced more challenging behavior problems in my personal teaching experience than some teachers (i.e., teaching eighth- and ninth-grade special education students), all teachers will probably face some type of power play challenge from their students at some point. Therefore, virtually every teacher will need some tactics to help in these situations, and having command of three or four of the tactics in this section can make the difference between an effective teacher and a teacher who, within a few short weeks, is seeking another line of work. Therefore, teachers are well advised to know how to manage a ticking time bomb, a power play challenge, or other emotionally charged situations without entering a power struggle with a student. These trigger avoidance ideas and behavioral Band-Aids are critical in almost every classroom today.

Strategy 10

Peer Pressure to Improve Behavior

Relationships that students have with their peers are a critical influence on behavior of students of all ages. However, for students in grade four and above, peer influence may be the most important influence on a student's behavior (Bender, 2007). When students begin puberty, the influence of the peer group increases rather drastically, and teachers can use that influence to improve behavior (Salend, Whittaker, & Reeder, 1992; Tanaka & Reid, 1997).

The peer pressure strategy, sometimes referred to as *peer confrontation*, is a powerful disciplinary strategy that involves holding a discussion of a student's problematic behaviors with his peers in the classroom. For attention-seeking students and students with other overt or even severe disciplinary problems, the last thing they want to see is their behavior critically analyzed by their peers. This strategy is therefore appropriate when peers have the most influence on behavior, generally from grades four through high school (Gable, 1995; Sandler, Arnold, Gable, & Strain, 1987). The teacher can use this strategy in a wide variety of disciplinary situations, including aggressive behavior and other highly emotional situations.

To understand the power of the peer pressure strategy, one need only consider the importance of perception during puberty and in the early teen and teen years. Perception during the elementary, middle, and secondary school years is one key to student behavior. Specifically, the identity of adolescents is heavily tied to what they believe others perceive about them. In fact, kids at this age often feel as if their entire lives are something of a play or performance that they put on for their peers. This is the time at which personal appearance becomes increasingly important, and one component of personal appearance is a student's desire to look quite different from her parents. Early adolescents begin to dress and act much more like each other, and this should yield insight on who truly influences students' behavior during those years.

> Peer confrontation is a powerful disciplinary strategy that involves holding a discussion of a student's problematic behaviors with his peers in the classroom.

The peer confrontation strategy is useful during this phase of development because it harnesses the growing influence of the peers in fostering appropriate behavior. In particular, teachers use the peer confrontation strategy for three reasons: (1) to remove the audience for inappropriate behaviors, (2) to elicit the appropriate behavior through the use of peer pressure, and (3) to help students develop an understanding of their own behavior.

> For students with overt or even severe disciplinary problems, the last thing they want to see is their behavior critically analyzed by their peers.

WHEN SHOULD I TRY PEER CONFRONTATION?

Almost every elementary, middle, or high school teacher has seen kids who show off through misbehavior—including defiant and aggressive behavior. Young adolescents who misbehave are often rewarded by peer-group admiration, and this can lead to increased behavior problems in the classroom. If you have students who are using their defiance as a means to earn attention from their peers or play off the attention of other students in your class, and if you wish to get rid of the "audience" for misbehavior and get that audience working for you rather than against you, the peer confrontation strategy is your best option.

Unlike some of the other strategies covered in this book, the peer confrontation strategy is useful for situations in which students are angry or heavily emotionally involved in other ways. Even when students are fighting, after they are separated, the teacher can implement a peer confrontation strategy. Also, for kids who consistently bully others, who overtly act out, or who are seeking attention, this strategy is useful.

However, there are some students for whom this strategy is not appropriate. Of course, the teacher should avoid the strategy if he can use instead the preventative tactics in Section I, but he should also avoid peer pressure if a particular child seems devastated by even the smallest degree of class attention or embarrassment. Many teachers have had the experience of teaching intensely shy students or students who would feel particularly sensitive to any open discussion of their behavior. Although some embarrassment will be the natural by-product of this strategy, the strategy is intended primarily to remove the audience that supports misbehavior (through peer attention, etc.) and help kids analyze their behavior and find ways to get their needs met without misbehavior. Embarrassment is not intended as the primary result of this strategy, and if a child is particularly easy to embarrass, this is probably not an appropriate strategy for that situation.

STEPS FOR IMPLEMENTING PEER CONFRONTATION: A CASE STUDY

Peer pressure is a simple, though powerful strategy for every teacher to use. It involves a six-step process, and takes only minimal class time. The teacher actually does steps 2 through 5 in the class, and they should take no more than two or three minutes of class time, making this a very efficient way to manage disruptive behavior. To best demonstrate this strategy, a classroom case study is below.

Steps in the Peer Pressure Strategy

1. Collect baseline data

2. Inquire about a problem with the peer group

3. Analyze the problem behavior

4. Identify alternative behaviors to meet the student's needs

5. Elicit the student's willingness to try one of the alternatives

6. Compare baseline and intervention data

When a student consistently interrupts the class or demonstrates a problematic behavior, the teacher should take some type of baseline data on how often it occurs. A simple frequency count will usually suffice for this. For example, Ms. Waller teaches a seventh-grade English literature class in which a student named Chas Palmer enjoys widespread audience attention for cursing in class. Needless to say, each time Chas curses in class, the class snickers until Ms. Waller can re-establish control. Five weeks ago, as a result of Chas's cursing, Ms. Waller sent him to the principal, and the next week, she called his parents in for a conference, with little results.

Step 1: Collect Baseline Data

Baseline data is essential when students consistently misbehave in the classroom, and all subsequent strategies I recommend in this book for individually targeted interventions begin with collection of baseline data on the behavior problem. In this example, Ms. Waller decides to take a more proactive step, use a peer confrontation approach, and that begins with Ms. Waller collecting several days' worth of baseline data. Figure 10.1 presents a four-day, baseline frequency count of how many times Chas cursed in the English lit class, showing that Chas disrupted the class by cursing an average of 4.5 times in each class. To collect this information, Ms. Waller merely had to mark on her notepad each time Chas cursed, and then instructed Chas to hush and return to work. Collecting these data therefore did not disturb the ongoing instruction.

Figure 10.1:   Chas's Cursing Behavior Intervention

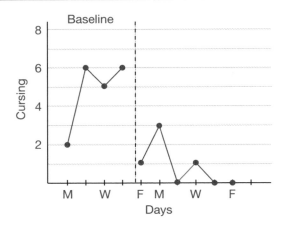

Step 2: Inquire About a Problem Behavior With the Peer Group

This is the first step done in the class and therefore takes up class time. When Chas first curses in class, Ms. Waller begins a problem-solving discussion of Chas's behavior by asking a question that defuses the situation and removes the class's attention from Chas's cursing by focusing on the specific behavior problem. The sample dialogue below provides examples of what Ms. Waller may say when Chas curses as well as the types of responses that other students in the class may give. In a voice loud enough to get every student's attention, Ms. Waller begins the strategy by saying,

> Wait a minute, everyone. We just saw an inappropriate behavior that disrupted our work. What problem behavior did we all just see?

With that question, Ms. Waller is focusing the class on the misbehavior that stopped the classwork rather than on Chas, specifically. Other statements she could use include

> We're going to stop class right now because something important just happened that interrupted our work time. Can anyone describe the behavior problem that just happened, please?

The desired response is to have another student in the class accurately describe the behavior problem that disrupted the class—Chas's cursing—without specifically criticizing Chas. The statements the teacher makes should therefore focus not only on the behavior problem but also highlight that offense as an offense to the class.

Go to www.learningsciences.com/bookresources to download figures and tables.

Of course, the students will not realize what this new procedure is the first time the teacher attempts it. Students may accurately identify the behavior, but Ms. Waller might get a response such as,

> Chas is being a jerk.

Clearly, this is not where Ms. Waller wants the discussion to go. Therefore, she stops this with the statement,

> No! We do not call other students names in this class. I want to know what behavior just occurred that stopped us from doing our work.

Note in the dialogue here that when another class member calls Chas a name, Ms. Waller actually comes to Chas's defense, and that results in considerable power for the teacher in the next few moments, in Chas's eyes.

Prior to moving on with the procedure, let's analyze the process up to this point. Thus far, Chas disrupted class and yet Ms. Waller didn't even look in his direction. Rather, she removed the audience for Chas's misbehavior because the class is, at that point, engaging with Ms. Waller and discussing Chas's problem behavior. Further, when another class member called Chas a name, she defended Chas! At this point, Chas is expecting some punishment, but he hasn't received it. Each of these factors is a positive result of this procedure and empowers the teacher in dealing with Chas's problem behavior.

Step 3: Analyze the Problem Behavior

Ms. Waller asks a student to give her a one-sentence description of the specific behavior problem, rather than a direct criticism of Chas. The student says,

> Somebody just cussed in class.

Ms. Waller moves the discussion on to analyze why a student might do that behavior. She may ask one of the following questions:

> Can anyone guess why Chas might do that?

> Why would someone do that?

Chas's peers offer some guesses as to why Chas misbehaved, and those shed light on what Chas needs and hopes to gain through his misbehavior. Students may say,

> Chas just likes making us laugh.

> Chas can't do the work and needed help so he avoided it.

Both of these are possible reasons for Chad's misbehavior, so Ms. Waller would thank each student offering these possible reasons. Of course, Chas is listening to his peers critically analyze his misbehavior. Further, Chas's peers have identified several possible needs including the possible need for attention or help with the work. Ms. Waller wants the rest of the class to participate by stating possible reasons for the misbehavior, so she encourages them to answer for a minute or two. Still somewhat puzzled, Chas listens to the discussion, and by this point Ms. Waller has the class critically analyzing a misbehavior rather than snickering and serving as an audience for that inappropriate behavior. Again, this is a powerful deterrent and further empowers Ms. Waller by removing Chas's audience. Note also that Ms. Waller still hasn't engaged with Chas about his misbehavior.

Step 4: Identify Alternative Behaviors to Meet the Student's Needs

Ms. Waller invites the class to continue their problem solving about Chas's behavior by suggesting other options for Chas to use when he wants attention or needs help with the work. She can elicit these options by the following types of statements:

> Can we suggest other things someone could do if he needs help? We are not here to criticize anyone, but we do want to help everyone control their temper and stop cussing. Can someone suggest what a student may want to do when he feels he is getting angry?

Ideally, responses from the class will involve more constructive options for Chas to use. Possible answers from the class may include:

> He could put his head down for a minute and calm down. Raise his hand and ask for help.

Again, let's analyze what has happened in the class to this point. First of all, in a situation where Chas thought he would get a great deal of positive attention from his peers, they instead analyzed his behavior coolly and critically. Next, Chas heard Ms. Waller defend him when another class member called him a name. This alone can have powerful effects with some troubled students. Then, in a situation in which Chas thought he would get punished, Ms. Waller showed that by stopping others from doing their work, his offense was an offense against the class. This is very punishing for most preadolescents and adolescents, who do not generally engage in misbehavior to offend others in the class (though they may wish to offend the teacher!).

Step 5: Elicit the Student's Participation

This step takes time away from the class, but the teacher may also do this outside of class. However, the step is critical to the process overall. In fact, this step represents a critical decision on the part of the teacher. Ideally, Ms. Waller wants to elicit Chas's agreement to use one of the alternative behaviors generated in the class discussion, and at some point she must engage with Chas to request that he consider using that alternative. Her goal is to briefly discuss the problem behavior and the behavioral options with Chas and get him to buy into trying the solution(s) that the class offered. She can accomplish this within the class setting by merely turning to Chas immediately after the class completes the two- to three-minute problem-solving discussion above, and requesting that he try these ideas. This is how the procedure is implemented in the efficacy research, and it is shown to work in public school classrooms (Gable, 1995; Tanaka & Reid, 1997).

However, in the real world of teaching this may be a bit idealized. For some behaviors (e.g., fighting and overt name calling), certain disruptive students may be too emotionally charged to participate in the discussion immediately after hearing the class analyze their behavior. Therefore, Ms. Waller must make a choice about when to invite Chas's participation in the solutions offered. If Chas seems calm during the class discussion, then Ms. Waller can continue the procedure in class by moving on to this next step and invite Chas to consider putting his head down rather than cursing, or asking for help if he needs it.

Alternatively, if Chas is still highly charged, angry, or appears frustrated, Ms. Waller may choose to wait until the end of the class period and then pull Chas aside for this final debriefing step. For most problem behaviors, a later individual conversation with the student will work best because students will often be angry immediately after the removal of their audience.

However, the decision on when to hold this brief conference with the student is solely up to the teacher. If, in Ms. Waller's view, Chas is not angry or overly excited after the class analyzes and discusses his behavior, she may complete the process then by turning to him in class and saying,

> Chas, would you like to try putting your head down or raising your hand? We'd all like to help you stop cussing so we can continue our work.

Again, note the last phrase of this statement. Ms. Waller again emphasizes the need of the class not to be disrupted. If Chas indicates a willingness to try the alternative options offered, Ms. Waller can conclude the in-class procedure merely by indicating that the class should return to their work.

In using the peer pressure strategy in class, Ms. Waller might expect to undergo this same type of dialogue four to six times, relative to Chas's cursing behavior, over a four- to ten-day period. In short, once will not be enough to curb a problematic behavior. However, both the class as a whole and Chas in particular will quickly master this strategy, with Chas realizing that each time he curses in class, the class will once again analyze and discuss his behavior. Unless he wants his classmates to discuss his behavior again, Chas will learn that he needs to curb his cursing and other attention-seeking behavior. For this reason, once Ms. Waller begins the intervention, she must be willing to see it through by stopping the class each time Chas disrupts the ongoing class work. Each session will take two to four minutes, and in some cases she may hold more than one such discussion in a single class period. However, soon the class will grow weary with Chas's misbehavior, and Chas will disrupt class less. In most cases in the research, a week or two of the intervention will be enough to stop students' misbehaviors.

Step 6: Compare the Baseline and Intervention Data

As stated previously, targeted interventions must involve specific data collection procedures, and they therefore involve comparing baseline and intervention data. The teacher can collect these data as easily as making a mark on a notepad each time a student disrupts class. Figure 10.1 shows baseline data for four days and a six-day intervention period. The data indicate that this intervention curbed Chas's cursing, reducing that behavior to less than once per class.

ADDITIONAL GUIDELINES FOR STRATEGY APPLICATION

The case study above presents the basics of the strategy and should be enough to allow teachers to apply this strategy in their classes. However, there are several variations and guidelines that may help, depending on the individual class.

First, if a teacher chooses to use this strategy as a targeted intervention with a particular student, the teacher may wish to expose the class to the strategy beforehand. Teachers could try this strategy first with students in the class other than the targeted student, targeting behaviors of students that are not the biggest behavior problem. In this fashion, the class learns how to participate in the technique before the teacher applies the strategy with the target student. Also, it is quite easy to use this strategy with two or three targeted students at the same time, and this can be an advantage when multiple students in the classroom demonstrate behavior problems.

Next, teachers should share the project with the principal and parents as soon as the student chooses not to cooperate. This keeps everyone informed and lets others know that the teacher is undertaking a serious intervention to help the student improve his behavior.

Finally, teachers should be sensitive to the impact of this strategy on the targeted students. If a student becomes highly uncomfortable and indicates that she feels the procedure is an effort of the class to gang up on her, the teacher may wish to discontinue this strategy and select another option. The intent with this strategy is to get the student to think objectively about her behavior and not to overtly embarrass her.

> The intent with this strategy is to get the student to think objectively about her behavior, and not to overtly embarrass her.

As I discussed above, it may be necessary in some cases to talk with the student after class, after he has calmed down a bit. Teachers may then show the baseline data to the student and encourage willing participation.

ADVANTAGES OF THE PEER CONFRONTATION PROCEDURE

There are a number of advantages of this procedure that make it a powerful option for the teacher to consider. First, the teacher can easily use this as a data-driven, highly targeted disciplinary procedure to focus on behavior problems of a particular student. In my experience, it is not uncommon to find that, although teachers frequently experience fairly severe disciplinary problems in the classroom, some teachers fail to undertake a highly targeted intervention to alleviate those disciplinary problems. In too many cases, when overt disruptive behavior occurs, some teachers merely "punt the problem" to the principal's office. While this may have been acceptable in the past, today's teachers live in a world where expectations are different; today's teachers live in a world of data.

In my workshops, I often make this point with a paraphrase of a popular movie's line: "Show me the data!" In short, in the 21st-century classroom, if a teacher cannot present a data chart from a behavioral intervention, that teacher can no longer claim to have intervened with the problem student. Also, in short, the standard for best disciplinary practices has now changed, and teachers can no longer avoid their responsibility for discipline by merely referring a problem to the administrator (Duncan, 2014). That is why the case study above is so critically important. Once Ms. Waller has collected baseline data, undertaken a targeted intervention to reduce Chas's inappropriate behavior, and developed a data chart to show the efficacy of that intervention, she has met the highest standard for management of disciplinary problems today.

As I indicate in the introduction of Section II, most of the strategies in this section are specifically focused, targeted interventions for overt behavioral problems. Rather than class-wide preventative applications, these strategies are focused on post-disruptive behavior responses, and target one student at a time. The remaining strategies in this book require teachers to take data through a baseline and intervention period in order to show the impact of their disciplinary efforts. If a teacher hasn't taken data on a baseline and intervention period, then the teacher hasn't done a disciplinary intervention.

Another advantage of this peer confrontation procedure is the ease of application for many types of behavior problems, including severe behaviors (cursing, lying, stealing, bullying, fighting, etc.). In this strategy, unlike peer mediation—for example—the teacher remains directly involved. Further, this procedure allows the teacher to avoid an overt power struggle with the offending student. Here, the teacher can discipline the student proactively, using the power of the peer group. This procedure is powerful because the teacher decisively removes the audience for misbehavior. Teachers using this procedure can get the class working on their side to promote positive behavior in the classroom.

> If a teacher hasn't taken data on a baseline and intervention period, then the teacher hasn't done a disciplinary intervention.

Time is another advantage. The first time a teacher does this procedure with the class, it will take approximately four or five minutes, but after several occurrences, teachers will see that the time drops to two to three minutes. Almost any classroom can profit from the brief periodic discussions of appropriate behavior that this procedure facilitates.

Perhaps the most important advantage of this strategy is that it offers teachers an optional response to misbehavior that not only avoids a power play but also holds open the opportunity for establishing a helping relationship with a student. When the teacher implements the strategy well, the behaving students will perceive her as assisting the offending student to develop a method to control his temper (or cursing, etc.). In fact, when kids get angry as a result of this strategy, they are more often angry at other class members than the teacher, for the teacher is seen as a helper.

One final point shows the true advantage of this strategy. Note that even if this procedure is a total flop as an intervention for Chas, and the intervention data show no decrease in cursing, at the very least, Ms. Waller's class has now learned a two- to three-minute problem-solving technique, and have on multiple occasions discussed appropriate and inappropriate class behaviors. What classroom in any public school today would not benefit from such a discussion? Also, the positive effects of this procedure on other class members shouldn't be overlooked. It is quite likely that, even if this procedure doesn't work for Chas, it may work for others; other students may begin to respond more appropriately in class over time, based on the intervention targeted at Chas. In some ways, classroom behavior is likely to improve even when the procedure doesn't work for the target student. Personally, I love recommending this intervention because "it works even when it doesn't work"!

> When peer pressure is done well, the teacher will be perceived as assisting the offending student to develop a method to control his temper.

SUMMARY

Peer confrontation is a powerful strategy that effectively removes the audience for misbehavior and gets the power of the peer group working to facilitate appropriate behavior. Research shows this strategy is highly effective in public school classrooms (Bender, 2007; Gable, 1995; Salend et al., 1992; Sousa, 2009; Tanaka & Reid, 1997), and teachers who witness recurring behavior problems from the same student or students are well advised to explore the use of this strategy.

Strategy 11

The Group Contingency Strategy

Group contingency is another disciplinary strategy that harnesses the power of the peers in the class to foster improved behavior. This strategy involves one or more students earning either rewards or punishments for an entire group of students (Bender, 2007; Jones, Boon, Fore, & Bender, 2009). While either positive or negative contingencies can work to improve behavior, most educators tend to be proponents for using positive contingencies rather than punishments. In particular, using a group-oriented reward system for supporting targeted, specific positive behaviors of individual children can elicit the input from the peer group in a positive fashion, and students actually encourage others to behave more appropriately (Jenson & Reavis, 1999; Salend, Whittaker, & Reeder, 1992).

In most group contingency situations, the targeted students generally find ways to improve their behavior, even habitual, highly disruptive, or aggressive behavior, because the power and influence of the peer group is brought to bear. Further, this strategy often results in building and strengthening a group identity within the class, and therefore leads to an improved class climate overall. Although this strategy has been around for a while, it is receiving increased attention because students are working collaboratively in their classes today more so than in years past. For that reason, every teacher should have this strategy as a disciplinary option for students exhibiting challenging behavior.

Beyond the choice of using either rewards or punishments, there are several additional choices teachers must make that involve different types of group contingencies (Jenson & Reavis, 1999). In the *individual/whole-group reward* approach, the behavior of one individual determines the reward for a group of students or for the entire class. In the *group/whole-group reward*, the teacher observes and records the specific target behaviors of every member of the group and bases the reward on the total group's behavior.

> Group contingency is a disciplinary strategy that involves one or more students earning either rewards or punishments for an entire group.

Of course, the teacher must make a choice about which approach to use, and charting the behavior of one student in the class is somewhat easier to do while teaching than charting behavior of multiple students. However, if a specific, well-defined behavior is targeted for several students, or even for all students in the class (e.g., disrespectful statements to others), teachers should find it relatively easy to note all such statements they hear. The teacher can do this by making a tally mark on an index card while continuing to teach. With this in mind, either type of group contingency can work in most classes.

STEPS IN A GROUP CONTINGENCY

Because implementation of group contingencies is somewhat easier when the teacher targets only one or two students to earn rewards for the larger group, the remaining discussion in this section focuses on the individual/whole-group reward approach. Most proponents of this approach describe this as a multi-step process (Bender, 2007; Jenson & Reavis, 1999; Salend et al., 1992). Here are six steps to implement a group contingency intervention:

Steps to Implement a Group Contingency

1. Target one specific behavior per target student
2. Collect baseline behavior data and hold individual student meetings
3. Discuss intervention with the class and establish reward groups
4. Practice class-wide support for appropriate behavior
5. Identify desirable contingencies and begin
6. Celebrate the data with the class

Step 1: Target One Specific Behavior per Target Student

Teachers are generally very good at accurately describing a targeted behavior, but problems may arise when a teacher has to select only one behavior as a target behavior, because many students who demonstrate behavior problems often display an array of inappropriate behaviors. For example, verbal aggression, physical aggression, and cursing often go together, and for intervention purposes, the teacher may have to focus on only one. While the teacher can undertake interventions to decrease many problem behaviors at once, these are often much more complicated, time-consuming, and longer-term interventions.

To address this issue, I usually recommend that the teacher target one of the more serious but nevertheless frequent behaviors. For example, if an aggressive student is demonstrating verbal aggression, physical aggression, and cursing, I would recommend using verbal aggression as the target behavior. First of all, it typically is more frequent than physical aggression and therefore offers more opportunities to intervene with rewards or punishments. Also, verbal aggression almost always precedes physical aggression, and using verbal aggression as a target may decrease physical aggression as well. Finally, verbal aggression is usually considered a more serious behavior than merely cursing, because verbal aggression is typically directed at someone else, whereas cursing may not be.

However, the teacher should target the behavior or behaviors that, in the teacher's judgment, offer the greatest likelihood of success in the intervention. Further, once the teacher sees some success on one target behavior, she can then modify the intervention to focus on other behaviors, as necessary.

Step 2: Collect Baseline Behavior Data and Hold Individual Student Meetings

The teacher should hold a meeting with the target student and discuss that behavior and how it might negatively impact the student or the class as a whole. If possible, the teacher should elicit buy-in from the student by pointing out that the student can earn rewards for the entire class or group of students and will probably become quite popular in the class. This motivation is one reason this intervention is so effective. After this discussion, the teachers should begin to collect baseline data on the behavior problem, and collect such data for four to five days.

Step 3: Discuss Intervention With the Class and Establish Reward Groups

At some point, the teacher must describe the intervention to the class. Of course, students in any classroom can usually tell when a teacher is taking specific types of data, so teachers should discuss this with the class fairly soon after completing baseline data, and possibly sooner if the class asks about what the teacher is doing. Of course, for the group contingency to be most effective, all class members should participate. I recommend teachers explain these interventions to the class, and let them know what group they are in, while taking care not to embarrass the target students.

The teacher should establish the groups for which the target student may earn rewards. In some cases, teachers may wish to have a target student earn rewards for the entire class, while in others, different students may earn rewards for different groups of students in the class.

Step 4: Practice Class-Wide Support for Appropriate Behavior

This strategy, like several others, is intended to harness the influence of the peer group and use that influence to foster appropriate behavior among the target students. Once the teacher establishes groups and specifies the target behaviors, the teacher should discuss with the class some supportive ground rules about the types of things that students in the reward groups might say to target students to remind them to behave appropriately. Because of inappropriate conversation models seen in the media today, it is not uncommon to find students who do not know how to make a polite request. The teacher should therefore directly teach the skill of politely requesting to the students in the class. Teachers may wish to post some models of polite requesting in the classroom and discuss those with the class. These could include

> Tamara, please remember to do your work quickly.

> Royce, please remember that this is work time, and our group wants to win the prize for today.

> Amanda, could you please work more quietly so that I can finish my work on time?

In addition, teachers should remind the students to use an appropriate tone of voice when making their polite requests to the target students. Finally, teachers should tell students to ignore any angry remarks made by any group member in response to a polite request for better behavior. In such a situation, the teacher should step in and deal directly with the angry student.

> Because of inappropriate conversation models seen in the media today, it is not uncommon to find students who do not know how to make a polite request.

Step 5: Identify Desirable Contingencies and Begin

Selecting a contingency that motivates both the target students and the group is critical. When identifying each reward group, teachers may ask the group or groups which reward they would like. Of course, not all imaginable rewards are possible, so teachers may wish to begin with a list of possible rewards (e.g., going to recess two minutes early for a week, five extra minutes of computer time at the end of the day, pizza party in two weeks).

Step 6: Celebrate the Data With the Class

Success should always be celebrated, and most group contingencies are successful in reducing inappropriate behavior. Students at almost any level can understand the basics of an *x-y* axis data chart, that presents the days during the baseline and intervention as the *x* axis (across the bottom of the chart), and the actual count of inappropriate behavior on the *y* axis (on the left side of the chart, running bottom to top). Using this type of chart the teacher can easily summarize the data from the intervention. Further, when the intervention is successful, such charted data will create a positive impact class-wide, so I recommend that teachers share and celebrate the charted-data results of the intervention with the class. In most cases, these group contingency interventions will be successful and will present the teacher with an opportunity to praise the misbehaving student in front of the entire class several times during the project. That alone can become a powerful incentive for some students who may not have received before such positive recognition in front of the entire class.

Further, the teacher should share with the parents those charted data in every case and share with the guidance counselor and principal, as necessary. Sharing data of this nature is the mark of a dedicated teacher who understands how to address class management issues in the 21st century.

> Group contingency interventions are often successful and will present the teacher with an opportunity to praise the misbehaving student in front of the entire class several times during the project.

A CASE STUDY OF A GROUP CONTINGENCY INTERVENTION

Here is a case study using two target students in a fourth-grade class. The teacher, Mrs. Duval, has two students in the class who require a targeted behavioral intervention. Billy needs to decrease his verbally aggressive statements, and Kanesha needs to increase her attention in class. The first step in the group contingency process, Target One Specific Behavior per Target Student, is relatively easy in this case. For each student, the target behaviors are obvious to Mrs. Duval because she is having to call each student down nearly daily for these behaviors.

For Billy, Mrs. Duval begins a count of verbally aggressive statements using the simple approach of tally marks each time Billy gets into an argument. She collects data throughout the school day. For Kanesha, Mrs. Duval makes a tally mark each time she has to remind her to pay attention, which she does when Kenesha's eyes are closed in class or when Kenesha puts her head on her desk. Mrs. Duval continues this data collection for three days. Then she transfers the data to an *x-y* axis chart for each student, as shown in Figure 11.1.

The next step, meeting with the students, takes place the Friday after the teacher collects the baseline data. In that meeting, attended by both Kenesha and Billy, Mrs. Duval explains the group contingency by asking, "How would you guys like to earn rewards that the whole class can enjoy?" She then explains the process, and both students seem eager to participate. In this discussion, Mrs. Duval shares with the students the baseline data. (Generally, I recommend that teachers show baseline data to students and then discuss with them the negative consequences of their bad behavior. Actually showing baseline data to students emphasizes for them, in a very concrete way, that teachers are concerned with the behaviors in question.)

Next, Mrs. Duval discusses the target behavior with each target student while emphasizing the importance of changing that behavior. She is able to get both Kenesha and Billy to set a personal goal for behavioral change. Each states that the goal is to reduce the number of occurrences of misbehavior each day.

Figure 11.1:   Group Contingency Interventions

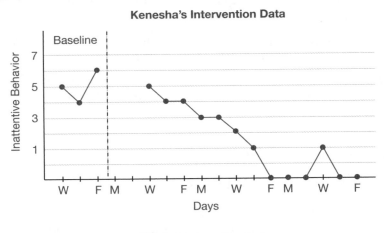

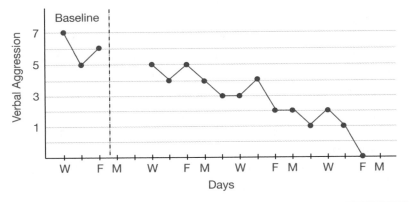

These goals suggest that both students are buying into the behavior change project.

The following Monday, Mrs. Duval holds a class meeting and explains that Billy and Kenesha want help from the class and the class could earn rewards for helping these students change their behavior. Next, she divides the class into two equal groups. Each group is half the class, and Mrs. Duval makes certain that she divides the more active students equally between the groups. Mrs. Duval then flips a coin to assign one group as "Billy's Support Group" and the other as "Kenesha's Support Group."

Mrs. Duval realizes that the language she uses when discussing the group contingency with the class will be critical. Mrs. Duval carefully phrases the project as something that Billy and Kenesha want to do to earn rewards for the class. She says,

Billy asked for some help controlling his anger, so I'll be noting each time he makes an angry statement, and when that count goes down, Billy will win ten minutes of extra computer time for his entire group! Kanesha has also asked for help in staying awake, so I'll be noting how many times she puts her head on her desk, and when she reduces her inattention behavior, she'll win the same reward for her group.

After a ten-minute discussion of the project on Monday, the class continues with their work. On Tuesday, Mrs. Duval provides fifteen minutes of training by first providing an example of a polite request, and then having students present examples of polite requests. She has several class members role-play inappropriate behavior, while others make a request for improved behavior, in a polite manner. Finally, at the end of that training on Tuesday, each of the two groups select their reward, contingent on the target student meeting his daily goal. Billy's support group chooses a two-minute head start in going to lunch. Kenesha's support group chooses five minutes of free time at the end of the day. Mrs. Duval does not take any data that Monday and Tuesday, because they are both training days for the intervention.

Mrs. Duval begins the intervention and her intervention data collection on Wednesday and she sees immediate results, as shown by the intervention data in Figure 11.1. Both Billy's and Kenesha's behavior improved, but, as in all targeted interventions, the behavior change was not constant. For example, on the first Friday after the intervention began, both Billy and Kenesha failed to reduce their inappropriate behavior, and therefore failed to earn the reward for their support groups. In that instance, Mrs. Duval heard several students make appropriate requests for both Billy and Kenesha to try harder the next week. The next week, both students did try harder, and in general there was a significant reduction in inappropriate behaviors over the next two weeks.

After only two and a half weeks, Mrs. Duval wants to "celebrate the data" with her students, so in addition to the ongoing daily reinforcement, she states that if both Billy and Kenesha could go the entire next week and reduce their inappropriate behavior on most days during that week, the entire class will win a pizza party the following Friday. Further, Billy and Kenesha will be party hosts because their good work will have earned that reward for the entire class! As the data in Figure 11.1 show, both Kenesha and Billy do achieve their goal on most days during the last week of the intervention.

It is hard to overestimate the importance of this type of targeted intervention. First, both Billy and Kenesha, as demonstrated by their inappropriate behavior, are not the types of students whom other class members frequently praised prior to this intervention. Rather, they are probably disruptive students who are not highly valued as class members. However, after this intervention, both show their value to the class by earning rewards for their peers, and the teacher's celebration at the end of this targeted intervention emphasizes how special Bill and Kenesha are to the class as a whole.

OTHER GROUP CONTINGENCY OPTIONS

Like many behavioral interventions, group contingencies give teachers many options for improving behavior across the class. For example, teachers may identify a target behavior for everyone in the class. Also, teachers may reward groups differentially, based on the target student's behavior. If students do not show any inappropriate behaviors on a given day, the teacher may double the reward (e.g., from five minutes to ten minutes of game time on the computer).

As another option, teachers may wish to intervene with only one student at a time and offer the possibility that that student can earn rewards for the entire class. Finally, teachers may choose to vary the rewards or even offer a mystery reward as in the example below. This can add an additional level of excitement to the procedure.

EFFICACY RESEARCH ON GROUP CONTINGENCIES

Research frequently documents the efficacy of all variations of the group contingency strategy (Jenson & Reavis, 1999; Jones et al., 2009; Salend et al., 1992). This research shows the efficacy of both individual/whole-group contingencies and group/whole-group contingencies, using both whole-group and single-subject research designs.

For example, to reduce verbally disrespectful behavior in class, Jones and her co-workers (2009) use a Mystery Hero group contingency with seven middle-school students with learning disabilities or attention disorders. Jones tells each student in the group that the behavior of one of the students, the Mystery Hero she selected for that day, could earn a reward for the entire group, but only if that student reduces the number of verbally disrespectful statements from the count on the previous day. During the class, the teacher notes on an index card whenever she hears a verbally disrespectful statement from the Mystery Hero. Of course, the students don't know who the Mystery Hero is on any given day, so all students have to modify their behavior. However, at the end of the day, Jones announces the Mystery Hero, and she checks that student's behavior against the previous day's count. If the student earns a reward, the teacher produces a paper bag that holds Mystery Rewards cards, which describe rewards such as game time for the group or a credit toward a pizza party for the entire class.

> Research has frequently documented the efficacy of all variations of the group contingency strategy.

The results of this intervention show that the intervention significantly reduces verbally disrespectful statements every member of the class makes. In that sense, this intervention also increases the positive class climate throughout the project.

SUMMARY

Depending on the goals of the teacher and needs of the class, the group contingency strategy may be one of the most effective strategies in this book because it often has many positive consequences that reach beyond the actual intervention effects. Not only does it curb inappropriate behavior for the targeted student, it also builds a sense of community within the class, and that can help foster a much more positive class climate. In group contingencies, students who have a history of being punished in school often find themselves praised by their classmates for earning desirable rewards for their group, and that can be a powerful experience for many students. In fact, such peer praise can be one of the most memorable and most positive experiences some students ever have. This is certainly an intervention teachers should use, and seeing a highly disruptive student not only become less disruptive but also receive praise from his peers is a powerful motivation for teachers to undertake the work involved in this intervention. Simply put: this feels great for the teacher too!

Strategy 12

Self-Regulation and Goal Setting

SELF-REGULATION AND SELF-MONITORING

In contrast to the peer influence strategies, self-regulation strategy is more focused on students' control of their own emotions and behavior. Self-regulation seems to have become a buzzword in some educational circles today, particularly in Canada, where self-regulation has become a major disciplinary focus (Hoffman, 2010; Marzano, 2003; Preston, 2014; Shanker, 2010; Wells, 2013). As a discipline concept, self-regulation is best understood as the ability of students to understand and control their own emotions, stress levels, and behaviors in the classroom and other environments (Hoffman, 2010). This practice fosters the development of a mind/body awareness among students and urges them to assess their own stress levels and learn to control their behavior. Students in this approach often seek to decrease agitation through breathing exercises, moving away from habits that increase stress, and generally becoming more aware of how they feel and how those feelings impact their behaviors. In one sense, this strategy is similar to the mindfulness concept I discussed (see Strategy 6, Quiet Time and Meditation).

Stuart Shanker, a distinguished research professor of philosophy and psychology at York University, is the conceptual leader of the self-regulation initiative in Canada (Shanker, 2009, 2010; Wells, 2013). The self-regulation movement is growing in Canada, in large measure because of Dr. Shanker's work and the Canadian Self-Regulation Initiative (http://www.self-regulation.ca/about-us/canadian-self-regulation-initiative-csri/).

Self-regulation has received research support from recent studies that indicate increased awareness of emotional state, increased engagement with learning tasks, and fewer behavioral problems in students who have learned to be more aware of their own stress levels (Hoffman, 2010; Shanker, 2009; Wells, 2013). This practice has also been supported by research in the neurosciences on the functioning of the human brain. When a child's brain is overstimulated, the frontal lobe areas that allow a child to control her behavior begin to shut down (Shanker, 2010; Wells, 2013), and other brain regions associated with the fight-or-flight response become more active. In stressful situations, students literally become less able to reason with adults about their behavior and its consequences and more likely to become overtly emotional or potentially violent. The self-regulation initiative seeks to make students more aware of their own stress levels and the causes for that stress, and make students thereby able to control their own moods, emotions, and behaviors.

> In stressful situations, students literally become less able to reason with adults about their behavior and its consequences, and more likely to become overtly emotional or potentially violent.

While the term self-regulation is relatively new (Shanker, 2009), the concept of having students assess and then assume responsibility for their own behavior is not. In the 1980s, a great deal of research focused on self-monitoring to improve attention behavior in students (Bender, 2007). In particular, Daniel Hallahan was one of the early researchers to research the attention problems among students with learning disabilities (Hallahan & Sapona, 1983; Mathes & Bender, 1996; Snider, 1987). He and his coworkers at the University of Virginia developed and provided a way to teach attention skills by training students to systematically and habitually check in to the happenings in the classroom. By following a relatively simple self-monitoring procedure, teachers learned to assist students to pay attention and accomplish more work in the same time frame.

The self-monitoring procedure involved using a timer of some sort that, every forty-five seconds or so, cued a target student to ask the question, "Was I paying attention?" The teacher instructed the student to answer that question on a self-monitoring form and then return to work (Hallahan & Sapona, 1983; Snider, 1987). As the teacher weaned the student from this procedure, he, in most cases had developed the habit of mental checking in and thereby improved his attention behavior. That same self-monitoring procedure was then expanded to other behaviors such as having students monitor their own class readiness behaviors (e.g., having pencil and paper, bringing in homework, etc.; see Bender, 2007).

The concept underlying the research on both self-regulation and self-monitoring is the same; by learning to frequently assess one's own mental state or assess and control one's own moods or emotions, students can be empowered to take charge of their own behavior (Bender, 2007). Further, in addition to becoming aware of their own emotions and behaviors, students are taught to set goals to improve their behavior in the classroom. Therefore, proponents of this behavioral approach recommend a number of ideas for building skills that help students monitor their moods, emotions, and behaviors, and based on that self-assessment, help students improve them.

> While the term self-regulation is relatively new, the concept of having students assess and then assume responsibility for their own behavior is not.

GAMES AND ACTIVITIES TO TEACH SELF-REGULATION

The focus within the Canadian self-regulation initiative has been self-regulation tactics for young children. For those children, teachers can use a variety of classroom games in order to teach self-regulation skills (Hoffman, 2010). Claire Cameron Ponitz of the University of Virginia and Megan McClelland from Oregon State University recommend the following games to help students learn to regulate their behavior (Hoffman, 2010).

Red Light, Green Light. Children line up along one wall, and pretend to be cars. One child (or the teacher) serves as the stoplight. When the stoplight yells, "Green light" the children may walk quickly toward the goalpost set up in the other end of the classroom, but when the stoplight yells, "Red light" the children must stop. If a child doesn't immediately stop, he has to return to the starting line. To make this complicated, if the stoplight yells, "Yellow light" the students may move but must walk slowly toward the goal. In this game, children must learn to pay attention, follow directions, and wait their turn, all of which are self-regulation skills.

> A variety of classroom games can be used to teach young students self-regulation skills.

Simon Says. This is similar to the game above, in that one student or the teacher gives directions to the others. The instructions can be simple or complex and may say "jump," "take two steps forward," or "hop on your right foot three times." Children follow the directions only if they hear "Simon says" at the beginning of the command. The last person standing becomes Simon for the next round. Again, students are practicing self-regulation because they have to pay attention and follow directions only when appropriate.

Other childhood games can help reinforce self-regulation behaviors. For example, in *Hide and Seek*, students learn to stay quiet and wait patiently, and *jump rope* teaches students to anticipate and time their movements as necessary to succeed in the activity. *Role-playing* also helps students by helping them consider their actions in the context of what their character must do (Hoffman, 2010).

In addition to games, some teachers have used classroom displays to stress emotional awareness (Wells, 2013). For example, a graphic bulletin board display can help remind students to check their feelings in the classroom, and even a relatively simple reminder such as this can help alleviate some behavior problems. Teachers might consider using a display of the desired arousal level in class, as shown in Figure 12.1. The circle can be divided into thirds and labeled in bold on the three inside sections.

The poster title at the top could ask, "How Am I Feeling?" The label "Just Right! Ready to Learn" is at the top third of the circle in bold print, and smaller text below in that section lists descriptors of that feeling: "Calm, Relaxed, Focused." The bold label "Stressed!" is on the right of the circle with the descriptors:

Figure 12.1:   Check Your Feelings! Poster

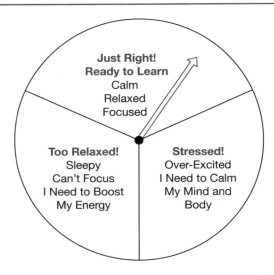

"Over-Excited, I Need to Calm My Mind and Body." The left portion bold label says, "Too Relaxed!" The descriptors here say, "Sleepy, Can't Focus, I Need to Boost My Energy." Teachers can affix a large dial hand (like a minute hand on a watch) that students can move to indicate their feelings. Teachers should refer to the poster when a student seems to be getting too aroused or angry in the class, and maybe have that student adjust the hand to reflect his feelings. Like the simple games and activities above, this display will help children develop the habit of checking their feelings and, eventually, develop self-regulation skills.

SELF-REGULATION STRATEGIES FOR MORE INTENSE CLASSROOM SITUATIONS

An Anger Thermometer

While simple games do help students learn self-regulation, the realities of the classroom often require more intensive tactics. In particular, when students become angry or verbally aggressive in the classroom, this calls for specific individual interventions. To help students with anger-based behavioral problems, Elias (2004) developed the "anger thermometer," which allows very young to middle school students to rate their own level of anger. Many students with overt behavior problems have difficulty controlling their emotions in emotionally charged situations and they often display aggression. For those students, the anger thermometer works very well.

Go to www.learningsciences.com/bookresources to download figures and tables.

In this strategy, the graphic of a giant thermometer is used as a rating scale and allows students to self-monitor their own emotional intensity, and in turn to reflect a bit on their behavioral response to their own intense emotions. The temperature indicator on the thermometer must move in order to allow a student to adjust the thermometer to his level of anger. The teacher could also make an anger thermometer as a bulletin board display for anyone in the class to use as needed, like the Check Your Feelings! Poster above.

Also, teachers may wish to create individual thermometers made from a laminated piece of cardboard and then place them on individual students' desks. Most classes will have several students who might need such a thermometer, but not every child will benefit from this idea. Most teachers will need no more than perhaps five such individual thermometers. When a target student is angry, she would be expected to show on the thermometer her level of anger and then seek the help of the teacher, prior to acting on her intense emotions. An adapted anger thermometer is in Figure 12.2.

Here, the highest-intensity anger is scaled as "Ready to Explode!" anger, while the lowest is "I'm Dead." Teachers might put beside each level of the scale specific things for students to do. For example, if a student is feeling Ready to Explode! anger, the teacher may require him to show that indicator on the thermometer and then speak directly with her or go to another area of the room. This self-rating assists students in regulating their emotional intensity as well as controlling their behaviors.

Figure 12.2: The Anger Thermometer

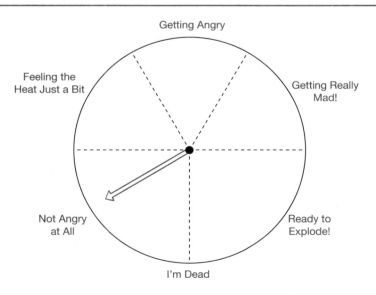

Go to www.learningsciences.com/bookresources to download figures and tables.

The ZIPPER Strategy

The ZIPPER strategy involves teaching self-reflective behavior during intense emotional situations (Smith, Siegel, O'Connor, & Thomas, 1994), which is useful for highly aggressive or easily enraged students from grade four through high school. In particular, for explosively violent students, this self-regulation strategy can often provide them with a degree of behavior control that they have never before achieved. The steps involved in this strategy are in Figure 12.3. The term ZIPPER is an acronym indicating what students should do when they feel intense anger. Again, knowing these steps will help a student self-regulate and often empower students whose behavior has seemingly been totally out of control.

Figure 12.3:   The ZIPPER Strategy

Z	Zip your mouth	Stop! Take a deep breath before you do anything!
I	Identify the problem	What do I feel? What do I need? What is the problem?
P	Pause	Can I pause and remove myself from the situation?
P	Put yourself in charge	I will put myself in control of my own actions!
E	Explore choices	What are my choices? What can I do? Can I leave and go talk to the teacher?
R	Reset	Reset the situation! Pick a good option!

A CASE STUDY ON SELF-REGULATION: USING THE ANGER THERMOMETER

Angela is an above-average student with anger issues and often displays hostility. Mr. Palmer, a veteran fourth-grade teacher, notes that Angela gets into verbal altercations several times each day. On one occasion in the second week of the school term, Angela gets so angry she hits another girl in class.

Mr. Palmer has been conducting morning meetings for several years, and on two occasions in the first two weeks, the class discusses anger, and specifically Angela's anger. In each case, Angela does not really participate. To develop a more effective intervention, Mr. Palmer keeps a formal baseline count of Angela's aggressive verbal behavior for the first eight days, by noting all the times he has to break up a verbal altercation involving Angela. The data show that she has some type of argument an average of 3.25 times each day and physical fights twice in that time.

Mr. Palmer presents Angela with an anger thermometer and explains:

Angela, you know you've been getting into arguments daily, and that prevents you from getting your work done. I've got an idea that I need you to try. I'm going to use it with a number of folks in the class, but you'll be the first. Would you do that?

While some students would overtly resist being the only one in class with such a tool, Angela says she will try it. Mr. Palmer then shows her an anger thermometer like the one in Figure 12.2 and then continues the instructions:

Everybody gets angry from time to time, Angela, but I want you to learn to control that anger. When you begin to get angry at someone, you have permission to get your anger thermometer out of your desk, adjust it to the level of anger, and then hold it high so I can see it, even if I'm leading an activity in front of the class, okay? After you do that, I want you to take five deep breaths without saying anything to anyone, even if someone is arguing with you. After I see you do that, I'll know you are in control, and then I'm going to call you up to help me in some way. I may have you help me teach the class for a few moments, or I may send you to do an errand for me at the office. The important thing is to set the thermometer, hold it up for me to see, and take five deep breaths without saying anything to anyone! This will help you control your anger and not get you into trouble.

While I'm sure other class members will see that thermometer, we won't tell them about it, and you'll be the only one using it. Also, after class each day, we'll make time to discuss why you felt angry that day, and we'll try to resolve any problems. I want you to do well in my class because you certainly have the academic background to do very well here!

Angela then indicates her desire to do well and have fewer arguments, and Mr. Palmer responds:

I'm glad you want to get better control of your feelings too. Let's do this: Let's set a goal of trying to get angry only twice a day, rather than all the time. In fact, every day you get angry only once, I'll make sure you have some free time at the end of the period, even when other class members don't. If you like, you can get on the class computer for five minutes whenever you go all day and get angry only once!

In this case, the intervention involves helping Angela learn to self-regulate her anger and also provides reinforcement for improved behavior. Of course, during this targeted intervention, Mr. Palmer continues to count the number of verbal altercations and fights involving Angela. These data, along with the baseline data, are in Figure 12.4.

As the chart indicates, the anger thermometer intervention coupled with reinforcement for reducing verbal aggression was enough to make Angela more aware of when she was becoming angry. Overall, this targeted self-regulation intervention

Figure 12.4:   Angela's Self-Regulation Intervention Data

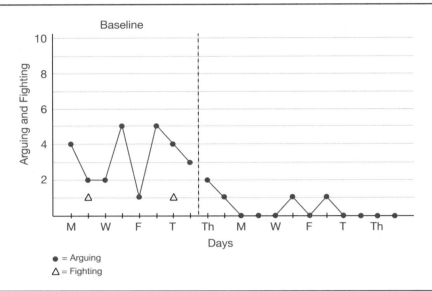

reduced the number of behavioral problems she displayed in class to less than one per day, and eliminated fighting altogether. This was a real success for Angela because it was the first time she learned that there are ways to control her own anger.

While this intervention is very effective for older students, it is also very useful for students in lower grades. In contrast, the ZIPPER strategy is somewhat more dependent on students' verbal fluency and their ability to determine their own feelings. It is therefore generally recommended for students in grade four and above. However, teachers should feel free to use any self-regulation strategies they feel might work in any given situation.

EFFICACY RESEARCH FOR SELF-REGULATION

In this context, I suggest that the basis for today's emphasis on self-regulation lay within the earlier research on self-monitoring, and taken together, the research on self-regulation tactics have proven to be quite effective (Bender, 2007; Elias, 2004; Hoffman, 2010; Mathes & Bender, 1996; Marzano, 2003; Preston, 2014; Shanker, 2010; Snider, 1987; Wells, 2013). In particular, Marzano (2003) reports that self-control strategies have an average effect size of –.597 documenting a significant and strong inverse relationship between use of these self-regulation strategies and inappropriate classroom behavior. (Note: an effect size is a mathematical measure of the amount of impact of an intervention summarized across multiple research studies; typically, effect sizes over .40 are considered highly effective.)

Of course, when teachers choose to use a self-regulation strategy, such as those above, they should plan on conducting a baseline count of the target behavior and then continue that count after they introduce the intervention. The example above, for the anger thermometer intervention, can serve as a model for collecting data for the ZIPPER intervention, as well, and again, teachers will be expected in today's classroom to collect such data on the interventions they undertake.

SUMMARY

Self-regulation interventions have roots in research done over the past thirty years, and that research has consistently been quite positive. Students can and should, from the earliest ages, be trained to become aware of their feelings and ultimately regulate those feelings and their behaviors. Further, for students with self-control issues, these self-regulation tactics might represent some of the few tactics teachers can implement to help out-of-control students. In my opinion, virtually all teachers should be undertaking these interventions on a fairly regular basis in their classes, targeted at those students who seem to consistently disrupt class in various ways. This is how effective teachers manage behavior in today's world.

Strategy 13

The Personal Responsibility Strategy

Personal responsibility is another buzzword in both politics and education today, and this is often reflected in discussions of classroom disciplinary procedures. In fact, teaching students that they have personal responsibility for their own behavior and their participation in class has become something of a trend in education (Bender, 2007; Marzano, 2003; Pleasant Valley Community Schools, 2014; Sousa, 2009). Moreover, many students who demonstrate problem behaviors could benefit greatly from instruction on their responsibilities for their own behavior and their classroom interactions. Marzano (2003, 2007) has been a strong advocate of teaching students about their responsibilities for appropriate behavior, and advocates tactics such as self-regulation of behavior (discussed previously) and written statements on personal behavior.

In my previous work, I've recommended that teachers implement a specific disciplinary strategy, the Responsibility Strategy or personal responsibility strategy, to curb inappropriate behaviors (Bender, 2007). The responsibility strategy focuses on helping a student understand his responsibility for classroom interactions as well as helping the students gain attention for positive behaviors and contributions to the class. This involves assisting the student in identifying his contributions and responsibilities to teachers, classmates, and the school, giving the student a task based on those responsibilities, and then helping the student take pride in meeting those responsibilities. The tactic is based on the assumption that in many cases, if a student is given a responsibility of which he can be proud, then he will seek to meet that responsibility.

> Teaching students that they have personal responsibility for their own behavior and their participation in class has become something of a trend in education.

WHY GIVE A BEHAVIOR-PROBLEM KID RESPONSIBILITY?

Most of us remember dusting the erasers, cleaning the blackboard for teachers, and doing other teacher's helper jobs as privileges in the classrooms of our youth. We can even remember how important and involved those relatively mundane tasks made us feel, because we took pride in helping and getting to do something that not all of the students in the class could do. Of course, students with behavior problems did not get to do those jobs, because those tasks were usually used as privileges or rewards for good behavior. In fact, in presenting this idea around the country, I have realized that many teachers feel it may be inappropriate to reward misbehavior by using these aggressive and defiant kids for special tasks or responsibilities. Indeed, rewarding misbehavior with a serious responsibility does seem to go against basic behavioral training, which usually involves rewarding only positive behaviors.

Nevertheless, with some students, offering an attention-generating task as a personal responsibility is just the ticket to turn negative behavior into positive behavior, and thereby improve the student's behavior overall. Even aggressive and defiant students—students who typically don't respond to more moderate forms of reward and punishment—may be good candidates for this strategy. By the time you consider using the responsibility strategies for a student with behavior problems, you have probably already tried everything else—so, at that point, you have nothing to lose by giving the offending student a serious responsibility.

Of course, this is not to suggest that the responsibility strategy is right for all students. Teachers need to consider the student's motivations for misbehavior in order to effectively use this strategy. In fact, some students with severe behavior problems such as defiance, acting-out behaviors, aggressive behaviors, attention-seeking behaviors, or oppositional behaviors may intentionally choose not to meet their responsibilities. In some cases, negative attention directed toward a student's misbehavior is somehow a payoff for that particular student. Consequently, these students demonstrate very inappropriate behaviors consistently in the classroom because they get attention for those behaviors.

> By the time you consider using the responsibility strategies for a student with behavior problems, you have probably already tried everything else—so, at that point, you have nothing to lose.

Some students may feel that they derive a certain amount of personal power from oppositional or defiant behavior. For example, during misbehavior, the attention of the entire class is usually centered on the misbehaving student, and this meets some deep-seated need for attention. This is a powerful position for a student to be in, as she, at that moment, is the center of the class! In fact, highly oppositional students often find that most of their recognition comes from situations in which they misbehave, and they have never understood that gaining attention for positive behaviors in the classroom can, likewise, meet their need for attention. In these cases, the teacher's job is to teach them about their positive contribution, their responsibility, to the class. Clearly, there are students who demonstrate misbehavior, and in some cases highly disruptive behavior, specifically to get attention. For those

> Many students with severe behavior problems such as defiance, acting-out behaviors, aggressive behaviors, attention-seeking behaviors, or oppositional behaviors, are motivated as much by a desire for attention as by their anger.

students, providing an alternative set of responsibilities of which they can be proud will help alleviate the misbehavior.

RESPONSIBILITY STRATEGY EXAMPLES

There are several examples in literature showing that increasing students' responsibilities does improve their behavior (Bender, 2007; Kelman, 2013; Sousa, 2009). As one example, several schools in California recently explored giving more responsibility to the entire student body by completely eliminating bells as a signal to change classes (Kelman, 2013). In those schools, educators wished to present a more collegial, college campus atmosphere, so they eliminated bells between periods and gave the responsibility for getting to class on time directly to the students. Anecdotal reports indicated that students responded quite favorably to this, showing up on time for their next class almost all the time. Teachers also reported many other behavioral improvements among many students (Kelman, 2013) suggesting that when students are treated like adults, they are more likely to respond like adults. In those schools, when students were presented with increased responsibility for their own scheduling, they responded quite well (Kelman, 2013).

Here is another example. Dr. Bob Brooks is a psychologist and a former administrator of a lock-down school unit in a psychiatric hospital for disruptive students. He frequently shares an example about a student who, for some reason, broke lightbulbs everywhere (Bender, 2007). All lights in the school were endangered! Further, that student really didn't care what disciplinary measures were used to punish him for this behavior, showing that this was an extreme example of an oppositional, attention seeking behavior. This frustrated Dr. Brooks, as it would any educator.

After much reflection, Dr. Brooks realized that he had not directly invited that student to make a positive contribution to the school. To his credit, he took a chance and invited the student to become the "Lightbulb Monitor" for the entire school! Specifically, every morning, the student was to roam the school, visit each room, flick on the lights, and assure that each and every lightbulb was working properly. If lightbulbs were out, the student had the responsibility of reporting the problem to the office. This involved some degree of positive attention—of bragging rights—for that student, and the student loved being the only student with that school-wide responsibility. He loved going into a room of his peers each morning and checking the lights while the teacher checked attendance. His peers saw that he was given special privileges, along with his special responsibility, and that attention from his peers made a very positive difference in this student's behavior. Over time, this positive responsibility ended the rash of broken lightbulbs, but perhaps more importantly, this student had a personal responsibility, a meaningful contribution he made to the school each day. Because of that contribution, the student received much positive attention daily from teachers and his peers.

USING THE RESPONSIBILITY STRATEGY

In some cases, behavioral problems can seem untouchable or nonresponsive to any intervention, and that is exactly when the Responsibility Strategy should be implemented. Educators may have some students that really don't care what their punishment might be. Some students demonstrate the attitude of "Another suspension? Another talk with my mom? Really?" In a broader sense, many students seem particularly unconnected with the school environment or dissociated from others in the class, and in all of these cases, educators sometimes feel lost as to how to intervene.

In short, educators should do this when nothing else works. When students demonstrate behavior problems very frequently, when it seems as though the same type of problem was dealt with yesterday—or maybe even fifteen minutes ago—it is time to ask, has this student been given a responsibility to perform or something positive to do for her class (Bender, 2007)? In those cases, a specific set of responsibilities, individually selected for the student, may result in reconnecting the student emotionally to the school and having that student take personal responsibility for her own behavior.

The Responsibility Strategy works for students across the public school grades and often works for students who are angry, aggressive, or oppositional (Bender, 2007). Once the immediate behavioral problem is dealt with (using one of the Band-Aids I discussed previously), the teacher should reflect with the student on how the student can assist in the class, using his specialized knowledge or leadership skills in the classroom to make a positive contribution to the class.

I should note that this strategy has been successfully used with one group of students who seem nonresponsive to almost every other intervention—gang members. Gang members are primarily socialized to the norms of their gangs, and/or small gang-like groups within the school. However, when gang members can be used to positively contribute to their class or school (perhaps they have the responsibility of policing the playground or hallways under the supervision of teachers), they respond positively to this responsibility (Bender, 2007). If teachers can identify responsibilities that allow gang members to demonstrate their power in positive ways without putting other students at risk, this can be a very effective strategy because it acknowledges the power of the gang member in a way that the teacher finds acceptable.

> The Responsibility Strategy has been successfully used with one group of students who seem nonresponsive to almost every other intervention—gang members.

This strategy is not recommended for the occasionally violent student, or for students who seem unpredictable in terms of when they might become violent. Students who generally behave fairly well but occasionally blow up into a display of violent behavior require other strategies and often respond best to meditation or relaxation strategies I describe elsewhere in this book.

IMPLEMENTING RESPONSIBILITY STRATEGIES

There are a number of specific steps for implementing the responsibility strategy, and teachers need to carefully consider these implementation guidelines prior to usage within the class. Here are the specific steps:

Steps for Implementing the Responsibility Strategy

1. Step back and reflect

2. Seek a responsibility for the student

3. Meet with the student and invite participation

4. Jointly choose a responsibility

5. Develop a description and monitoring plan

6. Present the intervention to the school administrator

7. Compare baseline and intervention data

Step 1: Step Back and Reflect

When you see the same student demonstrating repeated behavior problems, manage the immediate violence, disruption, or other problem by using one of the Band-Aid strategies earlier. For example, you may merely inform the student in a relatively soft voice that you and she will need to schedule a conference about the misbehavior. Then turn away from the student and attempt to get the others in class to refocus on the classwork at hand.

Next, begin a baseline count of the number of disruptive behaviors demonstrated by the student. Baseline data is critical, as I discussed previously, for documenting how serious the behavior problem is and showing the efficacy of any intervention that you implement later.

Third, reflect on the student's relationship with you and others in the school. Has the student had any positive relationships in the class? Does the student have any contributions she can make for others in the class? It may also be effective to mentally take several steps back and ask, "How have I invited this student to positively contribute to this class today?"

A wise teacher should try to find ways to make students feel special—by inviting specific positive contributions to the class regularly, but this is much more challenging when the student in question seems to misbehave all the time. Still, such invitations are critical. The teacher phrases her reflective statement above very carefully: note the use of the term *invited* as well as the direct responsibility for the invitation. Have you, the teacher, *invited* that offending student to make a positive contribution today? Has that student been invited to demonstrate her talents and leadership skills or been given opportunities to present a positive self to the class? In some cases, the answer is probably that the student hasn't been effectively invited to make an appropriate and meaningful contribution, because time and numbers of students often prevent such interactions. Therefore, wise teachers will try to find ways to involve a student—to make the student feel special—by inviting her to contribute in an appropriate way.

Step 2: Seek a Responsibility for the Student

Consider the student's hobbies, interests, and desires, and identify several possible tasks that would be positive contributions to the class. Preferably, these should be tasks for which the student is uniquely qualified, and will take pride, as was the previous case with the lightbulb monitor. Also consider how to get the student to want to undertake the responsibility, and it should be a task that the student can perform once or several times daily.

The possible task options are almost endless, and the actual task assigned to a student is relatively unimportant; almost any necessary task will do. However, two things are critical. First, the student and others must value the task, giving the student bragging rights for the opportunity to do the task. Next, the student must believe that the task is important for others in the class. The student should be made to feel like a contributing partner in a task that she values. The following job ideas might help you get started.

Tutor students in a lower grade.	Work as a peer buddy.
Be a homework helper to a sibling.	Empty the trash cans in class.
Be a clean room helper.	Serve as Playground Monitor.

Often the student's actions, hobbies, and interests may suggest specific tasks. For example, the student earlier was fixated on lightbulbs, and the role of Lightbulb Monitor was perfectly appropriate for him. Try to consider a student's hobbies and interests as well as the needs of your class or your school. Does your school need writers for the school newspaper, reporters for the video news each morning, or pictures taken? Could you use someone to report gang graffiti on or near the school? Might some of the aggressive students in the school be used (when supervised by teachers) to notify teachers about verbal fights on the playground? If planned appropriately, any of these tasks could represent an effective contribution to the school and a positive responsibility for a disruptive student.

Of course, in selecting the responsibility, consider issues such as the student's confidentiality, privacy, safety, and legal liability. For example, don't appoint a Bathroom Monitor unless you want students peeking into bathroom stalls. Further, no student's responsibility should require that she leave campus or get involved in physical altercations that have already begun between other students. The principal, because of required training in school law and policy, might be the appropriate contact when considering responsibilities that involve students leaving the classroom. Also, supervision should always be available for any student completing her responsibility.

Step 3: Meet With the Student and Invite Participation

In this meeting, show the baseline data to the student and discuss how such misbehavior is hurting the student's success in class. In some cases, merely by showing baseline data to a student on her disruptive behavior, the teacher demonstrates that he is taking the problem very seriously.

Next, discuss why students might misbehave, providing a list of possible reasons. Emphasize in every way how important the student is to the class, because your overall goal is to elicit the student's willingness to try and gain attention through positive things that she can do for the class. At that point, present your ideas on what the student might like to contribute, and show the student both why those contributions (i.e., task responsibilities) are important and how they involve bragging rights.

Step 4: Jointly Choose a Responsibility

Student buy-in is critical for the success of this strategy. If the student continues to reject the idea of gaining attention through doing an important task for the class, the teacher needs to choose another disciplinary intervention. However, most students can be persuaded to at least try to positively contribute to the class, and the goal of the teacher is to elicit that student participation. You want the student to actually buy in to performing the responsibility and hopefully grow into that responsibility.

It is critical that this task selection be a joint selection between the student and teacher. The student must be interested in doing the responsibility, and the teacher represents the interests of the class in having the task performed. Both must therefore agree on the importance of the selected responsibility.

Step 5: Develop a Description and Monitoring Plan

Invite the student to write down a one-paragraph description of the responsibility, carefully stating exactly which task she will perform and how often. Give the student some time to do that, and then continue the meeting with the student by helping to edit the written statement, as necessary. That paragraph description of the responsibility then becomes a part of a signed contract between you and the student. This simply written plan should present the details of the task, state exactly when and how it is to be performed, and how you might monitor the task. You and the student should both sign this agreement. Figure 13.1 presents a form that may be used for this contract.

Figure 13.1:   Responsibility Strategy Agreement

Student: _____   Date: _____

Teacher: _____   Class Period: _____

Description of Behavior Problem:

_____

Responsibility Selected:

I, _____, agree to make a positive contribution to our class by:

_____

_____

_____

_____

Monitoring Plan: This task will be monitored by:

Intervention Follow-Up Session: We understand we will meet in three weeks to discuss follow-up for this responsibility.

Date and Time of Follow-Up Meeting: _____

Signatures: With our signatures below, we agree to abide by this contract and avoid future conflict by taking the action(s) above.

Student: _____   Date: _____

Teacher: _____   Date: _____

Principal's Signature: _____   Date: _____

Step 6: Present the Intervention to the School Administrator

Presenting the chosen responsibility and the signed contract to the school administrator will help highlight the importance of the responsibility to the student. It also serves to keep the school administrator informed as to why the student might be doing various tasks around campus.

Step 7: Compare Baseline and Intervention Data

Again, unless a teacher presents data on a baseline and a subsequent intervention to curb misbehavior, that teacher has not fulfilled her responsibility in today's classrooms. The standard for teachers today is higher than ever before in terms of this requirement. To state again: unless a teacher presents data (baseline and intervention), that teacher has not attempted to deal with the behavior problem. The final step in this targeted intervention is comparison of the baseline and intervention data to determine the efficacy of the responsibility strategy intervention for the target student.

A RESPONSIBILITY STRATEGY CASE STUDY

Figure 13.2 presents a completed Responsibility Strategy Agreement. In this example, Tremain, a fifth-grade student, is often engaged in verbal aggression or even fighting during recess time at school. The teacher notes that other students do not want to play with Tremain, because he is so aggressive, so they never choose him to be on their side in softball or dodgeball.

Unless a teacher presents data on a baseline and a subsequent intervention to curb misbehavior, that teacher has not fulfilled his or her responsibility in today's classrooms.

Figure 13.2:   Responsibility Strategy Agreement

Student: Tremain Johnson   Date: 10/14/14

Teacher: Mrs. Cass   Class Period: Recess

Description of Behavior Problem:

Tremain is involved in aggression often on the playground. He called other students names four times and got into two fights in one week.

Responsibility Selected:

I, *Tremain Johnson,* agree to make a positive contribution to our class by:

At the beginning of recess every day, I will get my yellow playground monitor jacket and the clipboard from Mrs. Cass. I will be the only playground monitor at recess, and I will have the only yellow jacket. I will help Mrs. Cass, and carefully monitor our section of the playground for any name calling, arguments, or fights. I will remain on the recess area for the fourth and fifth grade. If I see something that might start a fight, I'll write the students' names down and report them to Mrs. Cass immediately. If I don't see any fights or arguments, I will write that down and date the notation. I will then hand in that paper to Mrs. Cass at the end of recess and hang up my yellow jacket.

Monitoring Plan: This task will be monitored by:

Mrs. Cass will explain my role as playground monitor to the class. Then, after each recess, she will ask me for my written report at the end of that recess. She has promised to remind me to hang up my jacket.

Intervention Follow-Up Session: We understand we will meet in three weeks to discuss follow-up for this responsibility.

Date and Time of Follow-Up Meeting: November 9, 2014, in the morning just before school

Signatures: With our signatures below, we agree to abide by this contract and avoid future conflict by taking the action(s) above.

Student: Tremain Johnson   Date: 10/15/14

Teacher: Mrs. Teresa Cass   Date: 10/15/14

Principal: Ms. Vickie Mosely   Date: 10/17/14

Go to www.learningsciences.com/bookresources to download figures and tables.

The teacher, Mrs. Cass, during a five-day baseline count, notes seven separate instances in which Tremain shouts something aggressive or gets into a fight on the playground during recess, so clearly some type of targeted intervention is in order.

Upon reflection, Mrs. Cass notes that Tremain is always aware of hostile words from other students, and he can detect fights and hostility before they break out. She also thinks that helping monitor aggression on the playground might be something Tremain would like to do. She holds a meeting with him and explains how important it is to decrease his fighting on the playground, and she then asks for his help.

His responsibility would be to wear a yellow jacket on the playground with the words "Playground Monitor" on the back. He would carry a clipboard, and make a note each time he hears someone say something mean or aggressive, carefully noting the student's name and location. He would then report that immediately to Mrs. Cass.

Much to the delight of Mrs. Cass, this intervention seemed to work for Tremain. Figure 13.3 presents both baseline and intervention data on Tremain's aggression during the recess period, and the data clearly show a marked decline in Tremain's aggression. In fact, during the intervention period, Tremain engaged in aggression only once in eight days, and that is a significant decline in aggressive behavior.

Readers interested in this personal responsibility strategy might wish to review an additional case study using strategy. In addition to the case study above, the case study in Strategy 17 (Response to Intervention for Behavioral Change) of this text presents an example of using a personal responsibility strategy to improve a student's classroom behavior. Specifically, the personal responsibility strategy is used as a second intervention in Section 17.

Figure 13.3:   Tremain's Aggressive Behavior Intervention Data

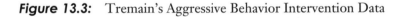

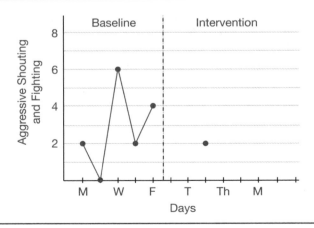

RESEARCH ON INCREASING STUDENTS' RESPONSIBILITIES

This strategy will work in your class, even when other strategies won't. In addition to the anecdotal research above, this strategy has been demonstrated to be effective in various research studies (Lazerson, Foster, Brown, & Hummel, 1988; Maher, 1984). In the early research on this strategy, Maher (1982, 1984) used adolescents with significant behavioral problems as tutors for students with mental disabilities in lower grade levels. His tutors were some of the worst behaving students in schools, and it was somewhat unnerving to give those students responsibility for teaching other students. The possibility for victimization was quite real. However, using intense supervision, Dr. Maher was able to undertake this study.

In Maher's study (1982), an experimental group of troubled adolescents was assigned as tutors and another randomly selected group of troubled students was assigned to receive peer counseling. After a number of tutoring sessions, the behavior of the tutors improved markedly, compared to the control group (the students receiving peer counseling). Data indicate that the number of disciplinary problems for the tutors in the experimental group went down drastically and their attendance improved. The tutoring even assisted them academically.

Also, anecdotal observations suggest that the responsibility of tutoring seemed to be the deciding factor. By virtue of tutoring, these kids were seen as leaders in some sense, and the behavior-problem tutors began to take responsibility for their students by protecting the younger tutees on the playground and even playing and interacting with them.

These results were quite surprising in 1982, so Dr. Maher repeated this experimental study in 1984, and the results of the second experiment were exactly the same. In short, the responsibility for tutoring gave these behavior-problem adolescents something they had—and in all probability, never had before—a meaningful contribution to offer to others in the school. These results were later replicated by others (Lazerson et al., 1988).

In combination, these anecdotal and experimental results indicate that providing a serious responsibility to troubled students, a responsibility that involves visibility and bragging rights, can make them take responsibility for their own behavior. This is a very effective intervention for many students with significant behavior problems (Bender, 2007).

> These anecdotal and experimental results indicate that providing a serious responsibility to troubled students can make them take responsibility for their own behavior.

SUMMARY

As indicated in the research and the preceding case study, this strategy will decrease problem behaviors for many students, though it is not appropriate for all students. Teachers should carefully consider the student's reasons for misbehavior prior to engaging in this particular intervention. However, if a student is seeking attention through misbehavior, this type of strategy can be highly effective. Further, as the research indicates, this strategy works for students with very significant behavioral problems, and as such, it is a strategy that teachers should undertake for many students with overt behavior problems. If we can find a way, as educators, to help students make positive behavioral contributions to the class, we can alleviate many behavior problems, and this strategy is one tool for educators to consider.

Strategy 14

Video Monitoring to Improve Behavior

Disruptive students often interrupt the class process, and in many cases may not be aware of the effects their inappropriate behavior has on others in the classroom. They may not recognize or acknowledge that their behavior is inappropriate in any way! At times, students' misbehavior may even be a cause for disdain or even ridicule from classmates, and students may be wholly unaware of that disdain. Such a situation would be the perfect time to employ video monitoring as an intervention tactic to improve the target student's behavior. In a video monitoring intervention, the teacher videos the behavior of the target student and then analyzes the behavior in a series of meetings with the student (Bender, 2007; Buggey, 1999).

By capturing a student's behavior on video, teachers have multiple options. First, teachers may edit the video to show the target student behaving appropriately. They can then use those video examples as a basis for discussions of appropriate and inappropriate behavior (Creer & Miklich, 1970). Today's digital editing capabilities, an option offered on most new computers, makes such video editing relatively easy.

Alternatively, rather than show positive behavior, the teacher may also edit the video to demonstrate the inappropriate behavior of the student. Such a video could then become the basis for a daily discussion of how the student responded inappropriately to others in the classroom and the negative consequences that followed such misbehavior (Bender, 2007). Also, the teacher can capture the reactions of peers to inappropriate behavior and discuss this with the target student, making that student more aware of the impact of the inappropriate behavior on others in the class. In some cases, class members may respond negatively to inappropriate behavior, and showing that to the offending student may motivate that student to work toward improving his behavior. Some students may believe that they improve their social status with their inappropriate behavior, even if the majority

> Teachers may edit the video to show the student behaving appropriately and use those examples as a basis for discussions of appropriate and inappropriate behavior.

of their classmates react negatively. If those subtle, negative reactions from other class members could be demonstrated to the misbehaving student, positive behavior change might result.

Of course, permission for videoing a particular student has to be solicited in advance, but this typically presents no particular problem. Students are very frequently videoed in classes today because class projects and various other achievements are often pictured on the class or school website. Many schools solicit permission from all of the parents for such video monitoring at the beginning of the year, and certainly videoing a student in order to improve her behavior should be included in such a blanket permission. This would give the teacher another effective option to curbing inappropriate behavior.

USING VIDEO MONITORING

Video monitoring works with many attention-seeking students and also for those with severe behavioral issues. It is useful across the grade levels but probably has more impact in the middle elementary grades and higher, where the influence of the peer group is greater.

It is also possible to use this strategy as a communication tool with parents. In some cases, family members of the misbehaving student may downplay the importance of behavioral problems. At many times during conferences with parents, teachers might sense that the parents do not share their concern relative to the problem behavior. Some parents may even pretend that no behavior problem exists or that the teacher is somehow picking on their child.

In those cases, video monitoring can become not only an effective intervention for the student, but also a mechanism for communication with the parents. By showing parents a behavior problem in class, teachers may find that the parents take the problem more seriously (Buggey, 1999). The video monitoring strategy calls a student's attention to her conduct problem in two ways, each of which supports and reinforces the other: (1) charting the occurrence of the behavior (whether a positive or negative behavior) and (2) using a television camera as a means of displaying the problem behavior directly to the student. This strategy therefore involves joint application of these two documentation methods—a hard copy chart of behavior and video record of behavior.

> Video monitoring probably has more impact in the middle elementary grades and higher, where the influence of the peer group is greater.

However, teachers should be cautioned. This tactic is not advised for those rare, often extreme behavioral problems, such as violent outbursts or occasional fighting. In those cases, the student is not usually in denial about the effects of the behavioral problems, and the behavior may be too rare to capture multiple examples on video. In such cases, other strategies, perhaps peer pressure or conflict resolution, would probably be more effective.

To state it another way, this strategy is not particularly effective for very low-frequency behaviors (i.e., those that occur only once or twice a week) for logistical reasons. It is difficult to capture seldom-occurring behavior problems on video. Rather, behavior problems such as constant attention-seeking behavior, verbal outbursts in class, arguing with other students, or constant joking in class are appropriate target behaviors for this intervention. In short, behavior problems that occur numerous times during a thirty- to fifty-minute instructional activity are the best candidates for this strategy.

Steps in Video Monitoring

1. Define the target behaviors.

2. Obtain permissions for video.

3. Determine a time frame and set up the video camera.

4. Edit the video.

5. Hold the first student conference.

6. Hold weekly student conferences.

7. Decrease the number of weekly conferences.

Step 1: Define the Target Behaviors

Teachers must determine if they wish to capture on the video inappropriate behavior, appropriate behavior, or both. There are some advantages to collecting video of both positive and negative behaviors, because the teacher-student discussion will then focus on both, making that conversation a bit more relaxed. However, this strategy can be time-consuming because video editing does take time. Targeting and capturing fewer behaviors overall will be more time efficient. After targeting two or three specific behaviors, teachers should write down the clear definitions for each and begin a baseline count for the target behavior(s).

> There are some advantages to collecting video of both positive and negative behaviors, because the teacher-student discussion will then focus on both, making that conversation a bit more relaxed.

Step 2: Obtain Permissions for Video

Teachers should verify permission, or obtain permission, to video the target student. As noted, almost all schools today have some digital video cameras available for teachers to use, and in many cases, that issue has already been addressed with school-wide permissions for video. Still, teachers should either ensure that permission has been obtained to video the student, or write a letter to the parents and obtain permission. I also recommend that teachers discuss the targeted behaviors and the overall video-based intervention with their administrator.

Step 3: Determine a Time Frame and Set Up the Video Camera

Teachers should identify a time frame for the videotaping—perhaps a forty-five-minute morning instructional period each day or the first twenty minutes of class in a particular subject, daily. As one consideration in selecting a time frame, teachers should consider when the targeted behaviors are likely to take place and the relative ease of setting up a video camera to capture those target behaviors during those times. After the teacher completes a baseline count, they will need to set up a video camera on a tripod to observe the student working at his desk and, if possible, several surrounding students. This provides an opportunity to show the target student the reactions of others to either his misbehavior or his appropriate behavior.

Finally, teachers should consider camera placement in terms of where the tripod is reasonably safe from harm (not in a walkway where it is likely to be turned over), yet able to capture subtle behaviors and even facial expressions of the students. The camera should be fifteen feet or so from the target student and centered on that student, but the view should also include perhaps one-fourth of the class members. Careful camera placement assures optimal video examples to use in the intervention phase. A remote control is preferable for turning the camera on because that lessens the potential impact of operating the camera. Data collection may then begin by running the video camera as the class proceeds with ongoing learning activities.

Initially, students will ask about the video camera, and teachers should be open about why it is there, while stressing the advantages of the video intervention. Something like this example may help:

> I want to understand why David gets angry in class and argues with other students so often. I want to see if you guys are picking on him, so I'll be videotaping the class several times, and then we'll talk about what is going on. Now, let's all get to work and just forget the camera is there.

Note that this discussion raises the possibility that David is not completely at fault, and therefore this phrasing might be more acceptable to him.

If students ask who might see the video, teachers might say something like, "Right now, I'll be looking at it, and I'll probably show some of it to David." In most cases, these statements are enough to help students feel comfortable, and they usually forget the camera is on after a few minutes.

> Initially, students will ask about the video camera, and teachers should be open about why it is there, while stressing the advantages of the video intervention.

Step 4: Edit the Video

Teachers will need to edit the video to isolate multiple examples of the target behaviors. This will take some time daily outside of class and may be a bit difficult at first. However, as teachers become more proficient in video usage and editing, they may find there are instructional benefits such as videotaping various class projects and reports.

For intervention purposes, I recommend that teachers select several examples of serious misbehavior as well as several examples of appropriate behavior. Each should be a clear example of the specific positive or negative behavior. Having both positive and negative behaviors often provides an opportunity for a richer discussion of the target student's behavior overall. Also, if teachers plan to show the video to parents, having both positive and inappropriate behavior on the video is a plus. Over the intervention time frame, teachers will likely concentrate more on the problem behaviors, but capturing several appropriate behavior examples will help in the initial student meetings.

After several days, there should be at least three or four examples of misbehavior and a few examples of appropriate behavior. An example of appropriate behavior might merely be a thirty- to forty-five-second time span of smooth class functioning, and two or more examples should be sufficient to model appropriate work for the target student. Teachers should capture and include in the edited video all inappropriate behaviors, of course. They should save all video examples in a digital file and discard any video that is not useful for the discussion. This should result in perhaps five to ten minutes of video with multiple positive and negative examples.

Teachers should also keep a written log of which inappropriate behaviors they chose to save, including the date, time, and class assignment in which the misbehavior took place. Because teachers will be saving examples of misbehavior from different days, the data in that log may become important in reporting on the behavior problems and/or the intervention results to the student, parents, or administrators.

Step 5: Hold the First Student Conference

The first student conference begins the intervention phase of this project. The meeting should begin with the teacher and student getting together outside of class. The first student conference is intended to accomplish several things, including

- Sharing examples of misbehavior and discussing them
- Sharing examples of appropriate behavior and discussing them
- Seeking a motivating reinforcement for good behavior
- Seeking a commitment from the student for behavioral improvement

Start the conference by saying something like, "David. I'd like to discuss what happened in class this week. Let's look at an example of when you got angry." After that, you should show one brief (thirty seconds to one minute) example of David's misbehavior and discuss it. Next, teachers may wish to show an example of appropriate behavior, and discuss that while complimenting the student for behaving appropriately. That should be followed by another discussion of the next example of inappropriate behavior.

Alternatively, with some students, it is of benefit to show several misbehavior examples up front, and then merely inquire, "David. What's going on here?" That type of approach allows the student to try and explain the misbehaviors together. In each case, the teacher should then respond by saying, "Here is what I think I see." The teacher can then accurately describe David's arguing behavior and carefully note any negative peer reactions to it, if any are observed on the video.

Again, using examples of both positive and negative behaviors will help frame the meetings on a more positive basis. Generally, the less confrontation the teacher and student have, the more likely it is that the teacher can eventually elicit a commitment from the student to try and change the behavior. The teacher might say, "I'd like to help you behave more appropriately, and I'd like to find a way for you to earn things you like for not arguing in class. What do you like to do in class?"

Having David identify some possible reinforcers is helpful, including things such as getting to line up first or getting more time at lunch. The teacher may then conclude the first meeting by saying,

> Okay, I understand that you will try not to get angry in class. I'll help by making an agreement with you: if you go an entire class period and get into only one argument or none, you will be rewarded by lining up first when we go to lunch and recess the next day. We'll plan to meet each week to discuss how this is going.

The teacher should consider the logistics of the student meetings. Most teachers find that the first student conference takes no more than fifteen minutes, whereas later meetings take considerably less time. Teachers should plan that meeting time for after class. Of course, after this first meeting, the teacher should continue keeping a daily record of the student's inappropriate target behaviors and record them daily on an *x-y* axis data chart.

Step 6: Hold Weekly Student Conferences

As in all interventions, no one can say how long this intervention must last to be effective. However, it is certain that merely videotaping a student and holding one meeting are not likely to elicit long-term behavioral change. I suggest that teachers commit to holding weekly meetings for at least four additional weeks after the first meeting. Therefore, teachers will continue to run the video camera, edit the video, and select examples of misbehavior and appropriate behavior to discuss.

However, if teachers do not see positive results by the second or third week, they may wish to further emphasize the importance of the intervention. They can accomplish this in several ways. First, teachers may modify the reinforcement offered while stressing to the student the importance of behavioral change. As another idea, teachers may wish to sign a written contract with the student that includes these agreements. The contract in Figure 13.1 can easily be modified for this purpose. Finally, teachers may invite the parents of the student, or a school administrator or counselor to attend a weekly meeting. At that meeting, teachers can review and discuss the video examples with all participants.

Step 7: Decrease the Number of Weekly Conferences

As the student's inappropriate behavior begins to decrease, teachers should decrease the number of weekly conferences. First, the teacher should praise the student for his behavioral improvement, and suggest that she begin to hold their conferences every two weeks or so for the next month. If the student's behavior continues to improve, the teacher should then be able to discontinue the intervention completely. However, as long as the weekly conferences continue, the teacher should continue to take daily counts of misbehavior.

RESEARCH ON VIDEO MONITORING

This video monitoring strategy is somewhat time-consuming because teachers will need time for video editing each week as well as time for the weekly meetings with the student. Therefore, teachers should use this strategy only after other strategies have been implemented without success or when students or their parents need to explicitly see the misbehavior to realize that a problem exists.

With those time concerns noted, there are times when this strategy is exactly the tactic needed to improve student behavior, and the limited research on this is positive (Buggey, 1999; Creer & Miklich, 1970). For example, Creer and Miklich (1970) implement a video monitoring strategy that focuses on capturing positive behaviors of several target students. As an intervention for noncompliance as well as occasional aggression, they videotape the students' behavior and then edit out all of the inappropriate behaviors. By showing the edited video to the aggressive and/or noncompliant students, they share models of appropriate behavior and repeatedly discuss the importance of appropriate behavior with the target students. Their results indicate that this technique works to significantly reduce the students' aggressive and noncompliant behavior.

> This strategy should only be used after other strategies have been implemented without success or when students or their parents need to explicitly see the misbehavior to realize that a problem exists.

SUMMARY

I have long been an advocate for this strategy (Bender, 2007), even though both research and practical examples of this strategy in schools are relatively rare. Nevertheless, it is likely that teachers will use this strategy increasingly in the future for several reasons. First, digital cameras are virtually everywhere in the modern world, including in classrooms. Security cameras are common in schools or on school buses. Further, students often use this digital recording technology themselves in today's classrooms. Also, teachers are increasingly doing digital video editing for personal or family videos as well as instructional purposes, particularly compared to the 1970s and 1980s when this strategy was first recommended.

Finally, nothing demonstrates inappropriate behavior as well as a digital video of that behavior, which is why police officers are increasingly mounting digital cameras in their cars as well as on their person. In short, while not used widely in schools previously, teachers are likely to use this disciplinary strategy much more in the future.

Strategy 15

The Let's Make a Deal! Strategy: Negotiating Power in the Classroom

From time to time, in various school situations, an entire classroom may be completely out of control, and teachers might need to do something rather drastic to reestablish influence in that class. I often say to educators that if I were allowed to assign students to classes, I could go into any school and create a completely unmanageable classroom! As any veteran teacher knows, some students challenge the disciplinary system much more frequently than others, and if those students comprise half the class or more, that class would be a challenge for even the most effective veteran teacher to manage.

Several years ago, I was presented with the following challenge. An inner-city school in New York was struggling with overall academic performance. Further, this school had very serious disciplinary problems, including gang-related problems and significant drug involvement. The school had recently replaced several teachers in the special education classes. I was invited to do a workshop on discipline for those teachers and specifically to consult with a brand-new teacher in one of the special education classes. In that rather extreme case, a newly graduated, first-year teacher had just been hired to teach one of the classes because a veteran teacher recently chose to retire midyear! To make matters even more interesting, it was only three months prior to the end of the school year!

> From time to time, in various school situations, an entire classroom may be completely out of control, and teachers might need to do something rather drastic to reestablish influence in that class.

Although I've faced a number of interesting challenges in my career doing workshops to strengthen discipline in schools, I quickly realized that this was going to be one of my most challenging tasks. What could I present to that brand-new teacher that would offer any possibility of her regaining control of that specific class, a class that had led a veteran teacher to retire early? Upon a bit more reflection, I began to feel somewhat guilty for those feelings. Although I had to conceptualize a few tactics for this situation, my job (in that instance) was completed with a one-day workshop, whereas the teachers with whom I was working had to face those middle school adolescents every single day for the rest of that year!

Upon much reflection, I determined that in an out-of-control classroom, a new teacher or perhaps even a newly transferred teacher will need to establish control over the classroom by quickly defining her role in the class. In fact, that process would, of necessity, involve some negotiation with students in the class, relative to the teacher's role in the class. In order to offer those teachers an option, and in particular to help a newly hired teacher quickly determine the power structure of the class, I developed a negotiation tactic based on sociometric charting of peer influences within that class (Bender, 2007; Busse, 2009; Elliott & Busse, 1991; Gresham, 2002). I called that strategy Let's Make a Deal!

Sociometric measures involve the assessment of social relationships in groups of individuals (Elliott & Busse, 1991; Gresham, 2002) and can be used to develop a quick understanding of who is most influential in the classroom. By developing a sociometric picture of peer influences among students in the class, it was my hope that the new teachers would at least begin to understand who the most powerful students were. The teachers could then negotiate with those students such things as choices of work, grading options, and so on.

> In an out-of-control classroom, a new teacher or perhaps even a newly transferred teacher will need to establish control over the classroom by quickly defining her role in the class.

THE PURPOSE AND PROCESS OF LET'S MAKE A DEAL!

The broad purpose of the Let's Make a Deal! strategy is to develop with the class a sociometric representation of the roles and responsibilities of various class members. Such a representation is sometimes referred to as a *sociogram*. The process of developing a sociogram should then present the teacher with a number of unique opportunities to help reestablish his influence in the classroom.

First, in this sociometric assessment process, the teacher has the opportunity to assist in defining for various class members a more positive role based on the strengths and perceptions of class members. Next, the teacher elicits input on the teacher's role from the students, which empowers the teacher somewhat. Finally, teachers can develop the opportunity to negotiate a power-sharing responsibility with one or more influential students in the class, which, in turn, gives those students a positive role responsibility, perhaps for the first time in their lives. In that sense, this can be an initial step within a responsibility strategy intervention, which I described earlier. Here are the steps in this Let's Make a Deal! strategy.

> The broad purpose of the Let's Make a Deal! strategy is to develop with the class a sociometric representation of the roles and responsibilities of various class members.

Ten Steps in Let's Make a Deal!

1. Identify the Power Kid
2. Elicit a self-description from another student
3. Discuss the descriptions
4. Focus on two other students and diagram those relationships
5. Select the Power Kid
6. Diagram others
7. Develop an "influence portrait"
8. Place yourself
9. Negotiate power
10. Write up the deal!

Step 1: Identify the Power Kid

Use some quick judgment during your first few days with the disruptive class and make some educated guess as to who the most influential student in the class is. Who leads the misbehavior? Who do other students defer to? This student, whom I call the "Power Kid," will help determine the relationships between you and all the students in the class. Once you identify the Power Kid, you must arrange a negotiation of power with that student, and, through him, the power and influence relationships with the remaining members of the class will fall into place.

Step 2: Elicit a Self-Description From Another Student

With the Power Kid in mind, select a student who may be sitting near him, and then tell the class that you want to draw a picture of the friendships and roles for each class member in order to help you understand the class better. Request that selected student (not the Power Kid) to go to the whiteboard and draw a circle in the center. That circle represents the student. Encourage her to give herself a descriptive name and/or several descriptive indicators of who she is and what role she plays in the classroom. Other class members can help, if they like, as long as all descriptors are positive in the student's perspective. Also, the student at the board, whom the descriptors are defining, must agree that each descriptor is accurate. That gives control to the student who is having her role in the class discussed.

For example, Zack might name himself as the class comedian by saying things like, "I like to make my friends laugh!" or "I'm the class entertainer." Alternatively, Maria may describe herself by a role she plays in class: "I'm everybody's Mom. I'm a peacemaker," or "I'm the best reader in class." Elicit positive descriptions and list their name in the circle on the board for the students, while ignoring all negative descriptions. Then review the descriptions and compliment the student on her positive role in the class.

Step 3: Discuss the Descriptions

Discuss the descriptors with others in the class, and elicit the other students' views of these descriptors for the student at the board. Again, ignore all negative comments and seek only positive comments; if possible, add to the descriptive statements any positive comments the class might make about the student's role. You may also wish to elicit certain comments on particular roles common in groups of students (e.g., class leader, class comedian, peacemaker, committee leader, best reader, best in math, the judge, class cop, the big man, etc.). Use the assistance of many students, particularly those who have identified roles for themselves along these lines.

Step 4: Focus on at Least Two Other Students and Diagram Those Relationships

Have several more students describe themselves and their roles in the class in positive terms. Before they draw their circle, have them determine how close they are socially to the first student. If they are close friends, their circle should be near the circle for the first student. If not, they should draw their circle farther away. Explain that the location will help students understand how the class works as a group and will give a picture of the friendships within the class. Be certain to instruct these first few students not to use the center of the board. Again, emphasize the positive aspects of the descriptions, and compliment the kids on their importance in the class.

Step 5: Select the Power Kid

Request that the Power Kid describe himself. Once the Power Kid sees you compliment the previous students, chances are good that he will want to participate. Be very obvious in noting any positive reactions of the class, and based on that anticipated reaction, suggest that the Power Kid place himself in the center of the board. Compliment him as a class leader, and inquire about what role responsibilities leadership entails. If possible, elicit a statement from this student about his influence in the class.

Step 6: Diagram Others

Now you can include all the other students. You can probably have two or three students at the whiteboard at a time, which saves time for the whole process. In small classes, say of ten students or less, do this with everyone in the class. In large classes, you might invite six or eight strategically selected students to participate, while the others conduct an assignment outside of class.

Step 7: Develop an "Influence Portrait"

When all participating students have circles and descriptors on the board, ask about close relationships and then draw lines and/or arrows to identify those friendships. Depict closer relationships in close proximity on the board, and you may need to move a few students after some class discussion. Explain to the students that this portrait represents the friendships and levels of influence within the class, and encourage them to suggest any additional modifications in the portrait as necessary.

Step 8: Place Yourself

The class has defined itself, and that information can be very useful to a teacher entering a tough disciplinary situation; but now, you should use this process to empower yourself. As a culmination for this activity, ask the class, "Who's missing? Who else has any influence in this class?" With this question, you can find out if they think to include you, the teacher. However, if you need to prompt them, ask them if you, as the teacher, have any positive role or responsibilities for what goes on. Next, ask them what that role might be. Elicit descriptions such as "Teaching us something important," "Making assignments," "Giving us grades," "Making school fun," and so on. You might wish to ask the class if you have a right to make assignments in class or for homework or assign role-plays, games, or work on the computer.

If successful, you are having the class admit openly that teachers have a role and some degree of influence in the class. For classes that have previously been totally out of control, this is the first step in the right direction. If the class says that you have no role, you may have to merely state that you do have some responsibilities, such as teaching and making assignments. If you can get the class to acknowledge your role as teacher, you have empowered yourself, to some degree. More accurately, the class has empowered you to do the things that you could not do in a class with no established disciplinary expectations.

Step 9: Negotiate Power

To re-establish control in a classroom in which teacher influence has been lost, you must be willing to negotiate a bit with the students. You must indicate a willingness to share power if you are to become empowered by the class. Maybe begin by saying, "I understand you don't like homework, but I have to make some assignments in order to do my job. What if I make homework assignments only three times a week?" In this manner, you may be able to negotiate your way into some influence in this difficult classroom situation where previously the teacher had none.

> In order to re-establish control in a classroom in which teacher influence has been lost, teachers must be willing to negotiate a bit with the students.

Also empower the Power Kid. Talk about your influence in the class, and mention that influential people in the class also have some responsibilities as well. You might indicate that you are willing to let the Power Kid even veto some assignments you make. This means that he can veto one assignment during any given week—any worksheet or homework (though not a test). That is real power in the classroom. This will mean that you must always have an alternative assignment in your desk, but it can also mean that you have earned some cooperation from the most influential student in the class, relative to overall class discipline. It will also improve class climate rather drastically if the teacher is not constantly fighting existing power relationships in the class. If the class requests another option or that another student share in the class power, consider that as an option as well. Perhaps that class should have two Power Kids, with specific responsibilities.

Step 10: Write Up the Deal!

To emphasize the responsibilities of the teacher and the Power Kid, write up the deal in a contract and have all the students sign it. List the roles of the class leaders (or multiple Power Kids), including their expected contributions and the veto (or other) powers that you have agreed to share. Also list the teacher's role and responsibilities. Make a paper copy of the diagram (the sociogram) from the whiteboard and attach it to the contract. The teacher can then refer to that agreement when students rebel against an assignment or task.

WHEN TO USE LET'S MAKE A DEAL!

Most veteran teachers, upon reflection, will agree that when a teacher negotiates and shares power with the students, she is merely acknowledging the reality of classrooms today—effective teachers negotiate with students all the time. Negotiation of power, using the process of constructing a sociogram is one way to do that openly, while having the class essentially empower the teacher through the discussion of the teacher's role. As I indicated in the preceding example, this strategy can be very useful in extreme situations where a class is out of control. With that noted, teachers might also wish to consider using this to make relationships obvious to class members, even in classes that are not out of control. Both teachers and students may be surprised by the views or roles that others seem to play in the class, and this sociometric technique will make all such roles apparent.

> Effective teachers negotiate with students all the time.

While sociometrics are often used in schools (Busse, 2009; Elliott & Busse, 1991; Gresham, 2002), this sociometric procedure has not been researched or previously used. In fact, this is the one strategy in this book for which there is no evidence of efficacy. Because I devised this strategy in response to a particular need only a few years ago (Bender, 2007), there is no supportive research here. However, in view of Marzano's (2007) emphasis on withitness, as I discuss throughout this book, we might note that it is impossible to be with it when one enters an out-of-control classroom with little insight into the dynamics of the peer influences in that class. In that sense, this sociometric process will, at a minimum, help the teacher gain quick insight into those relationships. It may also help renegotiate the power arrangements within the out-of-control classroom.

Further, to my knowledge there are no other guidelines anywhere for re-establishing discipline when a class is out of control. In that type of rather extreme situation, teachers may find that this emphasis on negotiated relationships and responsibilities is one way to re-establish some influence in the class.

SECTION III
Discipline Challenges in 21st-Century Classrooms

In discipline, as in every area of education, there are typically many ongoing influences or changes that teachers must deal with. While effective disciplinary tactics and strategies, once proven, do not typically change, other educational transitions can and do impact how teachers discipline students. This section presents five current challenges that impact how educators discipline in schools, and for each challenge, I describe at least one strategy. The challenges and strategies herein are

Strategy 16: Restorative Justice and Restorative Circles

Strategy 17: Response to Intervention for Behavioral Change

Strategy 18: Discipline in a Flipped Classroom

Strategy 19: Project-Based Learning to Enhance Class Discipline

Strategy 20: Apps, Laptops, and Technology for Enhancing Behavior

Strategy 16

Restorative Justice and Restorative Circles

DISPROPORTIONATE SUSPENSION AND EXPULSION

In January of 2014, the US Department of Education released a key policy letter from the Secretary of Education, Arne Duncan, that included some data on inequities in disciplinary practice in schools nationwide (Blad, 2014a, 2014b; Davis, 2014; Duncan, 2014). This policy letter resulted from joint work of the Department of Education and the Department of Justice, under the Supportive School Discipline Initiative of 2011 (US Department of Education, 2011). Data gathered by these agencies indicate that minority students are much more likely to receive disciplinary suspensions and expulsions than nonminority students and that these disciplinary practices result in a lack of school educational opportunities for those students (Blad, 2014a, 2014b).

For example, data collected from the 2011–2012 school year from all 97,000 public schools in the United States show that schools expel African American students three times as often as white students (Duncan, 2014; O'Brien, 2014). Overall, schools suspend 16.4 percent of African American students at some point, compared to only 4.6 percent for white students (O'Brien, 2014). Further, some other minority groups are likewise disproportionately disciplined in ways that result in loss of schooling. The data show that schools expel or suspend Native Alaskan students as well as students with disabilities at a much higher rate than their white counterparts (Duncan, 2014).

> Data gathered by the Department of Education and the Department of Justice have indicated that minority students are much more likely to receive disciplinary suspensions and expulsions than are nonminority students.

Most educators would agree that some behaviors are highly problematic and perhaps should result in suspension or even expulsion (e.g., repeated weapons violations on school grounds or behaviors that endanger other students). However, the discipline data show that many of those suspensions are for relatively minor rule violations such as being late to class (Duncan, 2014). In fact, many school exclusions from school for disciplinary reasons result from zero tolerance policies in schools relative to weapons violations, fighting, or class disruption, and most administrators want more flexibility in dealing with such rules violations. At the very least, schools should implement for those minor violations some disciplinary practices that do not involve exclusion from class (Davis, 2014; Duncan, 2014; US Department of Education, 2011). In this sense, expectations of teachers for behavior management are changing today, and that represents a challenge for all educators.

Because suspensions and expulsions effectively exclude those students from school, these disciplinary practices, when used disproportionately, may raise a civil rights issue involving denial of educational services to minority students (Davis, 2014; Duncan, 2014). In fact, high levels of suspension are also associated with higher dropout rates among certain minority groups (St. George, 2014), and high dropout rates are associated with increased levels of juvenile crime or even imprisonment for some groups. Clearly, these data present evidence of a disproportionate use of certain types of disciplinary practice based on students' race, and therein lies the challenge for educators. How can educators assure that schools apply disciplinary practices in a fair manner and minimize the students' exclusion from school?

> Expectations of teachers for behavior management are changing today, and that represents a challenge for all educators.

Secretary of Education Arne Duncan and Attorney General Eric Holder recently expressed their joint concerns on how exclusionary practices impact students over the long term. The phrase "school to prison" describes the fact that students with high numbers of suspensions and expulsions from school are much more likely to end up in prison (Duncan, 2014) than are other students. Of course, causality is an open question: there is ongoing debate about whether suspensions and expulsions, and the resulting loss of schooling, actually *cause* students to go to prison, or these are merely two results of some other cause.

While that question may be interesting intellectually, we cannot answer it in this context, and we must revert to what is known, based on the existing research. We know, for example, that many teachers and schools can do a more effective job in discipline than is currently being done. Teachers can become more involved and implement research-proven disciplinary strategies such as those herein and elsewhere (Marzano, 2007; Sousa, 2009), and therefore teachers can better help to manage rule infractions in the classroom.

> Many teachers and schools can do a more effective job in discipline than is currently being done; teachers can become more involved and can implement research-proven disciplinary strategies more frequently.

Because of data such as these from multiple studies, and the concern on disproportionate use of exclusionary discipline practices, Secretary of Education Arne Duncan encouraged schools to consider disciplinary practices that do not result in loss of school time. Rather, Secretary Duncan endorses alternative disciplinary practices that tend to restore the students' relationship with the school community.

RESTORATIVE JUSTICE IN SCHOOLS

Initially, restorative justice arose as a practice within the prison system, and for background purposes, teachers may wish to review the video on restorative circles from the University of Rochester (http://www.restorativecircles.org/video). More recently, several educational organizations have responded to these disciplinary concerns relative to disciplinary inequity with the introduction of new recommended disciplinary policies, based on the concept of restorative justice and restorative circles (Davis, 2014; O'Brien, 2014; St. George, 2014).

Specifically, the Advancement Project, American Federation of Teachers, National Education Association, and National Opportunity to Learn Campaign have jointly developed a disciplinary toolkit that recommends restorative justice disciplinary practices (O'Brien, 2014), defined as practices and activities that restore students' positive relationships to teachers and others in the school environment. The idea behind restorative practices is that these disciplinary policies and procedures, rather than simply removing a student from school, will actually help build healthy relationships and a sense of community among those in the school in order to prevent and address conflict and wrongdoing (O'Brien, 2014; St. George, 2014).

These restorative justice disciplinary practices are intended to allow students who have violated rules to take responsibility for their behavior while remaining in the school setting. Further restorative practices address the issues underlying the behavior rather than merely the presenting overt behavior problem that occurs on any given day (Davis, 2014).

Several authors describe an array of restorative disciplinary practices for educators to consider as alternatives to suspensions and/or expulsions (Davis, 2014; O'Brien, 2014).

Restorative Justice. Restorative justice provides an opportunity for the victim in a conflict to explain how the misbehavior of the wrongdoer harmed him, and the wrongdoer is likewise provided an opportunity to show how she will work to resolve the conflict. Such actions may include replacing funds that were stolen, apologies provided to others as needed, or some explanations and corrections that might help restore a person's reputation if the wrongdoer has been telling lies about a person.

> Restorative justice disciplinary practices are intended to allow students who have violated rules to take responsibility for their behavior while remaining in the school setting.

Community Service. Community service is another restorative practice option highlighted (O'Brien, 2014). In particular situations, if the wrongdoer cannot "restore" something, she may be expected to perform community service around the school or elsewhere to allow her to make a meaningful contribution to the community at large. Such service would be planned and supervised.

Restorative Circles. Restorative circles represent one application of the restorative practices construct that schools utilize widely (Davis 2014; O'Brien, 2014). These circles involve meeting with students with behavioral issues, their parents, and other students and involved teachers, in a morning meeting type of framework and using conflict resolution techniques to reach a mutually acceptable solution to the problem.

The circle process is intended to provide a protected discussion in which students, both victims and perpetrators, can open a dialogue with each other. Each is provided an opportunity to speak and listen to one another, allowing both students and educators to offer their own perspectives (Davis, 2014; O'Brien, 2014). It is obvious that the same concepts underlie both conflict resolution and the morning meeting strategies I described previously. Further, schools can use this circle process approach either as a preventative measure, to develop relationships and build community among those in the school, or as a targeted response to specific inappropriate behaviors.

Conflict Resolution and Peer Mediation. Conflict resolution programs and peer mediation techniques jointly serve as the basis for restorative practices in schools. The specific techniques and guidelines for peer mediation and conflict resolution serve as the basis for the restorative circle. Because these techniques are above, I will not be reviewing them here.

RESTORATIVE CIRCLES IN SCHOOLS

Teachers may use restorative circles, sometimes referred to as *talking circles*, with the entire class to improve class climate, or they may use them with students in conflict as a disciplinary intervention. Both types are in video examples, the links to which you can find below.

MetWest High School

MetWest High School in Oakland, California, uses restorative circles to build a sense of community among students as well as address behavioral problems in the school. In this use of the restorative circle, the entire class might be involved in an effort to build a better class climate overall, avoiding future disciplinary problems. You can watch a video showing an example of a restorative circle at this school at http://www.ousd.k12.ca.us/restorativejustice

An Administrator's Perspective

Victoria Halferty, M.S. Ed., earned degrees from the University of Georgia and the University of Scranton, Pennsylvania. In addition to rearing three children, she gained certification and taught special and general education (K–12) in three states.

I had the honor to teach Ms. Halferty in her undergraduate work, and I have followed her career since. She has taught students with special needs for thirteen years and spent the past five years as assistant principal at Reading Senior High School, in Reading, Pennsylvania, with significant disciplinary and instructional leadership responsibilities. I know her to be an effective professional educator and a no-nonsense disciplinarian with vast experience dealing with some of the toughest students in the schools. She has led the effort in several schools to institute restorative practices over the past six years and used restorative circles to reduce conflict among students. She is committed to this approach.

> After only two days of restorative practices in Bethlehem, Pennsylvania, in 2008, I discovered that what I once recognized as "old-fashioned, just plain talking and listening," is fundamentally effective for managing students with behavioral issues. What a wonderful, though hidden, discovery! The caring, effective listening skills of my family, and in particular of my grandparents—my most admired educators—were linked with my educational experiences by one very simple, fundamental guideline for lifetime learning: genuine conversational skills—reaching toward a common understanding with open listening and thoughtful speaking—is the most valuable factor in rich teaching and effective discipline. To have these conversations with students demonstrating behavioral problems, clearly defined and structured, will build communities supportive of appropriate behavior and learning, a precious goal indeed. After implementing restorative circles within my academic and behavioral practices as an educator, my need for writing referrals to the administration became very limited, as many behavioral problems melted away. My experience as a professional educator and lifelong learner was redefined with regards to my own personal responsibility for truly engaging my students, and developing the art of restorative and meaningful conversations.
>
> Restorative practices return us to an old and effective way of encouraging the human spirit toward growth. People who know they are able to speak honestly, freely, and thoughtfully to others within defined parameters are able to quickly build and develop mutual goals. These practices allow teachers to develop as the "lead" learners in the educational environment, and the students are able to develop as mutually dependent on one another for cooperative, cordial, and positive feedback while building knowledge! As this recognition of mutual learning grows, so does the capacity of the entire learning community!
>
> Restorative practices are not only necessary in the 21st-century classroom, they are essential in a time when the digital environment leaves the humanistic world in the past. Without intentional conversations toward behavioral improvement and meaningful learning, our professional efforts to foster appropriate behavior and to direct students toward lifelong learning is futile.

STEPS IN A RESTORATIVE CIRCLE INTERVENTION

As with most of these strategies, different schools implement this process in different ways, and the intended application of this process may determine how schools implement it. For improving class climate, the restorative circle functions much like the morning meetings I described. Alternatively, from a disciplinary perspective, a school may choose to use restorative circles as an immediate response to a behavioral outbreak, such as a fight in school or bullying episode, and many schools use this procedure in that fashion. In that application of the restorative circle process, schools do not typically collect and chart baseline and intervention data. Of course, the advantage of this application is that restorative circles can be an immediate teacher's response to a disciplinary altercation. In those instances, restorative circles serve the same disciplinary function as the practice of suspension.

However, to really document the impact of restorative circles, I recommend collecting baseline and intervention data whenever possible, particularly in recurring behavioral problems. In that fashion, teachers can not only document the impact, but build a strong track record of interventions they have used to alleviate a specific student's recurring behavior problems.

The eight steps below seem to be common to most targeted restorative circle interventions. We should note the similarity between these steps for conducting a restorative circle and the steps in the conflict resolution process.

Restorative Circle Steps

1. Collect baseline data or initial report.
2. Schedule the restorative circle.
3. Present initial data or narrative.
4. Main participants state their perspectives.
5. Point out areas of agreement.
6. Take responsibility.
7. Finalize alternative ways to relate.
8. Sign an agreement.

Step 1: Collect Baseline Data or Initial Report

Teachers must base the restorative circle on some type of data, and I recommend a baseline count of similar behavioral infractions. For example, if a student is frequently cursing and calling other students names in class, the teacher should tally those behaviors over a three- to five-day period, and then use that baseline to plan a restorative circle. In such a case, the circle may involve the student, the student's parents, the teacher, an administrator, and one or two members of the class whom the behavior offended. The count of baseline behaviors then becomes the reason for discussion during the restorative circle.

However, in some cases, teachers may wish to hold a restorative circle immediately after a behavioral problem, especially if the problem is of a serious nature. Fighting, having a weapon in school, or bullying may be instances in which teachers could initiate a restorative circle immediately after only one behavioral outburst. In those cases, the teacher should document in a short paragraph exactly what she saw or what other students told her about the behavioral problem. That narrative then becomes the launching point for the circle discussion. A sample narrative is in the forthcoming case study.

Step 2: Schedule the Restorative Circle

In most cases, teachers schedule a circle for after school, and the school administrator's office manages the logistics of scheduling. It is critical to have all involved students and their parents attend. The teacher should be there, and in addition almost all restorative circles involve an administrator. Depending on training, some schools have the guidance counselor or a school administrator actually conduct the restorative circle. Others who may be involved include special education teachers, school resource officers, and psychologists, as appropriate.

Step 3: Present Initial Data or Narrative

This step and the steps that follow take place during the restorative circle itself. Again, different schools manage restorative circles in different ways, but because this process is based on conflict resolution, many of the conflict resolution steps apply. First, the meeting facilitator (usually a school administrator or guidance counselor with specific training in conflict resolution) begins the meeting by presenting the initial data or narrative. He does this in a nonjudgmental, statement-of-facts manner because for parents and others who may not yet know of the behavior problem, this may be the first time they hear any details about a behavioral incident.

Step 4: Main Participants State Their Perspectives

The main participants in the conflict state their perspectives and add to the narrative. These will frequently disagree with the initial narrative, so the meeting facilitator makes notes on disagreements and points them out to participants. The facilitator gives each of the students in the conflict the opportunity to state her perception of the events without being interrupted by the other participants. If a student and a teacher are in conflict, the facilitator invites both to state their perspectives.

Depending on the situation, parents may be invited to share their perceptions of the conflict at this step. In many cases they have critical information to share. For example, they may note that their child has been complaining at home of an ongoing problem with the other person in the conflict. Although parents of the students in conflict are not required to verbally participate in any steps, the facilitator invites their contribution, beginning with this step and continuing in subsequent steps.

Step 5: Point Out Areas of Agreement

The meeting facilitator points out areas of agreement as positive steps toward restoring a positive relationship. Also, the facilitator might ask one or both of the participants if she or they understand how the other person may have perceived the conflict differently. In some cases, it might be useful to have participants take the other side of the argument or try to explain why the other combatant might have done what they did or said what they said.

Step 6: Take Responsibility

The meeting facilitator asks the participants if they would be willing to take responsibility for how the other party interpreted their actions. In some cases, the facilitator might ask students to apologize to the other party. Again, parents can be critical here, and may help motivate students to see the need to take responsibility for their actions.

Step 7: Finalize Alternative Ways to Relate

The meeting facilitator leads a brief brainstorming session to try to find a mutually acceptable interaction option that may reduce or eliminate conflict in the future. Then the group discusses each option and chooses one or more options.

Step 8: Sign an Agreement

The meeting facilitator asks the students in conflict to sign an agreement stating that they will manage the potential conflict that way in the future. The agreement includes the initial baseline data or initial report, specific perspectives of the students, and specific behavioral option or options the students chose.

If the conflict is between a student and a teacher, school administrators must consider any state rules or regulations that may apply when determining if teachers or other educators should sign such a document. In some states there may be union regulations that prohibit schools from asking teachers to sign such documents, and the school administrator should carefully consider what options or problems may be involved in having teachers or other educational professionals sign such a document.

A CASE STUDY: RESTORATIVE CIRCLE TO ELIMINATE FIGHTING

Again, different types of application of the restorative circle intervention yield different types of information. If teachers collect baseline data, they should present it—as evidence for the procedure—on an *x-y* axis chart of behavior. However, in most current applications of the restorative circle in schools, teachers do not collect baseline data, because schools are typically using this intervention as a quick response intervention to immediate problems. In such cases, only the restorative circle form provides the data, along with a written report of a follow-up meeting held several weeks after the restorative circle. A case study example of this type of report is in Figure 16.1.

The final part of this report shows that the planned follow-up to the restorative circle meeting is held about ten days after the restorative circle. Those notes show that the students have both honored their commitments and that no subsequent fights have taken place after the restorative circle. At this point, the principal considers the problem resolved, and it has been resolved without excluding the students from school through suspension. Further, when compared with a simple suspension for fighting, the more traditional punishment option used by schools, this restorative circle much more effectively addresses the problem of name-calling.

RESEARCH ON RESTORATIVE CIRCLES

In addition to the examples above, there is a strong research base for these disciplinary practices (Duncan, 2014; US Department of Education, 2011), part of which is in various sections above on conflict resolution and peer mediation. In a recent report on PBS, Principal Mathew Willis of Hinkley High School in Colorado indicates that restorative circles have transformed behavior in his high school. Specifically, restorative circles have drastically reduced fighting among students, and he reports a 48 percent reduction in suspensions based on use of restorative circles (http://www.youtube.com/watch?v=g8_94O4ExSA). Through their use of restorative circles, students have developed a sense of positive community and are taking more responsibility for their own behavior school-wide.

In general, all of these restorative justice strategies reduce discipline referrals to the principal's office and school violence and suspension/expulsion rates while simultaneously encouraging troubled students to take a leadership role in their schools and make a positive contribution to the school community (Duncan, 2014; O'Brien, 2014; St. George, 2014). As such, every school should explore the use of restorative justice as one aspect of their school-wide disciplinary practices.

All educators must realize that the expectation of 21st-century schools is the reduction and/or elimination of disciplinary practices that involve removal of

Figure 16.1: Case Study: A Restorative Circle Report

Date: 9/2/15   **Students Involved:** Fredo Sparks, Jason Attwood

Class or Location: Mr. Trent's History Class   **Date of Restorative Circle:** 9/5/15

Problem: fighting in class

Teacher's Perspective:
On September 2, 2015, at 1:30 P.M., I told the class to get out their history books. A moment later, I looked up and Jason was standing over Fredo's desk with Jason's book in the air, and then brought the book down against Fredo's head. I rushed over there, but by the time I got there Thomas was holding Jason, backing him away, and Fredo was on the floor with his forehead bleeding. I told Jason to sit down in an empty desk across the classroom and sent another student to get the principal and school nurse. We wiped Fredo's head with a paper towel.

Students' Perspectives:

Jason: He was looking at me funny, and I heard him call me a queer.

Fredo: Jason calls me names every day—queer, fag, and slimeball, and he won't stop. He called me slimeball that day, so I called him an asshole.

Areas of Agreement: The students both state that they have never been friends and have no desire to become friends. They "move in different circles." Also, they both see the dangers of spreading rumors round school and agree that it is undesirable to do so.

Options for Reducing Conflict:
The students decide that it is best to

    (1) Just ignore each other

    (2) Sit apart from each other in the two classes they have in common

    (3) Avoid each other on school campus (lunchroom, commons, library, etc.)

    (4) Not call each other names

    (5) Not talk about each other, even when the other one is not around

Commitment: By our signatures below, we agree to behave in the manner we've chosen and do the things listed above in order to eliminate any conflict between us.

     Fredo Sparks   *Jason Attwood*

Planned Follow-Up: Mr. Trent and Mr. Alston, the assistant principal, will meet with these two students after school in two weeks as a follow-up to this restorative circle. The purpose of that meeting is to review the students' behavior and their ongoing commitment to do the things above that they've agreed to do. Parents will be invited to come as soon as that meeting is scheduled.

Follow-Up Meeting: On the afternoon of September 18, 2015, Mr. Trent and Mr. Alston met with Fredo and Jason. Mr. Alston had the secretary call and invite the parents to the meeting. Mr. Alston noted that he'd not heard of any further conflict between the two students nor had Mr. Trent reported any. Both of the students affirmed that they had chosen to stay away from each other, and neither reported any on-going problems. Mr. Trent said that he hoped that one day, the two young men might become friends, but that that was up to them. Both reaffirmed their commitment to continue the specific options above to avoid conflict in the future.

---

students from the school community (Duncan, 2014; O'Brien, 2014). This national goal provides another rationale to explore the disciplinary strategies in this book. In short, if your school does not have some preventative, whole-school disciplinary measures in place, such as those in Section I, and if the administration utilizes frequent suspensions and expulsions for minor offenses, the school may be considered legally liable at some point in the future because it did not implement best practices in the area of discipline. Of course, no educator would knowingly allow himself to be placed in that position.

Strategy 17

Response to Intervention for Behavioral Change

The response to intervention (RTI) initiative has been under way worldwide since 2005, though most teachers became aware of RTI between 2005 and 2010 (Algozzine, Daunic, & Smith, 2012; Bender & Shores, 2007; Brown-Chidsey & Steege, 2005; Fuchs, Fuchs, & Vaughn, 2008). RTI began as an option to identify students for special education placements by documenting how students who were suspected of having disabilities were responding to well-designed, highly targeted individual interventions in reading. The RTI process depends on offering various levels of increasingly intensive instruction in order to meet the needs of the specific student with the problem. Following is an example of the RTI process for a student with a reading problem (Bender, 2012a, 2013).

AN EXAMPLE OF THE RTI PROCESS

Shonda has difficulty with multi-syllable words, which Ms. Foscue, her first-grade teacher, quickly notices. Ms. Foscue typically tutors Shonda after class twice a week on word attack skills and dealing with decoding of multi-syllable words, but that extra help—a type of help often provided by general education teachers—does not seem to be working. Ms. Foscue decides that Shonda needs more intensive instruction to assist her with that particular skill, perhaps fifteen to twenty minutes of additional instruction daily for four to six weeks, specifically on word attack and decoding skills for multiple-syllable words.

Ms. Foscue also realizes that three other students in her class are having the same decoding difficulty, so she decides to do a specific reading intervention for all four of these students daily. She works with Shonda and the other three students on a fifteen-minute intervention each day, while the rest of the class works with the paraprofessional on a science project. The intervention is highly targeted to focus on the specific reading skill in question—decoding of multi-syllable words. Also, to demonstrate efficacy of the instruction, Ms. Foscue assesses each of these four students weekly, specifically on that decoding skill, and charts their growth on that target skill over the four-week intervention period. She then decides who needs to continue the highly intensive intervention and who has mastered that skill and can therefore discontinue participation in the small group intervention.

After completing the intervention for four weeks, Ms. Foscue examines the charted data for Shonda and each of the other individual students. She finds that Shonda and two of the other students have now mastered that targeted skill and they are ready to discontinue the extra intervention. The data on the other student's weekly assessments show that he is not mastering the skill, and Ms. Foscue believes he needs an intervention that is even more intensive than the one she provided. Based on the individual achievement data chart for each student, Ms. Foscue discontinues the intervention for Shonda and the two other students, whereas she refers the third student (we'll call him Gerald) to the reading coach at the school. That reading coach might then undertake a more intensive reading/decoding intervention, perhaps 45 minutes of individual instruction each day for the next six weeks.

As this example shows, RTI is highly responsive instruction because the documented achievement of the individual student serves as the basis for making instructional decisions. Those decisions range from discontinuing the intervention when students have mastered the target skills, to increasing the intensity of instruction in another intervention (Bender, 2012a, 2013). The level of intensity of instruction is varied to match the needs of each individual student during the RTI process. Teachers regularly assess students and chart those assessment data to make decisions about efficacy of the intervention or determine if a more intensive intervention is necessary for an individual student.

A HISTORY OF RTI

Reading was the first area for the RTI emphasis, because the majority of students with learning disabilities, historically, have been identified based on disabilities in that skill area (Bender & Shores, 2007). More recently, RTI initiatives have increasingly included mathematics skills as well as RTI projects focused on improving behavior in the classroom (Algozzine et al., 2012; Bender, 2009; Bender & Crane, 2011). Of course, this section focuses on using the RTI process for behavioral improvement in the classroom.

Note that most RTI interventions take place as a function of general education, with general education teachers primarily responsible for administering these interventions. For this reason, the RTI effort has quickly grown far beyond a special education identification concern for reading disabilities. In fact, as the RTI initiative took off, students showed considerable improvement in reading, mathematics, and behavior when teachers applied intensive, highly targeted interventions. Other educators soon got on the bandwagon, and RTI became one of the most important school reform efforts in recent decades (Bender, 2012a).

The academic successes resulting from high-quality RTI efforts are quite profound. Hattie (2013), for example, reviews research on a wide variety of academic instructional strategies and identifies RTI as the third most important influence on academic achievement when compared to virtually all other educational interventions. I have personally written a number of books on RTI implementation (Bender, 2009, 2012a, 2012b, 2013; Bender & Crane, 2011). I have seen this instructional approach sweep across the nation, and few initiatives have been as profound in my thirty-three years of experience in education as has RTI.

> RTI quickly grew far beyond a special education identification concern, and the RTI initiative soon became one of the most important school reform efforts in recent decades.

THE STRUCTURE OF RTI: THE RTI INTERVENTION PYRAMID

In my workshops with teachers today, I like to emphasize, first and foremost, that RTI implementation is an effort to change a student's life; it is an effort to provide interventions, both academic and behavioral, that will change a student's trajectory of learning or behavior from a trajectory leading to failure in life to one leading to success. By describing RTI in this fashion, I've found that teachers will become more open to doing the work of RTI, because all teachers want their students to succeed.

More practically, RTI projects are often described as a series of interventions, increasing in intensity, that are designed to alleviate behavioral problems. An RTI pyramid is often used to describe the RTI process (Algozzine et al., 2012; Bender, 2009, 2013), and the three-tier pyramid in Figure 17.1 is the most common pyramid used (Bender 2009).

Figure 17.1: The RTI Pyramid Model

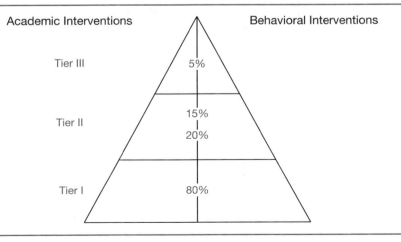

The RTI pyramid includes three tiers representing levels of intensity, as well as a vertical line from top to bottom that separates academic interventions on the left half of the pyramid from behavioral interventions on the right. RTI has, by this point, been implemented in several areas including reading, mathematics, and behavior (Bender, 2009).

The first tier at the bottom of this pyramid represents instruction and behavioral management in the general education class. This instruction might be considered as traditional whole-class instruction, and it includes the instruction typically provided in the class as well as some level of extra assistance when students need it. The percentage in this tier indicates that approximately 80 percent of students respond appropriately to that instruction and the normal class management procedures. Thus, about 80 percent of students in general education classes demonstrate behavioral problems that the general education teacher can manage relatively easily by using the typical teaching techniques (proximity control; loud, clear, and concise voice commands; repeated instructions; student conferences; etc.). Those students will need nothing more intensive than the typical class management techniques. Therefore, in these disciplinary cases, no specific targeted interventions are necessary to manage the behavioral problems, and teachers are not expected to take down data to document that the problems have been alleviated.

> RTI implementation is an effort to change a student's life; it is an effort to provide interventions, both academic and behavioral, that will change a student's trajectory of learning or behavior from a trajectory leading to failure in life to one leading to success.

Tier II represents the fact that approximately 20 percent of students might have problems that require a more intense, specific, and highly targeted intervention. In the previous example, Shonda needed this extra level of intensive, targeted instruction to master decoding multi-syllabic words. At this level, teachers are expected to use interventions specifically targeted at the exact academic skill or behavior problem demonstrated by the student. Teachers are likewise expected to take data on the skill or behavior problem during a baseline and intervention period in order to document the efficacy of the intervention.

Many representations of the pyramid present two percentages in this tier, indicating that whereas 20 percent of students may require such interventions, those interventions are expected to succeed with approximately 15 percent of the class.

This leaves approximately 5 percent of students who need a more intensive intervention to address their behavioral problems, and Tier III represents that 5 percent. In the earlier example, Gerald did not succeed during the Tier II reading intervention Ms. Foscue provided, so he needed a Tier III intervention that was more intensive. The numbering here can be a bit confusing; we should note that Tier III involves a second intervention, not a third intervention, because the first level of the pyramid is traditional instruction and not a specifically targeted intervention. However, for students who do not succeed in a Tier II intervention, teachers must apply a more intensive Tier III intervention in the ongoing effort to alleviate the behavior problem.

Therefore, at the end of a Tier III RTI process, the student's folder should contain descriptions of specific targeted problems, descriptions of two separate interventions addressed directly at those problems, and data charts showing how those interventions worked. At that point, if the Tier III intervention has not alleviated the behavior problem, the documentation of the RTI project should be forwarded to the Child Study Committee for the school, where a determination may be made as to the possibility of an emotional or behavioral disability. Another example of the RTI process for a behavioral problem is in the forthcoming case study.

RTI AND BEHAVIORAL CHANGE

Although schools have been developing behavioral improvement plans for students since the 1990s, the RTI initiative in behavior reinforces that effort in a profound way (Bender, 2009). In classrooms today, when a behavioral problem becomes frequent, general education teachers are expected to implement real, concrete interventions to alleviate those behavioral problems. Such interventions will, of necessity, be intensive, highly targeted interventions focused on specific behavior problems and administered individually. Further, data must be used to demonstrate the efficacy of those individual behavioral interventions, and in that sense, all of the interventions I previously described in this book could very well be components of an RTI project for a given student.

> In classrooms today, when a behavioral problem becomes frequent, general education teachers are expected to implement real, concrete interventions to alleviate those behavioral problems.

Of course, these intervention expectations do represent increased responsibilities for teachers in virtually every classroom, and therein lies the challenge of RTI implementation. Many teachers today are very effective in their class management and disciplinary skills without implementing specific, highly targeted behavioral change projects or taking down observational data on the efficacy of that project, and those teachers may well wonder why their responsibilities are changing regarding discipline in the class. It may be helpful to hear teachers discuss this increased role in academic work and behavioral improvement, and I recommend that all teachers watch a 10-minute video from Tigard High School in Portland, Oregon, which they can view at http://wn.com/implementing_response_to_intervention --tigard_high_school. After that video, teachers should discuss the restructuring of schools to meet these increased responsibilities for academic work and behavioral improvement.

Still, the message of this book is that expectations of both teachers and schools are changing in the area of behavioral management and discipline (Algozzine et al.,

2012; Duncan, 2014; Marzano, 2007). Future expectations of teachers will involve development of such individual interventions and documentation of the efficacy of those interventions. As I noted, if teachers cannot show baseline and intervention data for a recurring behavioral problem, their efforts represent 20th-century teaching standards and not the standards of today's classrooms. Here is an example.

CASE STUDY: AN RTI BEHAVIORAL CHANGE INTERVENTION

Alton is an eighth-grade student who often shouts in class, calls other students names, and disrupts Mr. Collins's social studies class. Sometimes, Alton shouts something funny in class, and other times, he merely shouts whatever is on his mind. Mr. Collins is a veteran teacher with fifteen years of experience in teaching, and he has attempted the usual array of disciplinary approaches to curb Alton's class disruptions. Specifically, he used proximity control by placing Alton's desk up front in the room near his own desk. He had the guidance counselor talk with Alton about his behavior, and he even called Alton's mother to a conference about the problem. Mr. Collins has not done a targeted intervention, because as I noted above, that has not been a general expectation for most teachers up to this point.

Mr. Collins, like all teachers, has had training in behavioral interventions and recently participated in a workshop on RTI. He knows that teacher expectations are changing relative to how they should handle behavior problems, and he wants to move in the right direction, not to mention do something to assist Alton. He decides to undertake an RTI project to address Alton's behavioral outbursts.

Alton's Tier II Intervention

As a first step, Mr. Collins writes a description of Alton's behavior problems (disruptive behavior, including calling others names, shouting in class, or other disruptions that require Mr. Collins to stop class). With that behavior in mind, Mr. Collins begins a baseline count, and five days of data show thirteen class disruptions that were significant enough for Mr. Collins to stop ongoing class work. On one day, Alton disturbed the class four times, and he averaged 2.6 disruptions per class that week. Clearly an ongoing behavior problem was evident.

Mr. Collins confers with the guidance counselor, Mrs. White, and Mrs. White recommends that Mr. Collins consider using a morning meeting intervention to build the sense of class community and help Alton understand how his disruptions are impacting class climate. This is possible, because the school schedule requires Mr. Collins to teach that social studies class four times weekly in seventy-five-minute sessions. In short, he could devote ten minutes to a morning meeting three times weekly, given the class schedule.

Mr. Collins implements a Tier II intervention using one of the whole-class/ whole-school interventions I described (see Strategy 2 in Section I). While the focus of the morning meeting discussions is expected to be the behavior of all class members and not just Alton's, Mr. Collins is sure that Alton's behavior will come up in the class discussions. Further, he believes it will help Alton to hear others describe his disruptions in negative terms. Figure 17.2 presents the data Mr. Collins collects on Alton's behavior.

Figure 17.2: Alton's Tier II Intervention Data

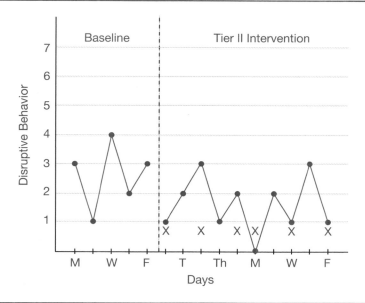

Note that the first five days present baseline data, whereas the next ten indicate how the morning meeting intervention impacted Alton's behavior. Data for those ten days of intervention show a total of 16 disruptions, and a daily average of 1.6 disruptions. The morning meetings did assist in reducing Alton's behavior somewhat, but the problem persisted.

Mr. Collins is sure he needs to do something further to assist Alton. He is convinced that if he cannot help Alton alleviate his class disruptions that Alton will not succeed in the next grade, when he goes to the local high school.

Alton's Tier III Intervention

While general education teachers are typically expected to conduct the Tier II intervention, Tier III behavioral interventions are often conducted by other general educators. When the RTI focus is behavioral change, school psychologists, master teachers, and guidance counselors usually play a role. Because Alton's behavior continues to be a problem, the guidance counselor, Mrs. White, and Mr. Collins decide two things. First, Mr. Collins will continue his morning meetings three times per week and continue to take down data on the frequency of Alton's disruptive behavior. Second, a Tier III intervention will begin, which involves a personal responsibility strategy intervention, as I described previously (see Strategy 13 in Section II).

In discussing Alton's behavior with Mrs. White, Mr. Collins mentioned Alton's shouting funny statements, and Mrs. White felt that some of Alton's disruptions might result from a desire for attention. Mr. Collins concurred in that assessment, but he also mentioned a strength of Alton—his skill with computers, and in particular his skills in online gaming.

Taking this into consideration, Mrs. White asks if Alton could have the responsibility of serving as the tech assistant in Mr. Collins's class. As tech assistant, Alton would be expected to help Mr. Collins set up any technology to be used during the daily lesson (smart board, laptop computers for other students, or finding web-based data for the class) as well as help other students in activities such as webquests or simulations used in various social studies lessons.

In a subsequent conference with Alton, Mr. Collins explains his need for help and asks if Alton would take on that role. Alton agrees, so Mr. Collins writes a description of Alton's new class responsibilities on the smart board and briefly discusses Alton's new job with the class.

In the Tier III intervention, Mr. Collins continues the morning meetings and continues to collect data on Alton's class disruptions over the next three weeks. Those data are in Figure 17.3. Note that no baseline data is collected at this point, because the data from the Tier II intervention can serve as Alton's baseline. As these data show, the combination of morning meetings and a responsibility strategy was intensive enough to nearly eliminate Alton's disruptive behavior by the end of the Tier III intervention. Data show 12 disruptions in these three weeks, averaging only 0.8 disruptions per day. This is more than a 66 percent decrease in class disruptions. These data therefore represent a success story for both Alton and Mr. Collins. More importantly, Alton is now much more likely to succeed when he moves into high school next year.

DOCUMENTATION IS CRITICAL: THE RTI BEHAVIORAL CHANGE NARRATIVE

As I mentioned, we live in a world of "show me the data!" When implementing an RTI procedure, data collection is critical, as is development of a complete description of the reason for the intervention, and the exact interventions attempted. Therefore, complete documentation of Mr. Collins's efforts would include more

Figure 17.3: Alton's Tier III Intervention Data

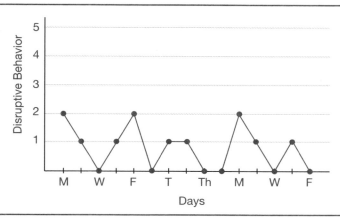

than the data charts in Figures 17.2 and 17.3. A narrative including all necessary descriptions for Alton's RTI behavioral change project is in Figure 17.4. That narrative, coupled with the data charts presented previously, represents the full RTI process for a behavioral change project.

Figure 17.4: Narrative of Alton's RTI Behavioral Change Project

Name: Alton Snyder   **Grade:** 7th   **Teacher:** Mr. Josh Collins

School: Toccoa Middle School   **Date:** 2/14/15

Observation of Behavior Problem:
I've noticed that Alton Snyder consistently disrupts my first period social studies class. He shouts answers that he believes are funny and sometimes calls other students names. I counted the number of times I had to discipline him for a week, and these data show a consistent number of class disruptions. I plan to discuss this with Mrs. White, our school guidance counselor.

Signed: Mr. Josh Collins   **Date:** 2/14/15

Tier II Intervention Plan:
Based on input from Mrs. White, I developed a Tier II intervention plan for Alton, based on the literature on morning meetings. Mrs. White gave me some reading materials for ideas on how the meeting should go, and I watched a couple of videos on morning meetings. I will hold morning meetings three times weekly (no more than a 10-minute meeting). I'll continue that for the next three weeks and chart Alton's class disruptions. I'll note on an index card on my desk those disruptions as a daily measure of his disruptive behaviors. I'll then discuss that intervention data with Mrs. White in three weeks.

Signed: Mr. Josh Collins   **Date:** 2/14/15

Tier II Data Summary and Recommendations (must include data chart):
Mr. Collins implemented the Tier II intervention for Alton, and he counted Alton's disruptions for three weeks. On at least six of the nine morning meetings in those three weeks, the class discussed Alton's class disruptions, represented by X on the specific day they

(continued)

discuss Alton's behavior disruptions. Alton heard his class say that while they enjoyed his humor and funny comments sometimes, they did not appreciate the number of his class disturbances. The data (see Figure 17.2) show that Alton's disruptions are decreasing, but he still disturbs the class too frequently, according to Mr. Collins.

Mr. Collins and I believe that we should undertake a Tier III intervention for Alton. We have to get his class disruption under control or he will not succeed in the high school environment next year. I gave Mr. Collins an article on the responsibility intervention strategy, and he developed an appropriate Tier III intervention for Alton.

Signed: Mrs. Amelia White   **Date:** 3/10/15

Tier III intervention plan:
I enjoyed reading about the responsibility strategy disciplinary idea, and I think I can undertake that with Alton. He will become my tech assistant and each day will help me and the other students with tech problems, such as computer set-up or the interface with the smart board.

I can even let him find simulations on the content we are covering and help other students as necessary. Alton has those types of skills, and this will provide him an opportunity to contribute to the class in a meaningful way. I'll begin that intervention immediately and continue to do the frequency count of his class disruptions.

I'll be discussing Alton's behavior with him individually as well as in the ongoing morning meetings. Also, Mrs. White and I plan to meet in four weeks to look at the success of this intervention.

Signed: Mr. Josh Collins   **Date:** 3/11/15

Tier III Intervention Results for Alton
On the evening of our monthly PTA meeting (4/2/15), Alton's mother, Mrs. Norma Snyder, asked how Alton was doing in class. Mr. Collins had great news to share, and he quickly found me. Together we shared the data with Mrs. Snyder. Alton's behavior had improved drastically in only three weeks of this Tier III intervention. Those data (in Figure 17.3) indicate that this intervention had all but eliminated Alton's class disruptions. While Alton occasionally did experience a rough day, Mr. Collins believes that the consistent class disruptions are a thing of the past and that his behavior was much improved.

The best news was that another one of Alton's teachers, Ms. Lovorn in Algebra I, found out about Alton being the tech assistant in Mr. Collins's class, and she made him the tech assistant in her class also. She reported that his behavior was much improved. At that point, I also pointed out to Alton's mom that this intervention would continue to assist Alton when he moves to high school next year, because he doesn't disrupt class nearly as often.

Mr. Collins will continue the morning meetings because they help many other students in his class with their behavior, beyond just Alton. Also he will keep Alton's tech assistant role going until the end of the year, but he will no longer need to take down behavioral data, since the problem is gone. It was wonderful to see Mr. Collins give such a great report to Mrs. Snyder!

Signed: Mrs. Amelia White   **Date:** 4/3/15

Go to www.learningsciences.com/bookresources to download figures and tables.

SUMMARY: CHANGING TEACHER EXPECTATIONS

As this case study demonstrates, general education teachers are expected to play an increased role in management of disciplinary problems than they have in the past, a fact that both educators and national leaders have stressed repeatedly (Algozzine et al., 2012; Duncan, 2014; US Department of Education, 2011). Of course, the same increased responsibilities are noted in the academic arena as well, and schools have undertaken significant restructuring to address these RTI responsibilities. Therefore, teachers must understand that RTI implementation will involve restructuring their teaching somewhat, as Mr. Collins did in the example above. Further, RTI involves restructuring schools overall to make RTI interventions available for students requiring them in reading, math, and behavioral improvement.

With that note, provision of educational services that make a real difference in students' lives is the very essence of teaching, as the teachers in the video from Tigard High School state. Also, the research on RTI shows that it is one of the most important things schools can do for students (Hattie, 2013). Today, RTI must be considered best practice across all school grades.

Strategy 18

Discipline in a Flipped Classroom

FLIPPING THE CLASSROOM

Within the past few years, a truly new instructional approach has received attention across the country: the flipped classroom (Flipped Learning Network [FLN], 2014; Flipped Learning Network & Sophia, 2014; Hamdan, McKnight, McKnight, & Arfstrom, 2013; Stansbury, 2013). While the traditional lesson plan model includes the expectation that the teacher is responsible for delivering initial instruction on new content to the students, the flipped class assumes that students will complete the initial instruction on new content on their own, usually as homework (Bergmann & Sams, 2014; Yarbro, Arfstrom, McKnight, & McKnight, 2014). That initial instruction would, in the flipped classroom, be undertaken prior to any classroom instruction on that content, by using video resources or interactive instructional computer programs covering the new content (Bergmann & Sams, 2014; 2012; Green, 2014; 2012).

In the flipped classroom, the class time that is no longer used for initial instruction can be used for instructional activities involving application of knowledge, including high levels of practical activities and/or practice time. Those activities, in the traditional instructional model, were often done as homework. The time, location, and responsibility for initial instruction and homework have all been flipped, leaving students with increased responsibility for their own initial learning of the content. Generally, flipping the class means that the student uses modern technologies (e.g., video demo lessons, web resources, interactive computer games and curricula) at home for initial instruction (FLN, 2014).

> In a flipped class, the time, the location, and responsibility for initial instruction and homework have all been flipped, leaving students with increased responsibility for their own initial learning of the content.

AN EXAMPLE OF A FLIPPED CLASS

A math teacher is teaching a lesson on linear equations ($5x + 5 = 40$; solve for x). The teacher uses a digital camera (or iPad) to create a brief video explanation of how to do that type of problem. These mini-lesson demos are usually five- to ten-minute demonstrations of one or two examples of the specific type of problem under study. The teacher then puts the video on a class or school website, making it available for students at home.

Teachers in flipped classrooms also use existing videos from sources such as Khan Academy, YouTube, or TeacherTube. This type of video presentation makes the video demo lesson available to students as well as their parents. The teacher makes the assignment for students to watch that video and learn how to do that specific type of problem. The initial instruction on that particular type of problem is done as homework, prior to studying that content in the class. Then, when they come to math class, the teacher asks if all students have completed that work, and follows with a quick quiz so students can demonstrate their understanding. That takes about only five to ten minutes of class time, and students can spend the remaining class time—the majority of time—on applying that knowledge through various projects or enjoyable group work involving that new skill (Bender, 2012a, 2013; Bergmann & Sams, 2012; FLN, 2014; Green, 2012).

FOUR PILLARS OF FLIP

Interest in the flipped classroom has grown exponentially in recent years, and a virtual community of educators has been formed that now exceeds over 20,000 (see Flippedclassroom.org and flippedlearning.org). Of course, all interested educators are invited to join that group. In one recent survey from the Flipped Learning Network, 78 percent of teachers indicate they have flipped at least one lesson, and of those, 96 percent indicate they would recommend this instructional approach to a colleague (FLN, 2014).

In recent years, that organization has moved the flipped learning concept beyond merely flipping initial instruction and homework time. The focus today involves student responsibilities for individual learning and teacher responsibilities for intentionally constructing a varied, effective learning environment to support student inquiry. To further those emphases, the organization recently created the four pillars of flipped learning (FLN, 2014; Yarbro et al., 2014), and these are now considered the basis for this practice. The four pillars are in Figure 18.1.

As these pillars of flipped learning emphasize, the dynamic of learning changes when educators flip the learning, moving from the physical space of the classroom to the individual space of the student. Further, teachers intentionally determine what material they need to directly teach in the first-person context and what material students should explore and learn on their own. Again, this shifts the responsibility of learning to the students, with more deliberate and intentional teacher support.

Figure 18.1:   Four Pillars of Flipped Learning: FLIP

F: Flexible Environments. Educators often physically rearrange their learning space to accommodate the lesson or unit, which may involve group work or independent study. Educators are also flexible in their expectations of student timelines for learning and how they assess students.

L: Learning Culture. There is a deliberate shift from a teacher-centered classroom to a student-centered approach, where in-class time is meant for exploring topics in greater depth and creating richer learning opportunities through various student-centered pedagogies. Students are actively involved in their own learning in a way that is personally meaningful.

I: Intentional Content. Educators believe the model is able to help students gain conceptual understanding as well as procedural fluency. They evaluate what they need to teach and what materials students should explore on their own.

P: Professional Educators. During class time, teachers observe their students, providing them with feedback relevant in the moment and assessing their work. While professional educators remain very important, they take on less visibly prominent roles in the flipped classroom.

COLLABORATIVE FLIPPING

It is not an overstatement to suggest that flipping the classroom had become something of a trend by 2014–2015 (FLN, 2014). Many teachers are flipping their classes in virtually all school subjects at many grade levels, typically from grade three through higher education classes (FLN, 2014). Bergmann and Sams (2014), the teachers credited with originating the flipped class idea, now recommend that teachers collaborate in flipping the class. Specifically, teachers can collaborate in the creation of the video lessons on the discrete subject matter. For example, if three teachers in the elementary grades collaborate to develop a video on long division, all three would develop the instructional ideas together and probably use better teaching pedagogy than any teacher working alone. They are also likely to take a bit more care in creating the video lesson, because they would realize that the audience would be larger than merely their own class (Bergmann & Sams, 2014).

As of 2015, there is not a strong empirical research base for the practice of flipping the class, but a great deal of anecdotal research indicates the efficacy of the flipped learning approach (Bergmann & Sams, 2014; FLN, 2014; Green, 2012; 2014; Hamdan et al., 2013; Stansbury, 2013). Flipping the class does seem to result in making students more engaged with the lesson and much more responsible for their own learning (Bergmann & Sams, 2012). The flipped classroom movement can therefore be viewed as one component of the emphasis on personal responsibility I describe in this book.

> Bergmann and Sams, the teachers credited with originating the flipped class idea, now recommend that teachers collaborate in flipping the class.

HOW MIGHT FLIPPING THE CLASS IMPACT DISCIPLINE?

While increased engagement with the content clearly seems to be a positive behavioral result of flipping (Green, 2012; Yarbro, 2014), any veteran teacher might well anticipate some of the types of discipline problems that could result from this new approach. First, while most students seem to respond positively to the flipped class idea (Bergmann & Sams, 2012; Green, 2012; Yarbro, 2014), others do not. Teachers may note that certain students consistently fail to do the homework and therefore learn nothing from the assigned videos or computer lessons. Of course, when those students come to class they will not be prepared to apply their new knowledge. They might display boredom or other, more overt behavior problems.

However, with those negative behaviors noted, it is also possible that flipping the classroom might have a positive impact on discipline, as some educators note (Bergmann & Sams, 2012; FLN, 2014; Green, 2012). For example, in whole-class instruction students who know the material may be bored and therefore demonstrate behavior problems during the initial instruction component of the traditional lesson. As another example, in social studies the American Revolution is covered a number of times across the grade levels, and students who master that content in grade seven may be bored in that unit in grade 10. In such cases, the students who have already mastered that content may misbehave in the traditional, teacher-led lesson.

However, in a flipped class approach, those students would be engaging in hands-on learning, simulations, or small group projects in the classroom, having reviewed the basic facts in the video lesson the previous evening. Those students are likely to be more highly engaged in the flipped class than in the traditional class, and that would lead to fewer discipline problems overall (Green, 2012).

A TEACHER'S REFLECTIONS: DISCIPLINE IN FLIPPED CLASSES

Going to the source is always advisable when considering questions that research does not address, and the flipped class, although effective academically, has not been evaluated from the perspective of class discipline yet. However, many teachers have experienced the flipped classroom directly and can shed light on this question. Kelsey Kempf, for example, has taught second-, sixth-, and eighth-grade mathematics at Linn-Mar Community School District in Marion, Iowa, for several years. She is currently working there as a technology integration coach and mathematics teacher. Ms. Kempf graduated from the University of Iowa in elementary education with a mathematics specialization, and she is now completing her master's degree in educational leadership at the University of Northern Iowa. She recently decided to flip her eighth-grade math class, and as a teacher who is new to flipped classes, she agreed to address the impact of flipped classes on class discipline.

> Flipping the classroom has been a powerful tool in my class. Flipping allows much more time working with students in small groups, and I am also able to provide more direct support to students as they work through their math problems. My eighth-grade students love the independence the flipped classroom provides.
>
> Prior to beginning a flipped math unit with a new class, it is important to address potential obstacles that may arise, and two major problems involve internet access and compliance with the expectation that students complete the homework of watching the videos. The last of these represents a disciplinary concern because students who don't complete their responsibility of watching demonstration videos as homework in the flipped classroom can present a disciplinary problem in class.
>
> Relative to internet access, I like to give my students a survey asking them if they have reliable internet at home, if they have a smartphone with internet access, if/when they have study hall, and how they get to and from school. These questions allow me to gauge their internet access, and help me determine if a flipped instructional unit would be practical with that particular group of students. If students do not have reliable internet access at home, I then consider if they have study hall, during which they can access the internet at school. They might also be able to watch demonstration videos before or after school, as another option, though this might require me to contact parents and make arrangements ahead of time.
>
> In terms of having students actually do the "initial instruction" videos at home, I've found that parents should be notified ahead of the flipped instructional unit and given information on how to help their child access the videos online. This allows parents to assist at home if a student has difficulties. Expectations for the unit must be made clear, in writing, for both the student and parent.
>
> Next, I've also begun to require that students take notes during the video they watch at home, as evidence that they watched it. Of course, some software platforms in education (Moodle is an example; see https://moodle.org/) allow teachers to create individual accounts and post quizzes for students to complete as they watch videos at home. This is another way to monitor engagement. It is important to hold students accountable for watching the videos, because one purpose of the flipped classroom model is having students take more responsibility for their own education.
>
> At the beginning of each class period, I first verify that each student has watched the required video. Students who are ready to work on the problems are able to work in the classroom where I am available to support them. Some days I let them work in pairs or groups, other days I have them work independently, and I often use working in groups as a reward. The disciplinary issues in these

instructional approaches are exactly the same as when these group instructional techniques are used in traditional classes.

The students who did not complete their work at home by watching the video are required to do so at the computer in the back of my classroom. This then results in an automatic "penalty," because the classwork that they miss as they watch the videos in my class will become homework for the next night, in addition to watching the next night's video. I've found that, for most students, this process works; not having to do any additional homework is a strong enough incentive to watch the videos before class, as expected in the flipped class model. For those students who do not find this to be motivating, I can require them to stay after school or watch videos in study hall, but overall, I have yet to run into a long-term issue with a student being unable and unwilling to watch the video as required. It just takes some proactive problem solving and parent contact.

With those potential discipline problems noted, there are some real behavioral advantages to flipping the class. First, while students are busy working on classwork, I am able to employ a wider variety of effective instructional strategies. For example, I can pull small groups to work with me at the teacher's work table. This may include remediation with struggling students or extensions of the lesson content with advanced students. At other times, I circulate around the room and check in with students as they work, answering questions and asking questions to extend their thinking. Thus, my teaching is much more timely and effective than in the traditional whole-group lesson.

Further, I've noticed a real behavioral advantage to flipping the lesson. Student engagement during class is always higher during my flipped lessons. Students are not simply absorbing information during class, as they would be in a whole-group lesson. Rather, they are "doing the math," and they are excited to have my support and the support of their classmates during this instructional time. Consistent, regular reminders that unfinished classwork becomes homework serves as a strong incentive to stay on task. Aside from letting students pick their partners or groups to work in, I also offer listening to music (as a class or on students' individual devices with earbuds) as additional incentives for students to complete work and demonstrate appropriate classroom behavior.

In these specific ways, I believe that flipping the classroom has resulted in somewhat fewer disciplinary problems overall, and I encourage other teachers to try this innovative approach.

A CASE STUDY: STUDENT ENGAGEMENT IN A FLIPPED CLASS

Given this growing emphasis on flipping the class and the potential impact on behavior, teachers are well advised to consider scenarios in which they might implement a flipped class to enhance student engagement. For this case study, we discuss the class of Ms. Stephens, a first-year middle school mathematics teacher. Like many first-year teachers, she is still getting a handle on class management, and while she is experiencing success in most of her math classes at grade seven, she does have a third period class that seems to be increasingly out of control.

In her third period class, she frequently has to call students back to task, seemingly much more often than her other classes, and she is worried that students are not as engaged as they should be. She often has to call out various students to get them back on task, but it is always for minor misbehaviors, which may include talking out, making jokes, or otherwise disrupting the class. She begins keeping a baseline count on how often she has to call out students in the class. Because many students are involved, she decided not to focus on only one or two students but rather count all her call outs in the class as a whole during her third period so she counted those for three days. In that sense, her subject for this intervention is not one student but rather the entire class. The data for the three-day baseline are presented in Figure 18.2.

Figure 18.2:   Student Redirections in a Flipped Class

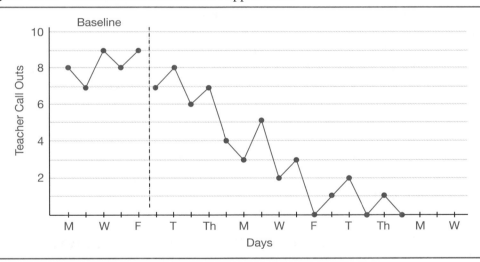

As these data show, there were an excessive number of times in which Ms. Stephens had to call one or more class members back to attention in the class. On average, she was making such redirections eight times daily in a fifty-minute period.

Ms. Stephens decides to do something different, and because she has heard of the flipped class approach, she gives that a try in her third period. If it works in that class, she is determined to implement it in her other classes as well.

She uses the video lessons she found in both Khan Academy (which has an extensive collection of lessons for mathematics), as well as several individual video lessons she found on TeacherTube. With those two sites as her initial instruction sources, she discovers that she can deliver all of the initial instruction for the topics she expects to cover during the next three weeks. She then devises a class project that requires application of those mathematical concepts and is determined to divide her class into two groups and use class time for that project. Of course, she plans a quick quiz daily. A quick quiz is a five-question quiz, taking five minutes or less at the beginning of the period, which can help ensure that all students have watched the video lesson that she assigned the previous evening. Students who fail the quiz are penalized several points, and then she instructs them to watch the video in the next ten minutes prior to joining their group. That daily quick quiz is enough to motivate most students to watch the video lessons at home.

Figure 18.2 shows the intervention data presenting the number of times Ms. Stephens had to call out the class, after she started the flipped lessons. Those data indicate that the number of times Ms. Stephens had to redirect the class fell dramatically as soon as she began the flipped classes. The evidence indicates that flipping the class resulted in increased student engagement with the lessons.

> A quick quiz is a five-question quiz, taking five minutes or less at the beginning of the period, which can help ensure that all students watched the video lesson.

While this case study is fictional, this type of result has certainly been shown in the anecdotal discussions of the flipped class instructional model. However, the behavioral impact of flipping the class is not exclusively positive. In this case study, for example, Ms. Stephens did not assess how often she had to speak to students who did not complete the assigned video homework. Further, when she shifted the basis of the class time to group work, there were, no doubt, some class management issues that arose simply from having multiple groups doing different tasks in the classroom. However, teachers interested in this approach can take comfort from the fact, noted above, that 96 percent of teachers who have tried flipping a class indicated that they would recommend this approach to a colleague.

EVIDENCE OF EFFICACY FOR THE FLIPPED CLASSROOM

As mentioned previously, the flipped classroom approach is so recent that there is no experimental research on this instructional approach, and certainly none on discipline within the flipped classroom. However, the available testimonies and other anecdotal evidence do indicate some positive impact of flipping the class in both academics and behavior (Flipped Learning Network, 2014: Flipped Learning Network & Sophia, 2014; Hamdan et al., 2013; Stansbury, 2013). The example of Clintondale High School in Michigan is often mentioned to illustrate these positive impacts (Green, 2012; Hamdan, et al., 2013).

As one example, Mr. Greg Green, the principal at Clintondale, encouraged his entire faculty to flip their classes in response to the fact that students' test scores were sinking and behavioral problems were increasing. Clearly something needed to be done, so the faculty agreed to flip their classes. The good news is that both academic performance and behavior improved rather drastically in only one year, after the entire faculty flipped their classes. The academic failure rate across the subject areas decreased dramatically, and the discipline problems dropped by 66 percent during the first year (Green, 2012, 2014). Mr. Green has received wide national attention, and he credits the entire transition of his school to the faculty (www.TechSmith.com).

> I believe it provides an engaging and interactive way for teachers to facilitate learning, rather than delivering content through lectures. This in turn gives students the opportunity to process the content in class, together, as a group! They can ask questions, they are more engaged in learning, they are less frustrated, and I've seen massive improvements in grades. I lay awake at night feeling like I have found a way to fix some of the huge problems we face in our education system. Now I just need to tell everyone who will listen.

SUMMARY

Based on the extensive anecdotal evidence on the efficacy of the flipped classrooms, I do encourage teachers and administrators to consider flipping their classes. Given the intensive use of technology in the flipped class and the increased engagement of students, this may represent the wave of future instruction. Of course, most of the rationale for the flipped class has always been described in terms of academics, but the anecdotal evidence does point to higher levels of engagement and fewer discipline problems. Certainly this strategy warrants ongoing exploration. I suggest that teachers identify the class in which they are most comfortable and try it! Like Mr. Green and thousands of other educators, you may find yourself becoming a true believer!

Strategy 19

Project-Based Learning to Enhance Class Discipline

PROJECT-BASED LEARNING

Project-Based Learning (PBL) is an instructional approach that has been around for several decades but received increased attention with the recent infusion of technology over the past five to ten years (Bender, 2012c; Larmer & Mergendoller, 2010; Oster, 2014). Advocates of PBL have argued in terms of improved academic instruction rather than improved discipline. However, there is some evidence to suggest that PBL does result in improved discipline in the schools (Bender, 2012c; Larmer & Mergendoller, 2010; Strobel & van Barneveld, 2008). Further, with increased use of PBL instruction, educators must consider the impact of this instructional approach on class discipline.

A DEFINITION OF PBL

In my recent book, I've defined PBL as

> using authentic, real-world projects, based on highly engaging questions or problems, to teach students academic content in the context of working cooperatively to solve the problem and develop the final project. PBL involves a student-driven inquiry using modern technologies to allow students to address authentic problems. In PBL instruction, the projects drive and structure the instruction, not lesson plans or units of instruction. PBL projects involve mapping projects to standards covered, and may replace instructional units and/or courses entirely.

> Publication of student work is the payoff of PBL! (Bender, 2012c; p. 8)

As this indicates, in PBL classes, students' choices drive the curriculum, not preset lesson plans or preplanned instructional units. Therefore, students in PBL classes, such as the flipped classes discussed previously, take much more responsibility for their own education and work much more independently. Of course, this does not mean that the students are wholly unsupervised; rather, the teacher's role in PBL is simply facilitative in nature (Bender, 2012c). In fact, one could even argue that in PBL, students may get more supervision because the teacher is spending much less time delivering instruction on new content.

I have suggested recently that PBL may be best understood as an updated version of differentiated instruction (Bender, 2012a, 2012c). Because students are much more in control of their activities in PBL classes, they are quite likely to select learning activities that allow them to use their particular styles of learning. Even in group projects, students select individual project activities that allow them to use their preferred learning strengths, and therefore, class activities are highly differentiated (Bender, 2012c).

PBL can involve either individual student projects or small group projects for students to complete (Bender, 2012c). In many cases, PBL involves some type of interdisciplinary instruction, because real-world projects rarely fall within the boundaries of a single academic subject. The critical aspects of PBL involve student voice and student choice, as students participate in solving real-world problems and devise projects that are published as widely as possible.

EXAMPLES OF PBL

Many examples of PBL are available on the internet, and a simple search of PBL projects yields examples for teachers to consider. Here is an example of PBL instruction involving a class garden project that was implemented by Ms. Alchier, an elementary teacher in Pittsburgh, Pennsylvania (Oster, 2014). The students had to initially identify which seeds might grow in the space behind the school. Those seeds were started in classroom flats and transplanted into the garden at the end of the year. During the summer, Ms. Alchier got help tending the garden from a local youth project, and the plants took off. By fall, the garden was filled with tomatoes, peppers, eggplants, radishes, beets, cabbage, corn, and beans. The garden project was directly tied to many areas of the students' curriculum, such as math, science, and reading. The kids measured the beds for planting and recorded what happened in the garden. At the end of each week, Ms. Alchier cooked using these garden products, and the students were able to enjoy what they helped produce.

A quick overview video on PBL is available from TeacherTube, and teachers may wish to review that introductory video (http://www.teachertube.com/video/project-based-learning-241506e). Another brief video I recommend is from the Edutopia website and is funded by the George Lucas Educational Foundation (http://www.teachertube.com/video/project-based-learning-208253).

To understand the PBL classroom more completely, I also recommend the following two videos. The first shows how several teachers work together in a PBL class, and the second is produced by students to show the strengths of PBL from their perspective.

Project Based Learning by Dean Shareski: http://www.youtube.com/watch?v=NPQ1gT_9rcw

PBL and the Mummified Chicken: http://www.youtube.com/watch?v=ovkW8M8vD5o

These videos present many aspects of PBL and also show the wide range of possible PBL structures. Not all schools using PBL have done away with overall course structure (as shown in the first video), but the Minnesota high school shown in the second video has, at least as far as the students are concerned. There, the students themselves propose projects they wish to undertake to master the required content. In fact, the "Mummified Chicken" probably represents the most extreme approach to PBL in that not only instructional units but also fundamental course structure has been tossed aside, with students negotiating their own projects and credits. Also interesting to note, while content coverage has traditionally been the responsibility of the teacher (i.e., mapping the content to assure coverage of all standards in any given year), note how in that example the students are given the responsibility to ensure content coverage of the standards! That is the only such example I've seen—in my career of over three decades in education—of students taking that responsibility!

STRUCTURING A PBL PROJECT

Teachers can structure PBL projects in a wide variety of ways, and to some degree the structure will depend on the task and the subject they will teach. In general, PBL projects tend to be somewhat interdisciplinary and involve significant use of technology. Therefore, the structure of PBL varies greatly. However, the major components of PBL projects tend to be similar from project to project. Figure 19.1 presents a PBL project that includes most of the common components, such as project/problem statement or narrative, driving question, list of initial artifacts, list of final artifacts, requirements for the final project, and a description of the publication planned for the final project.

Given that general description of the structure of a PBL project, one question that must be addressed is, how much of this description should a teacher develop prior to beginning the project in the class? In some cases in which students and teachers are not familiar with PBL, the teacher may wish to develop most or all of these components and present a PBL plan to the students. In cases where both teachers and students are very experienced with PBL, the teacher may present only the initial narrative and then hold group meetings in which the class develops the driving question, lists of artifacts, and other components of the PBL project.

Figure 19.1:   An Example of a PBL Project

Should Our Family Invest in Rental Real Estate?

The Problem: Your father recently inherited $35,000 and is considering investing in a duplex. He intends to rent out each side and use the income to build a long-term investment to pay for your college education. Your father knows construction and will evaluate the condition of the property overall. However, he asks you to give him an educated judgment on all costs and rental income. He needs evidence to show that the rent he generates will cover all costs and allow him to save enough money to fund your college account each year. He then asks that you compare that net rental income to the estimated interest income of 4 percent that he might generate if he invests the funds in the stock market.

Driving Question: Should the family purchase a duplex rental property?

Necessary Artifacts:
Worksheet/Excel Sheet of Purchase Costs: Include down payment of 20 percent on a duplex costing $80,000. What will be borrowed? How much are closing costs?

Worksheet/Excel Sheet of Operating Costs: Include information on mortgage note, estimated maintenance costs (at 15 percent of the rental payments), yearly taxes and insurance, and other potential costs.

Worksheet/Excel Sheet of Potential Income: What is the rental income from two-bed/two-bath apartments in that area of town? Estimate yearly rental income.

Written Log of Weekly Accomplishments: Your father asks you to present him a progress report each week during those two months.

Final Product: The final project must include the first three artifacts above (on computer) and a written document that summarizes all of that information and answers the question. This project is due in two months and will be presented to the family in a family meeting.

EVIDENCE OF EFFICACY FOR PBL

Unlike the lack of evidence for the flipped classroom approach, research is available on the efficacy of PBL instruction. In fact, research over the past two decades consistently demonstrates that PBL is more effective in increasing academic achievement than traditional instruction (Chen, 2014; Marzano, 2007; Marzano, Pickering, & Pollock, 2001; Mergendoller, Maxwell, & Bellisimo, 2007; Oster, 2014). Specifically, student engagement and academic achievement increases when teachers teach using PBL, indicating that PBL has a positive impact on both academics and behavior in the classroom.

> Research over the past two decades has consistently demonstrated that PBL is more effective in increasing academic achievement than traditional instruction.

There are many other benefits of PBL compared to traditional instruction. First, evidence indicates that skills in the use of 21st-century technologies increase in PBL classes, as do students' cooperative working skills (Bender, 2012c; Marzano,

2007; Oster, 2014; Strobel, & van Barneveld, 2008). In PBL instruction, students learn problem-solving skills within the content of the small project-oriented group work, and those skills are immediately transferrable to potential conflicts between students. In that sense, the very fabric of PBL instruction is designed to positively impact discipline (Bender, 2012c; Chen, 2014).

One early criticism of PBL is that this approach might be inappropriate for students with disabilities or behavioral challenges. The prevailing belief was that the expectation that students accept more responsibility for their own learning, or they manage their time within the context of less structured activities, made this instructional approach less effective for students with disabilities. However, research demonstrates the exact opposite. PBL is shown to be particularly effective for low-achieving students (Chen, 2014; Mergendoller et al., 2007) because those students (with teacher guidance) can determine which tasks to undertake and therefore how they can best master the required content.

In sum, research shows that PBL is more effective than traditional instruction overall and also improves behavior for many students by increasing engagement for most students in the classroom (Bender, 2012c; Chen, 2014; Marzano, 2007; Mergendoller et al., 2007; Oster, 2014; Strobel & van Barneveld, 2008). Based on this evidence, the impact of PBL on discipline within the class is something for all educators to consider.

WHAT DISCIPLINE PROBLEMS ARISE IN PBL INSTRUCTION?

PBL instruction makes students more responsible for their own learning, and, as the evidence shows, student engagement is considerably higher in PBL classes than traditional classrooms (Bender, 2012c). Again, this supports the trend in education to give more responsibility to students overall. Still, the very freedom that students experience in the PBL classroom represents an opportunity for misbehavior of all types.

Further, not all students respond well to the new responsibilities in PBL classes. Some students may have few social skills and that will lead to conflicts in small group projects, particularly while the teacher is across the classroom working with another PBL group. Also, even if students have acceptable social skills, some may not have the maturity to work independently or with reduced teacher supervision, as will be necessary in a PBL class. With immature students, discipline problems of all types are likely to increase somewhat during PBL instruction, though teachers can typically determine well in advance which students may need more supervision than others.

TEACHERS' REFLECTIONS ON DISCIPLINE IN PROJECT-BASED LEARNING

Sarah Edbauer and Jessica Shoup teach at the Fond du Lac STEM Academy in Fond du Lac, Wisconsin. The school is a multi-age, project-based, STEM-focused public school closely associated with the Fond du Lac School District. STEM has been recognized as an Exemplar School by the Partnership for 21st Century Skills. Sarah previously taught in traditional classrooms in grades K/1, 4, and 5 in Fond du Lac. She attended the University of Wisconsin Oshkosh and received a bachelor's degree in elementary education and is currently working toward a master's degree in administration from the University of Wisconsin. Jessica previously taught seventh-grade science and math in a traditional middle school in Charlotte, North Carolina. She attended Central Michigan University in elementary education. Jessica is a Nationally Board Certified Teacher and is working toward a master's degree in administration from Marian University. Sarah and Jessica shared the following thoughts on discipline in PBL classes.

> Project-based learning is a completely different teaching environment from the traditional classroom, and as teachers experienced in both, we realized that discussions about discipline and behavior would have to be significantly different as well for a project-based school such as the Fond du Lac STEM Academy. It has been a journey of discovery.
>
> Students at our school are in a multi-age setting. They are rarely grouped based on their grade level. Creating a collaborative culture is necessary for increased student achievement. We spend about six weeks at the beginning of the year to establish a safe, comfortable community within our school. The community is developed through hands-on, problem-solving activities. Creativity, collaboration, and critical thinking are all stressed and developed through each and every part of the process. Throughout, all students feel that they are equals and are willing to work with anyone in order to solve a problem or to create something. Many discipline problems cease to exist once this community of learners is established.
>
> We quickly learned that students need clear behavioral expectations. These expectations tend to be individualized, but always revolve around a set of school-based expectations. Our students spend several hours each day working on projects in a large group setting. Because of this, we need to review the expectations, which are intentionally taught at the beginning of the year and often thereafter. While working, students have to demonstrate self-control in order to see success. When a student is not meeting our school-based expectations, we record the behavior so we can track it and then work with the student individually to address what happened immediately.
>
> Another way we manage behavior in project-based learning is through specifically teaching our project process and working with students individually or in

small groups to follow up on individual learning. Because the students know the expectations of how to propose and follow through on projects, they must be focused and able to manage themselves independently. We build independence and working stamina from the beginning of the school and throughout the year. By intentionally teaching the students how to measure time and accountability through scheduling, they are able to build independence, switch activities, change work spaces, and work for sustained periods of time. This system was a process in itself to develop, and we have changed the system several times to be more teacher- or student-friendly, or to be more efficient overall.

We still take the time to reteach parts of the process in small or whole groups as necessary and work with the students to successfully complete the project process. The students have been flexible, proud, and willing to work with us on the development of our project process. Because they are involved in their project planning and build relationships with the adults at our school, they are more engaged in their work than the students we worked with in our previous, more traditional classrooms. We've learned that the emphasis on responsibility and choice in learning are two huge components in keeping students on-task in a project-based learning environment!

As we have worked to develop our behavior management system, we have learned the importance of reteaching consistently and constantly. Having clear, consistent expectations for our students to focus their minds on truly helps us with discipline in our project-based work. Students work together and monitor each other's behavior as well. They politely remind each other of how important their learning environments are and how important it is to keep them safe, comfortable places for each other to learn.

SUMMARY

PBL, like the flipped classroom instructional approach, is not typically discussed in the context of books on class management and discipline, and that is probably a mistake. One ironclad certainty in behavioral psychology is that environment heavily influences all behavior, and therefore discipline discussions should focus in part on the instructional environment in the classroom. This book is markedly different in focusing on several relatively new instructional approaches and discussing disciplinary issues within those classrooms, which is why I include this final section.

> One ironclad certainty in behavioral psychology is that all behavior is heavily influenced by environment, and therefore discipline discussions should focus in part on the instructional environment in the classroom.

With that noted, PBL does represent a decidedly different way to teach, with student choice and student voice largely determining what instructional activities students undertake and how they master the designated content. Discipline problems in this context, as in the flipped classroom, are different from the traditional class. When students have choices in the classroom, student engagement is much higher, and that positively impacts discipline.

As I mentioned, research strongly supports PBL instruction for improving academics and behavior in schools. For these reasons, many proponents of PBL, including this author, believe that PBL—perhaps combined with flipped classes— represents the instructional model for the 21st century, and educators are well advised to explore these instructional approaches as soon as possible. For schools struggling with disciplinary issues, this may be just the approach needed to turn the tide.

Strategy 20

Apps, Laptops, and Technology for Enhancing Behavior

INCREASING USE OF TECHNOLOGIES IN THE CLASSROOM

Use of technology in the classroom has increased rather dramatically in recent years for one simple reason: technology now dominates almost every aspect of modern life (Bender & Waller, 2013; Frey, Fisher, & Gonzales, 2011). For example, Frey and colleagues (2011) report that 19 percent of preschool children (ages 2–5) can operate a cell phone, while only 9 percent can tie their own shoes. Further, 65 percent of students who attend schools where cell phones are banned bring their cell phones to school every day anyway (Frey et al., 2011). For these reasons, it should surprise no one that upward of 90 percent of teachers now report using technology in some fashion every day in the classroom (Bender & Waller, 2013).

In schools today, it is not at all uncommon to see schools implement one-to-one computer initiatives, or programs in which every student in the school has and uses a personal computer for most educational tasks (Frey et al., 2011; Green, 2012). Further, research shows that such computer availability coupled with Wi-Fi capability across the school campus has a positive impact on school achievement (Bender & Waller, 2011, 2013; Frey et al., 2011; Marzano, 2007). Also, in a comprehensive review of all teaching methodologies, Hattie (2013) reports that computer-assisted instruction has a moderate to high impact on school achievement. However, modern classroom technology applications reach far beyond merely laptops or computers and often include cell phones, interactive whiteboards, digital video technologies in flipped classrooms, Wi-Fi capability, and virtually every other technology in modern life (Bergmann & Sams, 2014; Frey et al., 2011). Research shows that it is not only computer technology that increases achievement. Marzano, Pickering, and Pollock (2001), for example, indicate that appropriate use of interactive smart boards increase achievement by 17 percent.

While a full exploration of the positive impact of technology on teaching is far beyond the scope of this book, educators must consider implications of technology utilization for the area of class discipline. In this regard, there are a minimum of four major questions educators must consider, and, again, each of these could easily comprise an entire book:

1. How might increased technology use impact discipline?
2. Can technology teach more appropriate social behaviors?
3. Can technology help manage the entire class?
4. How can teachers help students avoid dangers that can come from the use of the internet and/or technology generally?

How Might Increased Technology Use Impact Discipline?

Almost every teacher who has required students to access the internet in schools sees certain disciplinary issues arise. For example, one need only imagine a highly distractible student working alone online and getting lost on the internet! For these children, every link seems to hold promise of just the right answer, even though their thoughts may have ranged far afield from the actual questions in the assignment. Within an online environment, almost everything is designed to look interesting. This internet world is a dream for a highly distractible child and a nightmare for virtually every teacher who has ever used computers in the classroom! Even for less-distractible students, how can a teacher be confident that every student is on task during a computer-based lesson, versus playing on Facebook or other social networking sites? Clearly, there are disciplinary questions involved when technology is infused within the lesson.

Research does suggest that technology has, overall, a positive impact on engagement (Bender & Waller, 2013; Marzano et al., 2001), and this increased time-on-task behavior results in higher achievement for students using technology overall (Marzano, 2007; Hattie, 2013). However, one message is clear from the research: the box is not enough (Bender & Waller, 2011; Bergmann & Sams, 2014). In short, merely having computers or other technologies available (i.e., a box for every student) does not result in achievement benefits; rather, teachers must use technology in creative instructional ways and fully integrate it into ongoing lessons based on research-proven instructional techniques in order to be effective (Bender & Waller, 2013; Marzano et al., 2001). Therefore, good teaching practice is critical, and such practice, supported by a range of technology, does increase student engagement and enhance learning (Bergmann & Sams, 2014; Marzano et al., 2001).

However, it is not a stretch to suggest that in 2015, we know more about the impact of classroom technologies on academic achievement than discipline within the classroom. Further, the discussions on the impact of technology tend to focus on the risky behaviors associated with computer and online capability (e.g., sexting, social networking, and online child predators, as I discuss below) rather than the more typical disciplinary issues within the class (e.g., student violence or aggression in the class or online).

Again, we should turn to an expert from the classroom. Rhonda Combs holds master's degrees from both West Virginia University and The Ohio State University. She is a lifelong learner with a background in educational consulting, teaching, and school administration. She is currently the Director of Early Learning and Elementary Education, Federal Programs and Technology Applications in Brooke County Schools, West Virginia.

Regarding the effects of the new teaching technologies such as smartphones, laptops, and interactive whiteboards on student behavior and discipline, I've observed a range of teaching innovations occurring in various classrooms. For example, in one of our middle school science classrooms, I observed students going back and forth between laptops, microscopes, learning circles, and conventional paper and pencil while conducting group experiments and assignments. The teacher was "freed" from direct instruction, so he was monitoring student work, providing some one-on-one support, and also setting up other learning activities on the Smart Board. Also, several of our social studies teachers now bring their lessons to life through sites such as Smithsonian's History Explorer by exposing students to artifacts and interactive lessons, and then discussions through online forums. In terms of class behavior and discipline, the students were excited by this instruction, and generally handled these new teaching formats very well.

In some of our special education classes, I have observed highly engaged autistic students using iPads for learning letters and beginning reading activities. Also, our behavior-challenged students were playing games on a Wii or a computer after earning "free" time from meeting their learning goals. Other learning-challenged students completed online reading activities that helped the teacher assess their reading fluency and comprehension.

Although these are obvious benefits from incorporating technology in the classrooms, there are also hurdles to overcome. Some teachers have reported that cell phone use, for instance, was distracting to the learning process. Several teachers struggled with transitioning from "controlling" the instruction to providing guidance while students engage in more self-paced learning based on the newer teaching technologies. Also, keeping updated on all of the new programs and resources is often overwhelming for both new and veteran teachers. In some cases, technology trainers will target learning sessions directly at students instead of teachers, to assure that students are not deprived of learning opportunities while teachers struggle to assimilate additional information. Trying to stay one step ahead of some of our students is another challenge for teachers, technology directors, administrators, and parents.

Regardless of these challenges, technology and the learning opportunities created by networking, sharing, researching, and publishing are an integral part of our students' lives. Teachers must supervise the learning, but it is the work of the whole school community to ensure that all students have equal access and are appropriately guided in utilizing these resources.

Although I have witnessed some instances of technology abuse by students and educators, I believe the majority are taking ownership of their learning in this fast-paced, interactive environment. We are currently transitioning to more one-on-one classes and are now using Smart Boards in all of our classrooms.

Clearly, today's classrooms are more active and engaging than they were even a few years ago, with students gathering information and accessing various learning tools that are readily available. Technology use is no longer confined to a central computer lab with limited interaction among students and teachers. Desktop computers have now largely been replaced with laptops, iPads, tablets, iPods, LeapPads, and Smart Boards, all allowing for more individualized learning and productivity.

I do find the various perspectives on technology use from the students, parents, teachers, administrators, and community members interesting—and diverse. Reactions to increased technology range all the way from "go back to pencils, paper, and chalkboards" or "we should ban cell phones" to excitement about one-to-one laptop programs. It has been an interesting journey to say the least—but this is just the beginning and educators have to work with the new technologies as they present themselves. After all, who can say what's next?

In our county, we just completed a summer program on robotics. We have formed a STEM club at one of our elementary schools, and our students now have access to virtual learning environments. All of this is sometimes overwhelming for educators, as we learn these technologies along with our students. So, it's not just the behaviors of the students that need to be monitored—it's also the behavior of teachers. We must all show enthusiasm, and the willingness to collaborate and grow in the use of these technologies right along with our students. As educators, we cannot close the door on what is to come.

Apps to Teach Social Behaviors

In addition to the new technology hardware Combs discussed, there are a number of apps and/or software programs that have been developed to improve school discipline (Mims, 2013; Thomas, 2014), though there is very little independent research showing the efficacy of such programs in terms of improving behavior. Still, every teacher today should have at least a passing knowledge of this area, as many of these programs are currently being used, with some success by individual teachers. Thomas (2014) presents a brief review of several additional apps or games that emphasize social skills, and teachers can use them to enhance behavior.

For example, *Social Skill Builder* (socialskillbuilder.com) is a relatively inexpensive set of gaming simulations for students with autism spectrum disorders, designed to teach social skills, problem solving, and critical thinking (Thomas, 2014). The programs use real-life stories to engage students, who then answer questions and make judgments in social situations. The software also provides ongoing assessment and progress monitoring, so teachers can track student progress and customize the program to highlight specific skills at different levels. Each program comes with built-in reinforcement and is differentiated for students ranging from nonreaders to proficient readers.

The Social Express (thesocialexpress.com) provides a series of animated episodes presenting social situations in the real world. In this context, teachers teach students to make choices in order to help characters negotiate their way through various social interactions, read facial expressions of others, follow social cues, and avoid negative social interactions. There is a fee associated with this program, but the program is appropriate from young childhood through young adulthood, and teachers can review a demo video on the website.

One exciting gaming program, *IF...*, became available in 2015. *IF...* is an online game/simulation to enhance social and behavioral skills. This program was developed by Trip Hawkins, a game creator known for very popular games such as *Medal of Honor, Madden NFL,* and *Desert Strike* (Takahashi, 2013; Thomas, 2014). *IF...* presents an online world called *Greenberry*, where the cats and canines cannot seem to get along. Young children can use that simulation environment to explore their own feelings and emotions as they help those in *Greenberry*, while learning social skills, relaxation skills, and conflict resolution skills.

IF... was developed for use with iPads and is intended primarily for students between grades one and six. The game allows those students to walk a mile in someone else's shoes, as their "animal person" runs into situations that help develop her character (Takahashi, 2013). Students learn to make moral choices and develop a compassionate attitude toward others. They also learn not to bully others or allow themselves to be bullied. This is a gaming environment that teachers in the primary and elementary grades might consider as an anti-bullying or social skills development program.

TECH-BASED BEHAVIOR-MANAGEMENT SYSTEMS

As the discussion above shows, many apps and social gaming programs are available for teachers to use to enhance social skills, conflict resolution skills, or improve behavior, and new programs are becoming available each month. However, software can do more than merely teach social skills; some programs are available to help educators establish entire class management systems.

There are literally hundreds of apps that teachers can use to assist with discipline, and a simple Google search on terms such as "apps for school discipline" will result in many apps to consider. For example, *Discipline Tracker* (manskersoftware .com/DT_New.htm) is an app that captures the discipline activity for every student in the school. The school district must enable the app, but once it is available, it allows educators to enter rule infractions, synthesize and analyze group discipline trends, develop intervention plans, and send emails to other teachers or parents. Also, it allows teachers to see what disciplinary problems a student may have demonstrated previously, and typically results in a more unified disciplinary effort from one year to the next.

Celly is a social networking app that students can use for the usual networking functions (https://play.google.com/store/apps/details?id=com.p2.android.celly& referrer=https://cel.ly/frontpage). However, Nielsen (2014) suggests this app as one way to establish an anonymous tip line for bullying. There are several easy steps. First, an administrator at the school sets up a Celly account. The group membership name should indicate the intended use of the network (e.g., *JonesHighSchoolBully*; Nielsen, 2014). The administrator sets the group membership to "open," allowing anyone to use the line, but should limit the chat function to administrators only (he can do this by setting the chat mode to Curated Chat). The administrator who establishes the account can then add other administrators to help monitor the line. Students who have a cell phone can text in the name of a bully, as an anonymous report, and students without a phone can use the Web to anonymously report bullying in the school (Nielsen, 2014). The app can be customized with various themes and avatars, as desired, making it a user-friendly option for schools (maybe use the school mascot as one avatar!).

Rich Kids 1.10 is a free disciplinary reward system for use with students between three and fifteen years old by either parents or teachers (Zero2Six Technology Co., Ltd.). This app is founded on motivating students toward good behavior and includes a variety of tasks for students to perform. For each task students complete, students receive pay in the form of "gold" coins that can be redeemed for a variety of prize coupons. The app helps mark daily success on classroom tasks with a check mark in each student's box.

Review360 is a commercially available behavior management platform developed by Pearson Education (http://www.pearsonclinical.com/education/ products/100000732/review360-behavior-matters.html?Pid=review360&Mod e=summary#tab-details). It is designed to reduce suspensions, implement anti-bullying systems, implement RTI interventions, and improve school climate. It ranges from data aggregation and analysis capabilities based primarily on office referrals, to intervention and progress monitoring for individual students with behavioral issues. Web-based professional development is built into the system for both teachers and administrators. Teachers make behavioral reports online, saving much paperwork. In that sense, this is compatible with RTI efforts. The app also includes a parent contact system that sends emails to parents on behavioral issues. Anecdotal evidence provided by Pearson suggests that suspensions and expulsions were reduced about 40 percent each year in one school district that has employed this system for several years (http://www.teachercast.net/pearson-review-360-iste-interview/).

However, with increasingly limited school funds, teachers may wish to consider one of several free, and very popular, class management systems such as ClassDojo (http://www.classdojo.com). ClassDojo is a behavioral and class management program that works with both iPad and Android devices (Mims, 2013). The program also interacts with other technology such as interactive whiteboards (Mims, 2013). This program can greatly assist teachers in a variety of class management tasks and help reward students across grade levels for appropriate behavior.

The program allows students to create avatars (digital representations of themselves), and those avatars are then rewarded appropriately. Students can even access the program after school to keep track of their rewards in class (Mims, 2013). The program itself presents a list of positive and negative behaviors and also allows teachers to create their own targeted behaviors for individual students, as necessary (Mims, 2013). Should misbehavior occur in class, the teacher can then merely click on a student's avatar during the class in order to award positive points or institute a response-cost type of punishment (called negative points). Other uses of ClassDojo include:

Improving class behavior

Counting/tracking student behavior

Identifying behavioral trends

Awarding points for positive behavior

Generating reports on student behavior

Communicating with parents/other teachers

Again, there are hundreds of apps for teachers and parents to use, and many provide the same functions for the classroom teacher. I recommend that teachers ask in their own school or district to find out which apps other teachers are using. Also, when considering an app, teachers should review the comments on any app they might consider, as those can be rich in information from other teachers about the actual application of the app. Further, given the efficacy of many of these apps, I believe it is critical in today's classrooms that teachers implement one or more of these apps in an ongoing effort to remain in line with current best practices. Below is one teacher's reflection on using one of the more popular free apps for discipline.

A Teacher's Reflection on ClassDojo

Angie Kilcrease has been teaching for a number of years at various districts in Texas and now serves as the technology director/instructional technologist with Boyd Independent School District. She recently received her master's in educational administration from Lamar University.

Giving my students positive motivation to do their homework, participate in classroom discussion, and set behavioral goals has been easier than ever this year with the implementation of ClassDojo in my math classroom. ClassDojo is a free behavioral management website that allows me to set customized classroom goals for each class period along with personalized individual goals for each student. It also has opened up an easier means of communication to parents with ClassDojo's weekly report to parents via email that shows the negative and positive points given to their child. Parents regularly email me to ask specific questions about their child's behavior based on the points given for that week. Also, it is not time consuming, which is the main struggle with providing positive and negative feedback on behavior to students and parents!

I am able to walk around my room with my iPad in hand and give immediate points for positive behavior such as turning in homework on time, good group discussion, giving a helping hand to another student, and being productive when finished with math homework. I can also issue negative points for being disrespectful, not turning in homework, not participating, or getting off task. I have students give me personal goals on behavior and provide the students with points for working toward those goals, such as talking instead of paying attention or not being negative toward math problems. My students love listening for the positive and negative sounds that ClassDojo gives when I award points, and this tool makes classroom discussions more competitive. I also have put the website on my Smart Board, and as students answer questions correctly, they are allowed to come up and give themselves positive points, and believe me when I say, all students love adding points beside their name.

I have also customized how I use ClassDojo with rewards in my classroom. ClassDojo allows students to create and edit avatars with their points, but I use several web-based software programs that use the same reward system. So rather than use the avatars, I give out reward coupons for every 10 positive points. Once every three to four weeks while the students are working independently, I call them up one by one and let them choose a coupon. The coupons include Friend Lunch (student and a friend can eat lunch in my classroom), Recognition Rockstar (positive phone call home from me), Big Gulp (bring a drink to class), Seat Swap (swap seats with a classmate for the day), and Big Dog (gets to sit in my rolling chair for a class period). What was most surprising to me was the majority of my students always choose Recognition Rockstar even if I had just called a few weeks ago! One of my students stated that, "Kids can see the rewards of their hard work, and it makes them want to work on the stuff more."

This has been a lot of fun for me this year and has allowed me to reach all those students that sometimes get overlooked because they do not stand out in a crowd. I have also had more positive contact with my parents than before, and this has helped greatly with some of my most at-risk students.

ClassDojo provides me with great reports and graphs and is very useful when meeting with parents. I am able to show hard data on the percentage of time a certain student turns in homework, is off-task, or is meeting the behavioral goals we have set out to work on for the year. In short, I enjoy teaching with ClassDojo.

DIGITAL CITIZENSHIP, RISKY BEHAVIORS, AND WHAT TO DO ABOUT THEM!

In addition to the classroom misbehaviors students may develop using new teaching technologies, there are many risky behaviors that technology facilitates, and today, virtually every parent and teacher is aware of these risky behaviors that students may engage in online. First, when every student in the class is interacting with a computer screen, how can any teacher be sure students are working on the lesson rather than playing on Facebook? How can teachers feel confident students are not playing games in the classroom or viewing inappropriate material online? Further, how can teachers (not to mention parents) protect students from the many dangers online such as pornography or online predators? Dangers range from cyberbullying, to sexting, to sharing personal information online, which makes personal data available to anyone worldwide!

With the instant, free, worldwide communication options inherent in these new technologies, the dangers of students' risky behaviors is magnified many times over. Young girls using an instant camera in 1975 could have given their boyfriend a picture of themselves in a bathing suit (or naked). Today that same picture in uploaded digital format would be available to anyone in the world with an internet connection. The impact and dangers of risky behavior are much greater in the modern world.

One suggestion is that schools respond to this set of risky behaviors via the concept of digital citizenship—teaching students that personal safety and appropriate use of these modern communications technologies is a personal responsibility of the students themselves. It is not an overstatement to say that, in general, schools have generally not responded well to this increased danger of risky behavior online. In one recent survey of teachers in the United States, nearly three-quarters of teachers indicate that they have never had formal internet safety training, even though 86 percent of those teachers report using web-based content in class, and 40 percent indicate that they sometimes assign online homework (Schaffhauser, 2014). Clearly, student safety demands that this quickly change.

> Schools have generally not responded well to this increased danger of risky behavior online.

To date, schools have responded in several different ways to this danger, but generally those responses take one of two forms: firewalling, or teaching internet safety and appropriate internet usage. Firewalling involves using settings within the computer technologies to block access to certain websites that may have objectionable content. Unfortunately this has several disadvantages. First, it is very hard to firewall all the possible internet sites to protect students today. Next, student computer savvy is often more sophisticated than the firewall developers. I've often said that if you show me a school firewall, and then give me access to the student body, within fifteen minutes I'll show you a student at that school who can break through that firewall. In fact, firewalls work only part of the time.

Firewalls can also prevent teachers and students from getting content online that has significant educational value. For example, while the website YouTube has some objectionable content, it also is loaded with excellent videos made by teachers that can facilitate flipped instruction. It is also loaded with other good content in almost any subject teachers can name.

As someone who has studied technology applications in schools (Bender & Waller, 2013), I generally support firewalls for only explicitly sexual content or violent content. I much prefer using technology implementation as a teaching moment for students. By implementing an "Appropriate Technology and Internet Usage" policy, schools can teach students about the dangers of the internet, including all of the wide range of problems that have arisen, like sexting, harassment, hate speech, and so on. I and my colleague, Laura Waller, recently provided an example of a contract with an appropriate usage policy, and an adapted version of that is in Figure 20.1.

In addition to an appropriate usage policy, teachers can also access an array of online resources that provide lessons on personal safety and responsible use of various technologies.

As one example, Google provides ten lessons on digital citizenship that teachers can access free (http://www.educatorstechnology.com/2014/07/10-great-digital-citizenship-lessons.html).

While these focus primarily on YouTube, they do emphasize topics such as cyberbullying, critical analysis of digital content, and personal safety/privacy.

Rather than pretend these risky behaviors don't exist in the digital world, educators should take the lead in teaching about the dangers of technology, and using this contract with all students in the school will provide teachers with the means to teach explicitly about these dangers. Certainly, this is more important for the safety and well-being of students than merely firewalling all possible objectionable internet sites.

Figure 20.1:   Appropriate Technology/Internet Usage Student Pledge

In order to enjoy the benefits of technology and support online educational options at my school, I agree to obey the following rules on appropriate use of these technologies.

1. I agree to use technology and the internet at school for appropriate educational purposes, as described and supervised by my teachers at school.

2. I will always show respect for other students, faculty, school administrators, and members of my community in my uses of technology, including laptop computers, social networking sites, digital cameras, online educational and other websites, and all other technologies both at home and at school.

3. I will not engage in any use of social networking or technology that is likely to offend, embarrass, or emotionally injure other students, faculty, school administrators, my parents, or others in the community.

4. I will carefully consider every text, picture, or video of myself and others that I share online. I will not share any information on my address or location, or other information that may compromise me or anyone else in my school or my community either now or at some future point.

5. I will not engage in any hate speech or online bullying of any sort. I will carefully avoid engaging in any form of harassment, intimidation, or bullying in all instances and in all school and community events.

6. I will not view inappropriate material of a sexual, violent, or vulgar nature online, either at school or at home. Should I open by accident any website that includes inappropriate material of this nature, I will immediately report the incident and website directly to my teacher.

7. I will report any and all hate speech, bullying, and cyber-based bullying to school authorities, including all incidents of bullying I see on campus and any bullying I see online. I will use the online, anonymous reporting system at my school in an honest manner for reporting these instances.

_____   _____
Student's Name   Date

_____   _____
Teacher   Date

Adapted from: Bender and Waller (2013).

SUMMARY

Again, a full discussion of the impact of technology on behavior is well beyond the scope of this book. However, I have provided the general answers to the three major questions posed earlier in the chapter.

How might increased technology use impact discipline? As discussed previously, technology does enhance engagement for most students, and that improves both behavior and academic performance. However, the concerns with technology distracting students are very real.

Go to www.learningsciences.com/bookresources to download figures and tables.

How can apps enhance a teacher's disciplinary efforts? While research is quite limited, a wide range of games, simulations, and apps are available to help manage and improve behavior in the classroom. I recommend that all teachers explore the use of programs such as ClassDojo or one of the gaming programs to enhance social skills and conflict resolution skills.

How can teachers help students avoid dangers that can come from the use of the internet and/or technology generally? Teachers must begin to specifically address digital citizenship much more in the classroom. While I support limited firewalls, I support more strongly teaching digitial citizenship and using appropriate usage policies, and I therefore encourage teachers to teach directly about the dangers and risky behaviors that increased technology use can facilitate. As educators, we should not miss that teachable moment as technology implementation continues to increase.

SECTION IV
A New Day in School Discipline: Conclusions and Recommendations

As I discussed throughout this book, it is not an overreach to suggest that educators are witnessing a new day in school discipline. Recent national educational policy statements, the RTI initiative, and an emphasis on strategies that build school climate all point to coming changes in disciplinary practices as well as increased disciplinary responsibilities for all teachers. Whereas teachers have not, by and large, actively intervened with individually targeted behavioral interventions or charted data on those interventions, such responsibilities are quickly becoming the expected norm for all teachers. That is one reason I wrote this book: to prepare educators for their increased responsibilities in this regard. I believe this may be the first book to take note of many of these very recent developments or incorporate these changes into a set of coherent disciplinary procedures.

As I promised, this book provides an array of disciplinary strategies for even the most challenging disciplinary problems within a differentiated discipline perspective, based on a three-tier need:

1. Whole-class/whole-school preventative disciplinary strategies

2. Trigger avoidance and Band-Aids for immediate response to discipline problems

3. Targeted, individual interventions for the most difficult disciplinary problems

I also noted the very recent demands of the US Department of Education as to reductions in the use of suspensions and expulsions, at least for relatively minor offenses (Duncan, 2014). Further, the expectation that RTI will be implemented to enhance teachers' management of behavior problems in the classroom will certainly change the landscape of teaching. Those factors, as much as anything, should help motivate teachers to understand that their disciplinary responsibilities will be increasing.

Within that context, here are my recommendations for teachers and administrators in every school, and in particular for those who may face significant disciplinary challenges school-wide.

1. ***Focus on Instruction:*** Schools should do professional development on positive behavior, and then implement at least one of the teaching approaches that foster such behavior. This book is rather unusual among the books on discipline in that it also focuses on instructional procedures as the basis for effective discipline. In particular, this book discusses a number of teaching approaches that have a positive impact on discipline, including using movement-based instruction, flipping the classroom, using project-based learning, and infusing of technology into the classroom. Any one or any combination of these instructional approaches is likely to result in fewer discipline problems because all of these tactics increase student engagement. That, in turn, will result in fewer discipline problems and increased teacher enjoyment of teaching.

   In today's world it is easy to imagine a flipped classroom infused with technology and using the majority of class time for project-based learning. I suspect that this exact combination is soon to become the best-practice model for almost all instruction.

2. ***Implement at Least One Preventative Strategy School-Wide:*** Educators around the United States, Canada, Australia, and New Zealand implement interventions such as restorative circles, quiet time, peer mediation, conflict resolution, adult mentoring, restorative circles, and any of the others in Section I. Further, many schools in those countries see significant decreases in disciplinary problems as a result of implementation of school-wide disciplinary strategies. This is true even in some schools in inner-city neighborhoods, which may face some significant disciplinary challenges. Even if discipline is not a major concern in your particular school, in today's world all schools should have at least one of these preventative interventions in place. Prevention must be emphasized much more and is certainly more time efficient than targeted interventions after problems occur! In simple terms, this is now best practice in education.

3. ***Teach Newer Teachers the Triggers and Band-Aids:*** Veteran teachers typically know how to manage a behavioral crisis in the classroom, but newer, recently graduated teachers may not have those skills. While school administrators may assume that newly graduated teachers can manage the minor, everyday behavioral concerns in the classroom, many beginning teachers have had little instruction or experience with more problematic behaviors. Managing students' fighting, weapons violations, or the emotional eruptions of bipolar students is not specifically taught

to most new teachers, so they will not have those skills when they enter the classroom. Particularly with new teachers, administrators should teach them these trigger avoidance strategies as well as the Band-Aids in Section II.

4. ***Implement RTI for Behavioral Improvement:*** Across the nation and around the world schools have implemented tiered instruction for reading and math, and many have used tiered interventions in the context of behavioral improvement plans. Most teachers are now aware of the tiered intervention concept, and schools should move quickly to implement the full RTI process for students with significant behavioral problems. This will result in teachers successfully managing more behavior problems in the classroom and referring fewer problems to the principal's office. Teachers can use many of the strategies in Section I and all of the strategies in Section II as targeted interventions, even if she initially implements the strategy as a whole-class tactic. While RTI implementation is always a three- to five-year process (Bender, 2009), RTI can do more to positively impact discipline in the classroom than any other strategy, which is why Hattie's research (2013) identifies RTI as one of the top three most influential things schools can do to foster success. Further, RTI now represents best practice in managing these disciplinary issues, so all teachers will be expected to undertake RTI interventions. This book should help them prepare for those increased responsibilities.

CONCLUSION

In closing, I'll merely note my sincerest hope that this book will assist educators facing disciplinary issues in their classes today. These are best practices in today's world, and I do recommend these strategies to you. Also, once again, I invite all educators to follow my Twitter account (@williambender1) or communicate directly with me on how these strategies work for you (or how and why they didn't!). I'd love to hear from you.

Finally, let me also thank you, as one educator to another, for the work you do. You are engaged in one of the most important and most critical jobs in the world—you are creating positive futures for the students in your charge, and I hope this book helps you, even if only a little, to do that. You have my undying respect for the role you play improving our world, so again, thanks for what you do!

Resources

Worksheets for
Disciplinary Strategies

Figure 1.1: Assessing Students' Comfort in the Class

Directions: On this sheet, circle the number that represents the extent to which you are worried about this.

	Not worried about this	Hardly worried about this	Worried about this	Very worried about this
Students picking on me	1	2	3	4
Failing in my schoolwork	1	2	3	4
The teacher not liking me	1	2	3	4
Being made fun of	1	2	3	4
Being different from others	1	2	3	4
Finding classmates for joint projects	1	2	3	4
Not understanding my work	1	2	3	4
Students picking a fight with me	1	2	3	4
Getting into trouble	1	2	3	4
Losing my way between classes	1	2	3	4
Working with peer buddies in class	1	2	3	4
Finding friends to sit with in the cafeteria	1	2	3	4
Being sent to the principal	1	2	3	4
Not knowing what is expected	1	2	3	4
Which clubs/teams to join	1	2	3	4

Figure 1.2: Parent Questionnaire on Class Climate

Directions: Answer each question with a yes or no, and then write a brief note on that particular question if you'd like. It is better to answer questions fairly quickly, without intense reflection.

How does the class feel? Welcoming? Intimidating? _____

Who is talking? Teacher? Students? _____

Is the teacher smiling? _____

Are the kids working on their assigned tasks? _____

Are multiple learning tasks ongoing? _____

Are any kids quietly whispering? Does the teacher respond? How? _____

_____

Do students seem happy? _____

Do students seem friendly toward each other? _____

Does the teacher speak respectfully to students? _____

Do students speak respectfully to each other? _____

Do you see any bullying in the class? _____

What disciplinary procedures are in evidence (e.g., rules posted, good behavior charts)?

_____

Are kids of different races working together? _____

Are there displays of student work in the class? _____

Do the students seek out the teacher for help with a problem? _____

Do the students seek out other students for help with a problem? _____

Is the classroom generally pleasing to look at? _____

Are you happy your child is in this class? Why? _____

Figure 8.1:   Peer Mediation Questionnaire

Mediation Participants Must Agree to Follow These Rules for Peer Mediation

1. Students will attempt to solve their problems through mediation and follow these rules for mediation.

2. Mediators are here to help students reach a mutually acceptable approach to conflict and not to impose a solution themselves.

3. No negative comments about others is allowed. Any shouting, cursing, verbal abuse, or physical violence will result in ending the session and a referral to the principal.

4. Students will not interrupt others. Students may write ideas down as others speak and share those ideas when it is their turn.

5. Students will tell the truth and honor the commitments they make in mediation.

6. Students will show respect for other disputants and the mediators at all times and keep all aspects of the mediation confidential.

Questions: Describe the conflict that you wish to resolve. State exactly who is involved and exactly what happened. It is usually better to answer questions without intense reflection.

State in only two lines exactly what the conflict is. _____

_____

Who is involved in this conflict? (More than one other person? If so, who?) _____

_____

What started the conflict? _____

_____

Did anyone involved in the conflict misunderstand the others? _____

_____

Can you suggest ways to resolve this conflict and avoid the same conflict in the future?

_____

_____

Figure 8.2: Peer Mediation Resolution Contract

Date: _____

Peer Mediator: _____

First Student Participant: Name _____ Grade _____

Second Student Participant: Name _____ Grade _____

Problem:

The two disputants listed above came to Peer Mediation with the following conflict: ____

_____

Solution Chosen:

The two disputants agreed to the following:

_____

_____

_____

_____

Contract Follow-Up Session: We understand that in three weeks, the mediator will sit with us again to hold a follow-up discussion of the solutions in this contract.

Date and Time of Follow-Up Mediation Session: _____

Signatures: With our signatures below, we agree to abide by this contract and avoid future conflict by taking the action(s) above.

Student One: _____ Date _____

Student Two: _____ Date _____

School Administrator's Signature: _____ Date _____

Figure 12.1: Check Your Feelings! Poster

Figure 12.2: The Anger Thermometer

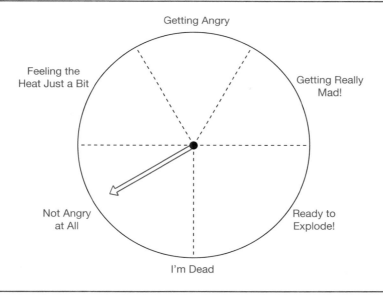

Figure 13.1: Responsibility Strategy Agreement

Student: _____   Date: _____

Teacher: _____   Class Period: _____

Description of Behavior Problem:

_____

Responsibility Selected:

I, _____, agree to make a positive contribution to our class by:

_____

_____

_____

_____

Monitoring Plan: This task will be monitored by:

Intervention Follow-Up Session: We understand we will meet in three weeks to discuss follow-up for this responsibility.

Date and Time of Follow-Up Meeting: _____

Signatures: With our signatures below, we agree to abide by this contract and avoid future conflict by taking the action(s) above.

Student: _____   Date: _____

Teacher: _____   Date: _____

Principal's Signature: _____   Date: _____

Figure 20.1:   Appropriate Technology/Internet Usage Student Pledge

In order to enjoy the benefits of technology and support online educational options at my school, I agree to obey the following rules on appropriate use of these technologies.

1. I agree to use technology and the internet at school for appropriate educational purposes, as described and supervised by my teachers at school.

2. I will always show respect for other students, faculty, school administrators, and members of my community in my uses of technology, including laptop computers, social networking sites, digital cameras, online educational and other websites, and all other technologies both at home and at school.

3. I will not engage in any use of social networking or technology that is likely to offend, embarrass, or emotionally injure other students, faculty, school administrators, my parents, or others in the community.

4. I will carefully consider every text, picture, or video of myself and others that I share online. I will not share any information on my address or location, or other information that may compromise me or anyone else in my school or my community either now or at some future point.

5. I will not engage in any hate speech or online bullying of any sort. I will carefully avoid engaging in any form of harassment, intimidation, or bullying in all instances and in all school and community events.

6. I will not view inappropriate material of a sexual, violent, or vulgar nature online, either at school or at home. Should I open by accident any website that includes inappropriate material of this nature, I will immediately report the incident and website directly to my teacher.

7. I will report any and all hate speech, bullying, and cyber-based bullying to school authorities, including all incidents of bullying I see on campus and any bullying I see online. I will use the online, anonymous reporting system at my school in an honest manner for reporting these instances.

_____   _____

Student's Name   Date

_____   _____

Teacher   Date

Adapted from: Bender and Waller (2013).

References

Albert, L. (1996). *Cooperative discipline*. Circle Pines, MN: American Guidance Service.

Algozzine, B., Daunic, A. P., & Smith, S. W. (2012). Classroom interventions and individual behavior plans. In C. F. Shores (Ed.), *Response to intervention* (pp. 133–152). Thousand Oaks, CA: Corwin Press.

Bender, W. N. (2007). *Relational discipline: Strategies for in-your-face kids* (Rev. 2nd ed.). Charlotte, NC: New Age.

Bender, W. N., & Shores, C. (2007). *Response to intervention: A practical guide for every teacher*. Thousand Oaks, CA: Corwin Press.

Bender, W. N. (2009). *Beyond the RTI pyramid: Solutions for the first years of implementation*. Bloomington, IN: Solution Tree.

Bender, W. N. (2012a). *RTI and differentiated reading*. Bloomington, IN: Solution Tree.

Bender, W. N. (2012b). *RTI in high school and middle school*. Bloomington, IN: Solution Tree.

Bender, W. N. (2012c). *Project based learning*: Differentiating instruction for the 21st century. Thousand Oaks, CA: Corwin Press.

Bender, W. N. (2013). *Differentiating math instruction, K–8: Common Core mathematics in the 21st century classroom* (3rd ed.). Thousand Oaks, CA: Corwin Press.

Bender, W. N., & Crane, D. (2011). *RTI in math: Practical guidelines for elementary teachers*. Bloomington, IN: Solution Tree Press.

Bender, W. N., & Waller, L. B. (2011). *The teaching revolution: RTI, technology, and differentiation transform teaching for the 21st century*. Thousand Oaks, CA: Corwin Press.

Bender, W. N., & Waller, L. B. (2013). *Cool tech tools for lower tech teachers: 20 tactics for every classroom*. Thousand Oaks, CA: Corwin Press.

Benelli, L. (2014). ADHD behavior, exercise, and ADHD children. *Ezine Articles*. Retrieved from http://ezinearticles.com/?ADHD-Behavior,-Exercise,-and-ADHD-Children&id=2859194

Bergmann, J., & Sams, A. (2012). *Flip your classroom: Reach every student in every class every day*. Alexandria, VA: Association for Supervision and Curriculum Development.

Bergmann, J., & Sams, A. (2014). Maximizing PLC time to flip your class. *District Administration*. Retrieved from http://www.districtadministration.com/article/maximizing-plc-time-flip-your-class

Blad, E. (2014a, January 8). New federal school discipline guidance addresses discrimination, suspensions. *Education Week*. Retrieved from http://blogs.edweek.org/edweek/rulesforengagement/2014/01/new_federal_school_discipline_guidance_addresses_discrimination_suspensions.html

Blad, E. (2014b, January 29). Maryland adopts new discipline rule to address racial disparities, suspensions. *Education Week*. Retrieved from http://blogs.edweek.org/edweek/rulesforengagement/2014/01/maryland_adopts_new_discipline_rule_to_address_racial_disparities_suspensions.html

Brand, S. (2011). *School climate*. Education.com. Retrieved from http://www.education.com/reference/article/school-climate/

Brown-Chidsey, R., & Steege, M. (2005). *Response to intervention: Principles and strategies for effective practice*. New York, NY: Guilford Press.

Buggey, T. (1999). Look! I'm on TV! *Teaching Exceptional Children, 31*, 27–30.

Busse, R. (2009). *Sociometric assessment*. Education.com. Retrieved from http://www.education.com/reference/article/sociometric-assessment/

Carter, J. L., & Russell, H. L. (1985). Use of EMG biofeedback procedures with learning disabled children in a clinical and an educational setting. *Journal of Learning Disabilities, 18*, 213–216.

Chapman, C. (2000). Brain compatible instruction: A presentation on a nationwide tele-satellite workshop. *Tactics for Brain Compatible Instruction*. The Teacher's Workshop, Bishop, GA.

Chen, I. (2014). *Can project-based learning close gaps in science education?* KQED.org. Retrieved from http://blogs.kqed.org/mindshift/2014/09/can-project-based-learning-close-gaps-in-science-education/

Christie, D. J., Dewitt, R. A., Kaltenbach, P., & Reed, D. (1984). Using EMG biofeedback to signal hyperactive children when to relax. *Exceptional Children, 20*, 547–548.

Clinton, G., & Miles, W. (1999). Mentoring programs: Fostering resilience in at-risk kids. In W. N. Bender, G. Clinton, & R. L. Bender (Eds.), *Violence prevention and reduction in schools*. Austin, TX: ProEd.

Cohen, R. (2014). *The benefits of peer mediation*. School Mediation Associates. Retrieved from http://www.schoolmediation.com/books/resolvingconflict/chapter3.html

Colvin, G., Ainge, D., & Nelson, R. (1997). How to defuse confrontations. *Exceptional Children, 64*, 47–51.

Creer, T. L., & Miklich, D. R. (1970). The application of a self-modeling procedure to modify inappropriate behavior: A preliminary report. *Behavior Research and Therapy, 8*, 91–92.

Dabbs, L. M. (2013). *The power of the morning meeting: 5 steps toward changing your classroom and school culture*. Edutopia.org. Retrieved from http://www.edutopia.org/blog/morning-meeting-changing-classroom-culture-lisa-dabbs

Davis, F. E. (2014). *8 tips for schools interested in restorative justice.* Edutopia.org. Retrieved from: http://www.edutopia.org/blog/restorative-justice-tips-for-schools-fania-davis

Drew, N. (2002). *Six steps for resolving conflicts.* Learning Peace. Retrieved from http://www.learningpeace.com/pages/LP_04.htm

Duncan, A. (2014). *A key policy letter from the education secretary and deputy secretary.* Washington, DC: US Department of Education. Retrieved from http://www2.ed.gov/policy/elsec/guid/secletter/140108.html

Dunn, D. (2010). *Peer mediation step by step process.* Retrieved from Askdjlyons.com.

Edutopia.org. (2014). *Infographic: Meditation in schools across America.* Edutopia.org. Retrieved from http://www.edutopia.org/stw-student-stress-meditation-schools-infographic

Elias, M. H. (2004). The connection between social-emotional learning and learning disabilities: Implications for intervention. *Learning Disability Quarterly, 27,* 53–61.

Elliott, S. N., & Busse, R. T. (1991). Social skills assessment and intervention with children and adolescents. *School Psychology International, 12,* 63–83.

Ellis, K. (2009). *Community begins with the morning meeting* [Online video]. Edutopia.org. Retrieved from http://www.edutopia.org/stw-louisville-sel-morning-meetings-video

Fleming, D. C., Ritchie, B., & Fleming, E. R. (1983). Foster the social adjustment of disturbed students. *Teaching Exceptional Children, 15,* 172–175.

Flipped Learning Network (FLN). (2014). *The four pillars of F-L-I-P.* Retrieved from http://www.flippedlearning. org/definition

Flipped Learning Network & Sophia. (2014). *Growth in flipped learning: Transitioning the focus from teachers to students for educational success.* Retrieved from http://www.flippedlearning.org/survey

Frey, N., Fisher, D., & Gonzales, A. (2011). *Literacy 2.0: Reading and writing in 21st century classrooms.* A topical book discussion presented at the annual AuthorSpeak Conference. Indianapolis, IN.

Fuchs, D., Fuchs, L., & Vaughn, S. (2008). Response to intervention: A framework for reading educators. Newark, DE: International Reading Association.

Gable, R. A. (1995). Use of peer confrontation to modify disruptive behavior in inclusion classrooms. *Preventing School Failure, 40*(1), 25–28.

Glasser, W. (1969). *Schools without failure.* New York, NY: Harper & Row.

Gold, J. (2013). *Morning meeting resources for teachers.* Mrsgoldsclass.com. Retrieved from http://www.mrsgoldsclass.com/MorningMeeting4Teachers.htm

Green, G. (2012). My view: Flipped classrooms give every student a chance to succeed. *CNN OnLine.* Retrieved from http://schoolsofthought.blogs.cnn.com/2012/01/18/my-view-flipped-classrooms-give-every-student-a-chance-to-succeed/

Green, G. (2014). Flipped classrooms get results at Clintondale High School [Online video]. *Techsmith*. Retrieved from http://www.techsmith.com/customer -stories-clintondale.html

Gresham, F. M. (2002). Best practices in social skills training. In A. Thomas & J. Grimes (Eds.), *Best practices in school psychology IV* (pp. 1029–1040). Bethesda, MD: National Association of School Psychologists.

Hall, N., Williams, J., & Hall, P. S. (2000). Fresh approaches with oppositional students. *Reclaiming Children and Youth, 8*, 219–236.

Hallahan, D. P., & Sapona, R. (1983). Self-monitoring of attention with learning disabled children: Past research and current issues. *Journal of Learning Disabilities, 16*, 616–620.

Hamdan, N., McKnight, P., McKnight, K., & Arfstrom, K. (2013). *A review of flipped learning*. Flipped Learning Network. Retrieved from http://www.flippedlearning .org/review

Harris, R. D. (2005). Unlocking the learning potential in peer mediation: An evaluation of peer mediator modeling and disputant learning. *Conflict Resolution Quarterly, 23*(2), 141–146.

Hattie, J. (2013). *Visible learning for teachers: Maximizing impact on learning*. Thousand Oaks, CA: Corwin Press.

Hoffman, T. (2010). *Self-regulation: The key to successful students?* Education.com. Retrieved from http://www.education.com/magazine/article/self-regulation -children/

Jenson, W. R., & Reavis, H. K. (1999). Using group contingencies to improve academic achievement. *Best Practices, 1*, 77–84.

Johnson, D. W., & Johnson, R. (2005). *Teaching students to be peacemakers* (4th ed.). Edina, MN: Interaction.

Jones, M., Boon, R., Fore, C., & Bender, W. (2009). Our mystery hero! A group contingency intervention for reducing verbally disrespectful behaviors. *Learning Disabilities: A Multidisciplinary Journal, 15*(2), 56–61.

Jones, T. (2000). *Conflict resolution education: Goals, models, benefits and implementation: A summary of research findings of the US Department of Education*. Philadelphia, PA: Temple University.

Katz, M. (1997). Overcoming childhood adversities: Lessons learned from those who have "beat the odds." *Intervention in School and Clinic, 32*, 205–210.

Kelman, B. (2013, June 20). CVUSD must reduce suspension rate. *The Desert Sun*. Retrieved from http://www.mydesert.com/article/20131201/NEWS04/ 312010024/?nclick_check=1

King, K., & Gurian, M. (2006). Teaching to the minds of boys. *Educational Leadership, 64*, 56–61.

Kirp, D. L. (2014, January 12). Meditation transforms roughest San Francisco schools. *San Francisco Chronicle*. Retrieved from http://www.sfgate.com/opinion/

openforum/article/Meditation-transforms-roughest-San-Francisco-5136942.php

Kriete, R. (2012). *The morning meeting book.* Turner's Falls, MA: The Northeast Foundation for Children. Also available at www.responsiveclassroom.org

Larmer, J., & Mergendoller, J. R. (2010). 7 essentials for project-based learning. *Educational Leadership, 68*(1), 34–37.

Layton, L. (2014, March 9). Socialization technique helps in academic achievement, trial study finds. *Washington Post.* Retrieved from http://www.washingtonpost.com/local/education/socialization-technique-helps-in-academic-achievement-trial-study-finds/2014/03/05/674d1e0e-a495-11e3-a5fa-55f0c77bf39c_story.html

Lazerson, D. B., Foster, H. L., Brown, S. I., & Hummel, J. W. (1988). The effectiveness of cross-age tutoring with truant, junior-high school students with learning disabilities. *Journal of Learning Disabilities, 21,* 253–255.

Lopata, C., Nida, R. E., Marabel, M. A. (2006). Progressive muscle relaxation: Preventing aggression in students with EBD. *Teaching Exceptional Children, 38,* 20–25.

Loukas, A. (2007). What is school climate? *Leadership Compass, 5*(1). Retrieved online from http://www.naesp.org/resources/2/Leadership_Compass/2007/LC2007v5n1a4.pdf

Lupin, N. (1977). *Peace, harmony, awareness.* Hingham, MA: Teaching Resources.

Machado, A. (2014). Should schools teach kids to meditate? *The Atlantic.* Retrieved from http://www.theatlantic.com/education/archive/2014/01/should-schools-teach-kids-to-meditate/283229/

Maher, C. A. (1982). Behavioral effects of using conduct problem adolescents as cross-age tutors. *Psychology in the Schools, 19,* 360–364.

Maher, C. A. (1984). Handicapped adolescents as cross-age tutors. Program description and evaluation. *Exceptional Children, 51,* 56–63.

Marzano, R. J. (2003). *Classroom management that works: Research-based strategies for every teacher.* Alexandria, VA: Association for Supervision and Curriculum Development.

Marzano, R. J. (2007). *The art and science of teaching: A comprehensive framework for effective instruction.* Alexandria, VA: Association for Supervision and Curriculum Development.

Marzano, R. J., Pickering, D. J., & Pollock, J. E. (2001). *Classroom instruction that works: Research-based strategies for increasing student achievement.* Alexandria, VA: Association for Supervision and Curriculum Development.

Mathes, M. O., & Bender, W. N. (1996). Effects of self-monitoring on children with attention deficit disorders who are receiving medical interventions. Implications for inclusive instruction. *Remedial and Special Education, 18,* 121–128.

McGuire, M. (1999). Connections and clear limits: Conflict resolution strategies for gang behavior and group violence. In W. Bender, G. Clinton, & R. Bender (Eds.), *Violence prevention and reduction in schools*, Austin, TX: ProEd.

McHenry, I. (2000). Conflict in schools: Fertile ground for moral growth. *Phi Delta Kappan*, *82*(3), 223–228.

McIntosh, K., Herman, K., Sanford, A., McGraw, K., & Florence, K. (2004). Teaching transitions: Techniques for promoting success between lessons. *Teaching Exceptional Children*, *37*, 26–31.

Mergendoller, J. R., Maxwell, N., & Bellisimo, Y. (2007). The effectiveness of problem based instruction: A comprehensive study of instructional methods and student characteristics. *Interdisciplinary Journal of Problem-Based Learning 1*(2), 49–69.

Miller, A., & Cunningham, K. (2011). *Classroom environment.* Education.com. Retrieved from http://www.education.com/reference/article/classroom-environment/

Mims, L. (2013). *Classroom behavior? There's an app for that.* Edutopia. Retrieved from http://www.edutopia.org/blog/classroom-behavior-classdojo-app-lisa-mims

National Crime Prevention Council. (2014). *Peer mediation in high schools.* Retrieved from http://www.ncpc.org/topics/bullying/strategies/strategy-peer-mediation-in-high-schools

Nielsen, L. (2014). *Set up anonymous bully reporting with Cel.ly.* Techlearning.com. Retrieved from http://www.techlearning.com/Default.aspx?tabid=67&entryid=8325

OBrien, A. (2014). *Inequities in student discipline: What to do about them.* Edutopia. Retrieved from http://www.edutopia.org/blog/inequities-student-discipline-what-to-do-anne-obrien?utm_source=twitter&utm_medium=post&utm_campaign=blog-inequities-discipline

Oster, D. (2014, September 27). School garden teaches students many lessons. *Pittsburgh Post-Gazette.* Retrieved from http://www.post-gazette.com/life/garden/2014/09/27/School-garden-teaches-students-many-lessons/stories/201409230198

Pianta, R., La Pero, K. M., Payne, C., Cox, M. J., & Bradley, R. (2002). The relationship of kindergarten classroom environment to teacher, family, and school characteristics and child outcomes. *Elementary School Journal*, *102*, 225–238.

Pleasant Valley Community Schools. (2014). *Personal responsibility (for students).* Retrieved from http://www.pleasval.k12.ia.us/studyskills/studentpersonalresponsibility.htm

Preston, C. (2014, January 19). Classroom behavior trackers. *The Organized Classroom Blog.* Retrieved from http://www.theorganizedclassroomblog.com/index.php/blog/classroom-behavior-trackers

Reed, K. (2011). Game changer: Phil Lawler's crusade to help children by improving physical education. *Human Kinetics*. Retrieved from http://www.humankinetics .com/excerpts/excerpts/classroom-behaviors

Robin, A., Schneider, M., & Dolnick, M. (1976). The turtle technique: An extended case study of self-control in the classroom. *Psychology in the Schools, 13*, 449–453.

Rohr, A. (2014, February 10). Bedford schools see fewer disciplinary problems under new system. *The News & Advance*. Retrieved from http://www.newsadvance.com/ news/local/bedford-schools-see-fewer-disciplinary-problems-under-new-system /article_8edc9214-91ef-11e3-9c4d-001a4bcf6878.html

Rowh, M. (2014). Schools learn to outsmart ADHD. *District Administration*. Retrieved from http://www.districtadministration.com/article/schools-learn-out smart-adhd

Rubenstein, G. (2014). *Louisville's CARE for Kids program starts with the heart*. Edutopia. Retrieved from http://www.edutopia.org/stw-louisville-sel-social -emotional-learning

Salend, S. J., & Sylvestre, S. (2005). Understanding and addressing oppositional and defiant class behaviors. *Teaching Exceptional Children, 37*, 32–39.

Salend, S. J., Whittaker, C. R., Reeder, E. (1992). Group evaluation: A collaborative, peer-mediated behavior management system. *Exceptional Children, 59*, 203–209.

Sandler, A. G., Arnold, L. B., Gable, R. A., & Strain, R. A. (1987). Effects of peer pressure on disruptive behavior of behavioral disordered classmates. *Behavioral Disorders, 12*, 104–110.

Schaffhauser, D. (2014; 7/7/14). Survey: Parents look to teachers for internet safety training. *The Journal*. Retrieved from http://thejournal.com/articles/2014/07/07/ survey-parents-look-to-teachers-for-internet-safety-training.aspx

Schneider, M. (1974). Turtle technique in the classroom. *Teaching Exceptional Children, 7*, 21–24.

Shanker, S. (2009). Enhancing the mental wellness of children. *Child & Family Professional, 12*(3).

Shanker, S. (2010) Self-regulation: Calm, alert and learning. *Education Canada, 50*(3).

Smith, S. W., Siegel, E. M., O'Connor, A. M., & Thomas, S. B. (1994). Effects of cognitive behavioral training on angry behavior and aggression of three elementary aged students. *Behavioral Disorders, 19*, 126–135.

Snider, V. (1987). Use of self-monitoring of attention with LD students: Research and application. *Learning Disability Quarterly, 10*, 139–151.

Sousa, D. A. (2009). *How the brain influences behavior: Management strategies for every classroom*. Thousand Oaks, CA: Corwin Press.

Stansbury, M. (2013, July 30). Does research support flipped learning? *eSchool News*. Retrieved from http://www.eschoolnews.com/2013/07/30/does-research-support -flipped-learning/

St. George, D. (2014, June 3). Schools get road map for improving discipline practices. *The Washington Post.* Retrieved from http://www.washingtonpost.com/local/edu cation/schools-get-road-map-for-improving-discipline-practices/2014/06/02/ da13257c-e8f2-11e3-8f90-73e071f3d637_story.html

Strobel, J., & van Barneveld, A. (2008). When is PBL more effective? A meta-synthesis of meta-analyses comparing PBL to conventional instruction. *International Journal of Problem-based Learning, 3*(1), 44–58.

Study Guides and Strategies. (2014). Peer mediation. Retrieved from http://www .studygs.net/peermed.htm

Takahashi, D. (2013). Trip Hawkins' new game helps kids learn about their feelings. *VentureBeat.* Retrieved from http://venturebeat.com/2013/12/15/trip-hawkins -new-game-aims-at-developing-social-and-emotional-intelligence-in-kids/

Tanaka, G., & Reid, K. (1997). Peer helpers: Encouraging kids to confide. *Educational Leadership, 55*(2), 29–32.

Thomas, R. (2014). *5 Apps to enhance students' social learning skills.* ASCD Edge. Retrieved from http://edge.ascd.org/_5-Apps-to-Enhance-Students-Social -Learning-Skills/blog/6564849/127586.html

Uhlig, K. (2014, January 30). Updated: Happy notes help Everest middle-schoolers start semester with a smile. *Wausau Daily Herald.* Retrieved from http://www .wausaudailyherald.com/article/20140129/WDH01/301290312/Happy-notes -help-Everest-middle-schoolers-start-semester-positive-note?nclick_check=1

US Department of Education. (2011). *Supportive school discipline initiative.* Retrieved from http://www2.ed.gov/policy/gen/guid/school-discipline/appendix-3-over view.pdf

Vanderwerf, L. (2014, January 4). Willmar Middle School developing mentoring program that aims to keep students in school. *West Central Tribune.* Retrieved 1/8/14 from: http://www.wctrib.com/content/willmar-middle-school-developing -mentoring-program-aims-keep-students-school

Walker, H., & Sylwester, B (1998). Reducing students refusal and resistance. *Teaching Exceptional Children, 30*(6), 52–58.

Walker, R. (1998, January). *Discipline without disruption.* A presentation appearing at The Tough Kid Professional Development Teleconference (W. N. Bender & P. Mclaughlin, Eds.), The University of Georgia, Athens.

Wells, K. (2013, November 30). Self-regulation technique helps students focus in class. *CBC News.* Retrieved from http://www.cbc.ca/news/canada/self-regulation -technique-helps-students-focus-in-class-1.2440688

Wilemon, T. (2014, January 22). Middle school students practice conflict resolution. *The Tennessean.* Retrieved from http://www.tennessean.com/article/20140122/ NEWS04/301220136/1970?nclick_check=1

Wolff, R., & Nagy, J. (2013). Section 6: Training for conflict resolution. *Community Tool Box.* Retrieved from http://ctb.ku.edu/en/table-of-contents/implement/ provide-information-enhance-skills/conflict-resolution/main

Yarbro, J., Arfstrom, K. M., McKnight, K., & McKnight, P. (2014). *Extension of a review of flipped learning.* Flipped Learning Network. Retrieved from http:// flippedlearning.org/cms/lib07/VA01923112/Centricity/Domain/41/Exten sion%20of%20FLipped%20Learning%20LIt%20Review%20June%202014 .pdf

Yell, M. L. (1988). The effects of jogging on the rates of selected target behaviors of behaviorally disordered students. *Behavioral Disorders, 13*, 273–279.

Zuna, N., & McDougall, D. (2004). Using positive behavioral support to manage avoidance of academic tasks. *Teaching Exceptional Children, 37*, 19–25.

Index